THE JEWISH CHILD:
Halakhic Perspectives

THE JEWISH CHILD:
Halakhic Perspectives

by

Shoshana Matzner-Bekerman

KTAV Publishing House, Inc.
New York

COPYRIGHT © 1984
SHOSHANA MATZNER-BEKERMAN

Library of Congress Cataloging in Publication Data

Matzner-Bekerman, Shoshana.
  The Jewish child.

  Includes bibliographical references and index.
  1. Children (Jewish law)   2. Jewish children.
I. Title.
BM727.M37   1984   296.3'87835874   83-19950
ISBN 0-88125-017-1
ISBN 0-88125-024-4 (pbk.)

MANUFACTURED IN THE UNITED STATES OF AMERICA

Dedicated to my parents
Abraham and Anna Matzner
*whose love and guidance
are the source of my inspiration*

Contents

	Introduction	1
	Part I The Foundations of Development	
1.	The Child in Judaism: An Overview	7
	The Role of the Child in Judaism	8
	The Child in the Jewish Family	11
	The Study of Children	14
	Stages of Development	16
	The Importance of the Individual	18
2.	"Be Fruitful and Multiply"	20
	Conception	20
	Artificial Insemination	22
	Pregnancy	23
	Abortion	28
	Contraception	30
3.	The Birth Process	31
	Prenatal Development	31
	Birth	35
	The Neonate	40
	Nonviolent Birth	40
	Postpartum Convalescence	42
4.	Welcoming the Newborn	43
	Berit Milah	43
	The Ceremony	45
	Halakhic Rulings and Special Cases	51
	Pidyon ha-Ben	54
	The Ceremony	56
	Halakhic Rulings and Special Cases	59
	The Blessing of Thanks	60
	A Jewish Girl Is Born	60
	Naming the Jewish Child	61

viii   *The Jewish Child: Halakhic Perspectives*

        When the Name Is Given 63
        Hebrew Names: Boys 64
        Hebrew Names: Girls 66

**Part II The First Five Years:
From Infant to Child**

5.   Infant and Child Care 71
        Personal Cleanliness and Hygiene 72
        Bathing 72
        Washing the Hands and Personal Hygiene .73
        Outings 74
        Clothing .74
        Care of the Teeth 75
        Care of the Nails 75
        Care of the Hair 75
        Exercise .76
        Sleep 76
        Nursing .77
        Natural Spacing 78
        Wetnurses 80
        Nursing on Sabbath and Holidays 80
        Diet of the Nursing Mother 81
        Play 83
        Infant Care on Sabbath and Holidays 85
        Bathing on the Sabbath 87
        Diaper Care 88
        Outings on the Sabbath 88
        Fast-Days 89
        Babysitters 89
        Summary 89

6.   Nutrition .92
        The Laws of Kashrut 92
        Recommended Eating Habits 93
        Weaning .94
        Solid Foods 95

	Halakhah Concerning Nutrition 98
	Feeding Children on the Sabbath 98
	Warming Food for a Child on the Sabbath . 99
	Sterilizing and Cleaning Bottles on Sabbath 99
	Passover 100
	Feeding Children on Fast-Days 100
	Conducting the Meals 100
	Foods to Avoid 101
	Summary 102
7.	Child Behavior 104
	The Sources of Behavior 105
	The Child's Basic Nature 106
	Development Stages and Moral Education 107
	Parent-Child Relations 110
	Deviant Behavior 114
	Summary 114
8.	Early Childhood Education 117
	Learning Readiness 117
	Parental Educational Obligations 120
	Torah Education and Reverence for God . 121
	Education in *Mitzvot* 122
	Parents as Educators 125
	Techniques of Early Childhood Education 127
	Honor the Child 128
	Setting an Example 129
	Summary 129
9.	Discipline 131
	The Concept of Discipline 131
	The Role of Discipline in Child-Rearing . . 132
	When to Discipline 133
	Methods of Discipline 136
	Summary 139
10.	Health and Disease 141

Guidelines for Health and the Prevention
of Disease 143
Exercise and Sleep 145
Fresh Air and Sunshine 145
Psychosocial Stress 146
Childhood Diseases 147
The Treatment of Disease 150
Medical Care on the Sabbath 151
Summary 153

Part III The Dimensions of Development

Introduction 159

11. Physical Development 161
   The Purpose of Physical Health 161
   Heredity and Environment 164
   Hereditary Influences 165
   Environmental Influences 166

12. Cognitive Development 169
   Developing the Child's Cognitive Potential 169
   The Judaic Philosophy of Cognition . . . 171
   The Stages of Cognitive Development . . 172

13. Emotional Development 179
   Fear 181
   Anxiety 182
   Anger and Aggression 183
   Hatred 185
   Jealousy 186
   Self-Esteem 186
   Affection 188
   Joy 190

14. Personality Development 191
   What Is the Personality? 191
   Temperamental Influences 193
   Environmental Influences 195

The Role of Torah and Halakhah in
Personality Development 198

Part IV Child Development in the Social Context

Introduction 203

15. Socialization 205
    Social Learning 205
    Peer Groups 207
    Sibling Relations 209
    Play 210

16. The Parent-Child Relationship 213
    Parental Duties 213
    Filial Duties 214
    Curbs on Parental Initiative 216
    Summary 218

17. Birthdays 222
    Bar and Bat Mitzvah 223
    Other Birthday Celebrations 224

18. Religious and Non-Religious Education . . . 226
    The Meaning of *Chinnukh* 226
    Parents as Teachers 229
    Preschool Education 230
    Education of Girls 231
    Education from Age Three to Six 232
    Formal Education 234
    Curriculum 236
    Methods of Education 239
    Discipline 244
    The Importance of the School in Judaism   245
    The Role of the Teacher 246
    Summary 249

19. The Rights of the Child in Jewish Law . . . 251

The Fetus in Jewish Law 251
Legal Definition of "Son" and "Daughter" 252
Legitimacy 253
Rights of the Firstborn 254
The Child's Right to Education and
  Support 256
Protection from Abuse 256
Equal Treatment 257
Property Rights 257
The Right to Participate in Religious
  Observances 258
Liability for Transgressions 259
Children's Rights in Matters of Betrothal . 260
Rights of Neglected or Abandoned
  Children 260
Orphans 261
Maturity 264
Conclusion 267

Notes 269
Index 307

Introduction

The purpose of this book is to present a clear overview of the Jewish sources on child-rearing and child-development. The materials gathered in this volume, providing a firm basis for understanding the core values and ideas embodied in Jewish child-rearing practices and traditions, are intended as a resource both for parents and for educators and other professionals involved with Jewish children.

Millions of parents and teachers throughout the world consult the writings of such leading authorities as Spock, Piaget, Erikson, and Freud for advice on raising children and for answers to their questions about child-development. Hospitals, medical schools, clinics, and universities are continually conducting research aimed at shedding new light on the physical, emotional, intellectual, and social development of children. Ironically, despite all of this interest and scientific activity, the earliest and most natural source on the rearing and development of children—the Bible—is neglected.

It is written in Psalms, "From the mouth of babes and sucklings hast Thou ordained strength."[1] This passage clearly points out the importance of the study of children and childhood, for accurate knowledge of the way children develop is the key to the attainment of mental health, ideal methods of education, and a sound society—indeed, of all aspects of human betterment.

The Talmud notes that one who teaches the child (Torah) is considered as if he bore the child.[2] In fact, a child's life is affected and influenced, in one way or another, by virtually everyone who has contact with him. Consequently it is vital that our attitudes and actions toward children be based on principles that are both ethical and beneficial.

A full understanding of the Jewish approach to child-rearing and child-development requires a familiarity with the Jewish sources on children through the ages, beginning with the Bible and including, as well, the Talmud and the post-talmudic Responsa and Codes. This vast body of literature, spanning thousands of years and originating in many different countries and cultural areas, is replete with references to child-rearing and child-development. I have sought in this book not merely to assemble these diverse materials in a coherent, systematic manner but to demonstrate, by comparing Jewish traditional views of children with the findings of modern psychology, that the approach they embody is often in consonance with the teachings of present-day experts on child-development.

My goal is to demonstrate the vitality and validity of the Jewish approach to child-rearing as a means of shaping our attitudes toward our children. Like the secular behavioral sciences, the Judaic approach to children is pragmatic—based on empirical observation and case studies—but it has, in addition, a special quality of its own. It is based upon and seeks to impart religious values, and it is derived from a divinely revealed system of life and law—Torah and Halakhah—designed to enable us to live in accordance with the desires of our Creator.

Whether we are parents or teachers, those of us who are committed to raising our children to be good Jews can only succeed if we are aware of the teachings on children afforded us by Judaic philosophy and law. Judaism knows that raising children is difficult. We are taught that "I will increase your toil"[3] refers to child-rearing,[4] as does "You will bear children with sorrow." But we are also taught that no human activity is more praiseworthy. "For I have known him [Abraham] in order that he may instruct his sons and his household after him, that they may keep the way of the Lord to do righteousness and justice, in order that the Lord may bring Abraham all that He spoke concerning him."[5] Indeed, rearing our children properly is our highest responsibility, and it is to the achievement of that goal that this book is dedicated.

It is essential to note that this book is meant as a reference to halakhic sources. Readers must consult the original halakhic source or a rabbi for any specific problem or question on child rearing.

Part I
The Foundations of Development

1
The Child in Judaism: An Overview

Since the time of our ancestors Abraham and Sarah, a common bond has united all Jewish parents in all four corners of the earth in every generation. This bond, the force that binds the major elements of Judaism together, has contributed to Jewish survival despite a history of exile, trauma, and oppression. Much has been said and written about the Jewish mother, the Jewish family, and even the Jewish father—sometimes with awe and respect, other times with exaggeration. If we were to summarize all that has been written on the subject, we could define the Jewish perspective on child-rearing and child-development with one word: *commitment*—a deeply rooted, unequivocal, imprinted commitment to children (whether one's own or those in the surrounding community). Varying with the historical situation, this commitment to satisfying the child's needs has taken many different forms according to the requirements of the time. At all times, however, the Jewish value of *giddul banim* (the upbringing of children) has stressed that effective child-rearing is based on developing the child as a living vehicle for the continuation of the Jewish heritage.

The conception of childhood in any society is shaped by three major factors: (1) the cultural ideology pertaining to children; (2) attitudes concerning the child as the object of parental affection and concern; and (3) the child as the object of formal study. In order to comprehend the Jewish perspective on child-rearing and child-development, we must look at each of these factors in the light of the Jewish sources on the subject.

THE ROLE OF THE CHILD IN JUDAISM

In Judaism, childhood is considered a period of purity, joy, and beauty to be valued and cherished. The Talmud states that "childhood is a garland of roses." To emphasize the concept further, one rabbi states of children that "their very breath is free of sin."[1]

Childhood is a symbol of creation, a time when the development of the human being is in its most crucial stage. Since the child is "not a thinker and is unable to distinguish good from evil,"[2] the parent has the ultimate responsibility of guiding the child. "And you shall teach them [the words of God] to your children . . . in order that you lengthen your days and your children's days upon the earth."[3] Moreover, as the Book of Proverbs states: "Listen my son to the instruction of your father, and forsake not the teachings of your mother."[4]

According to Rabbi Samson Raphael Hirsch, "The decisive age in education is just that period in which most people neglect education completely, and this is the period of childhood, the first years of life in which we must try to remove in advance any obstacles which might arise on the road towards the education of the children in future years."[5]

Childhood is the period in which the personality is molded and the physical and mental faculties develop. The process of human development, in essence, supplements the creation and mystery of the universe. Childhood is a time of joy and pain, happiness in development, and wonder at learning and exploring. The Talmud sums up the period of childhood in the following passage: "Better are the late fruits we ate in our childhood than the peaches we ate in our old age."[6]

Children are regarded as the hope of the future in every society, yet among the Jewish people this concept is enhanced by the view that children are a divine trust. This is stated in no uncertain terms in the Book of Psalms: "Children are an inheritance from the Lord, a reward for the fruit of the body."[7] The prophet Malachi notes that children are the "seed of the Lord."[8]

The Foundations of Development

The Jewish home provides the foundations for the child's emerging role as a good Jew. The parents set the stage for successful child-rearing by committing themselves to caring for the child and his future. Rabbi Yochanan tells the story of a man who planted a carob tree, which is known to bear fruit only after seventy years. When asked whether he thought he would live to eat from the tree, the man replied: "I am doing as my ancestors did. Just as they planted a carob tree for their children, I am planting for my sons."[9]

The principle underlying all aspects of the parent-child relationship is aimed at ensuring the continuation of the Jewish heritage from one generation to the next. This is aptly brought out in Psalms: "Instead of thy fathers shall be thy sons."[10]

Judaism has special esteem for children, considering them the hope for the future and the basis for the perpetuation of the Torah.

> Rabbi Meir said: When Israel stood before Mount Sinai to receive the Torah, the Holy One, blessed be He, said to them: "Shall I give you the Torah? Bring me good sureties that you will keep it, and then I will give it to you." They replied: "Sovereign of the Universe, our ancestors will be our guarantors." Said God to them: "Your sureties need sureties themselves. I have found fault with them." They answered, "Our prophets will be our sureties." God replied: "I have found fault with them also." Then the Israelites said: "Our children will be our sureties." To which God replied: "In truth these are good sureties. For their sake I will give it to you."[11]

Children are the vital links in the continuation of the unbroken chain of the Jewish heritage throughout the ages. It is said that the Shekhinah hovers over Israel when the spiritual heritage of the Almighty is transmitted from one generation to the next. "And I will establish My covenant between Me and thee and between thy seed after thee in their generation for an everlasting covenant; to be a God unto thee, and to thy seed after thee."[12] The Talmud comments on this verse that when the children follow the traditions of the parents, the Shekhinah is found among them, whereas if the children do not follow the parents' ways, where shall the Shekhinah rest—on trees and stones?[13]

The importance attached to children as a means of perpetuating the Torah places them on a separate level from other groups. The Midrash pronounces that "children receive the presence of the Shekhinah."[14]

> Rabbi Judah said: See how beloved are little children to God. When the Sanhedrin went into captivity, the Shekhinah did not go with them; when the watchers of the priests went into captivity, the Shekhinah did not go with them. But when the little children went into captivity, the Shekhinah went with them. For it says in Lamentations: "Her children are gone into captivity" [Lam. 1:5], and immediately after: "From Zion her splendor is departed" [Lam. 1:6].[15]

Another indicator of the special status of children in Judaism is the fact that God's relationship with the people of Israel is compared to that of parent and child: "You are the children of the Lord your God."[16]

This special relationship is especially evident when the text discusses the observance of the Jewish heritage: "My son, observe my sayings, and my commandments must thou treasure up with thee. . . . My son, attend unto my wisdom, to my understanding incline thou thy ear."[17]

Finally, we find clearly stated: "Beloved are the people of Israel, who were called the children of the Lord; an abundance of love is made known to them, for they were called the children of the Lord."[18] This passage has further implications for the role of the child in the Jewish family, because the emphasis on parental love and care is exemplified by the Lord's relationship with the people of Israel.

THE CHILD IN THE JEWISH FAMILY

"It is said that at the time the fetus is created in the mother's womb, there are three partners in his creation: the Lord, his father, and his mother."[19] The preceding Midrash links the unique relationship between the Lord, the parents, and the child as the basis for the principles underlying child-rearing in the Jewish family.

The child has occupied a central role in the Jewish family throughout the ages. In the Bible, we find that the first commandment which God gave man in the form of a blessing is *peru u-revu,* "be fruitful and multiply," in order to give meaning to the creation of the universe.[20]

The fundamental nature of this principle is stressed by the comments in the Talmud concerning the psychological importance of bearing children.[21] This is exemplified in the Bible by Rachel, who said to Jacob, "Give me children, or else I die."[22] When she gave birth to a son, she said: "God has gathered in my shame."[23]

Children are a blessing to the family: "The crown of old men are children's children, and the ornament of children are their fathers."[24]

The rewards in the parent-child relationship are reciprocal: "When the children are blessed, the parents by this very token are blessed."[25] To cite just two concrete examples, we find that Noah found favor in the eyes of the Lord on account of his offspring[26] and that Abraham was saved from the furnace on account of Jacob.[27]

Although, as we have noted, Judaism acknowledges the great challenge posed by the task of child-rearing (known as *tza'ar giddul banim*), parents are more than compensated for their toil, for "children are a bond of union between husband and wife."[28] Indeed, the entire nation benefits from the presence of children. When each family has children, there is no need for the process of *chalitzah* (release from the obligation of levirate marriage), and consequently there are fewer arguments and lawsuits over property, as each child receives what is his by birthright.[29]

The child in the Jewish family has been awarded love, compassion, and respect. In contrast, studies point out at other nations often considered children either as chattels, economic burdens or miniature adults. Tracing the history of childhood from the earliest times, several authors have noted the abuses carried out by the Greeks, Romans, Egyptians, Mesopotamians, Chinese, Indians, and other peoples, who killed, neglected, or sacrificed their children, drowned daughters, and practiced cannibalism or the newborn taboo. Maltreatment of children was not limited to prehistoric times or early civilizations—it occurred in "enlightened" European nations as late as the nineteenth century and is the bane of the most modern societies.[30] In contrast, as a noted author points out, the Jewish nation introduced humanitarianism to the world, as shown in its attitude toward children, especially in the condemnation of child sacrifice as illustrated by the story of Isaac.[31]

The cornerstone of the Judaic attitude toward children is the love and respect accorded by those who care for them as inscribed in Jewish law. This is a natural result of the conception that children are a divine trust. As we see in the Bible, Joseph said to his father, Jacob: "These are my sons whom the Lord hath given me."[32]

Since all human beings are created in the image of God, all children have the right to be loved and cared for. As the Talmud says, "Beloved is man, who was created in the image of God; an abundance of love is given to him, for he was created in the image of God."[33]

All human lives are considered holy, so much so that we find the ruling: "One desecrates the Sabbath for the sake of a baby of one day, but not for the dead body of David, King of Israel."[34] Thus, the sacredness of human life is applied to the infant as soon as he is born. Each individual has the right to feel that the world is created for his own sake.[35] As a logical consequence of this conception, each child is entitled to be loved and cared for in order that he may have the possibility of developing to his maximum capability.

Love for the child is essential, for "true compassion and true love exist only among children and for children."[36] In the Midrash we find the following observations:

> ... He has set the world in their heart" [Eccles. 3:2]. Rabbi Jonathan interpreted the words to refer to the love of children which God has put in men's hearts. Like a king who had two sons: the elder honored him, the younger was corrupt; and yet he loved the younger more than the elder.[37]
>
> Rabbi Issachar said of a child who says "Masha" for "Moses," "Ahran" for "Aaron," and "Aphron" for "Ephron" that God says, "Even his stammering I love."
>
> A child may jump over the holy name of God again and again and he is not punished; yea, even more, for God says, "His very jumping I love."[38]

How, then, are we to show our love to our children and at the same time provide guidance and discipline for their benefit? The Talmud provides the following answer: When dealing with a child, "be it ever your way to thrust off with the left hand and draw it to you with the right hand."[39] This principle has practical implications in all aspects of the parent-child relationship and provides an effective guideline for the rearing and development of children.

The practical implication of this guideline is the creation of an atmosphere of trust based on love as the foundation for the acquisition of the values of Judaism. In the Jewish family, the most tangible element of parental love is the great dedication and effort consecrated toward the child's education. The major educational institution for children mentioned in the Bible is the family (public education was not instituted until the days of Joshua ben Gamla in the first century C.E.). All family relationships were clearly defined in order to ensure the necessary atmosphere of love, respect, and mutual trust—now generally recognized as the essential psychological foundation for healthy mental development and learning.

THE STUDY OF CHILDREN

The commitment to the child as an individual who forms a link in the eternal chain of Judaism obliges us to study and understand the development of children. Whereas according to some authors, the concept of childhood was not fully developed in most societies up to the seventeenth century,[40] we find at the very basis of Jewish thought that the child is recognized as an individual with needs and rights different from those of the adult. The Bible singles out the *katan* ("minor") as not having the strength or knowledge that entails responsibility and obligation, and for this reason the Talmud considers the *katan* exempt from certain religious duties. The child is called as well *olal, taf, yonek,* and *tinnok* (feminine: *tinnoket*). The last of these means "suckling," but it became a term of endearment and was applied to children who had already passed the nursing stage.

Three basic factors shape the Jewish viewpoint on child development. The first is the necessity of studying and understanding the child's growth process, the second is the knowledge of the child's stages of development, and the third is the importance of each individual created by God. These guidelines have been reiterated in the contemporary field of child study.

In the tenth century, Bachya bar Joseph ibn Paquda wrote:

> It is our duty to study the beginning of the human being: his birth, the formation of the parts of his physical frame, the joining

together of his limbs, the use of each limb, and the necessity which caused his being made in his present form. Next, we should study man's advantages: his various temperaments, the faculties of his soul, the light of his intellect, his qualities—those that are essential and those that are accidental; his desires and the ultimate purpose of his being. When we have arrived at an understanding of the matters noted in regard to man, much of the mystery of the universe will become clear to us, since the one resembles the other.[41]

Translated into modern terminology, one discerns in this passage the outline of a contemporary child-development study on the topics of birth, physical development, emotional and intellectual development, personality formation, heredity and environment.

The responsibility for the way children develop in a society is shared by everyone who touches the lives of its children in some way. This obviously includes parents, teachers, and social workers, but it also includes policy makers and researchers whose work influences the society's conceptions of childhood and attitudes toward children. Anyone who affects a child's development has the power to build or to destroy. The developmental continuum consists of different dimensions: intellectual, social, emotional, and physical. Each of these has its own distinct processes, yet they are all basically intertwined. To work effectively with children, it is necessary to understand and take into account the various aspects of development. Although no single theory proposed by child psychologists explains all the changes that occur in the process of growth, the Halakhic perspective on child rearing encompasses all the dimensions of development, as we shall see in subsequent chapters.

The study of child development has yet another dimension in Judaism as expressed by Bachya ibn Paquda:

And thus some sages declared that philosophy is man's knowledge of himself; that is, knowledge of what has been mentioned in regard to the human being [his developmental process], so that through the evidence of divine wisdom displayed in himself, he will become cognizant of the Creator: as Job said, "From my flesh, I see God" [Job 19:26].[42]

The study of child development is itself considered something of value, for it makes us aware of the wonders of the process of human development and enhances our reverence for God, the Creator.

STAGES OF DEVELOPMENT

How does a child develop from an embryo to a fetus, a neonate, an infant, a toddler, a preschooler, a schoolchild, an adolescent, and finally an adult? Jewish sages have always recognized that development is a continuous process which proceeds stage by stage in an orderly sequence. Each stage marks a degree or level of maturity in the sequential cycle of development. The study of child-development involves the behavioral changes that accompany growth at each stage and takes into account individual differences determined by nature and the effects of environmental forces. Although these stages of development have been systematically formulated only recently by modern child-development theorists, we find a number of philosophical statements about the stages of development in the various branches of Jewish literature. According to the *Tikkune Zohar,* "A man's life has three periods: the period when his body develops, the period when his thought develops, and the period when his deeds develop."[43] A student of Piaget would define these three periods as the sensorimotor phase, the preoperational period (and phase of concrete operations), and finally the period of formal operations.

The Midrash offers the following characterization of the stages of life:

> At the age of one a child is like a king, and everyone embraces and kisses him. Between two and three years of age he is like a pig. He crawls on the floor, puts his hand into everything dirty, and whatever he finds, he deposits in his mouth. At ten years of age, he is like a kid, he dances and laughs all day. At the age of eighteen, he is like a horse, rejoicing in his youth and strength. When he is married, he is like an ass, carrying a burden. When he becomes a father, he runs about like a dog to obtain a livelihood for his family. When he becomes old, he is like a monkey; for he becomes childish and no one pays attention to him.[44]

Knowledge of the various phases of life is especially important in the process of education. A noted child psychologist used to say, "Never ready until the nervous system is ready."[45] The child's nervous system is manifested in his maturational age, and this is the criterion one must consider in attempting to teach the child—whether one is teaching how to scribble with crayons, or toilet training, or playing with a ball, or reading and writing. It is for this reason that Rav said to Rav Samuel bar Shilat: "Do not receive a pupil under the age of six years, but after that age stuff him like an ox."[46]

The Mishnah sets forth the following stages of development:

> At five years of age, one learns the Bible. At ten years one studies the Mishnah. At thirteen, the individual reaches the age of *mitzvot* [is responsible for obeying God's commandments]. At fifteen, one learns the Talmud. At eighteen, one is ripe for marriage. At twenty, one is ready to pursue [a vocation]. At thirty, one is at the height of his strength. At forty years of age, one has attained wisdom. At fifty, one is capable of giving advice. At sixty, one reaches old age. At seventy one turns gray. At eighty, one is venerable. At ninety, one is stooped. At one hundred years of age, a person is as if he were dead.[47]

Bachya ibn Paquda describes the stages of development from conception through the growth of the fetus in the mother's womb to the infant who "has emerged into the world—all its senses, except those of touch and taste, being weak." "Later on, the infant's physical faculties grow stronger, so that it is able to distinguish sights and sounds." "The offspring passes from infancy to childhood."[48]

These stages of development are relatively stable characteristics, and imply a universality of sequence in growth. Every child's growth obeys laws of development applying to the whole human species as well as patterns unique to himself. The knowledge of the universal aspects of development enables us to appreciate human diversity. The factor of individuality is so strong that each child is unique at any given stage of development despite the central trends of human growth.

THE IMPORTANCE OF THE INDIVIDUAL

The Judaic concept of human nature envisages man as a creature of the earth and at the same time a child of the Lord infused with the divine spirit. Each individual has the potentiality for good or evil. Each person is physically and mentally unique. It is noted in the Talmud that "when man makes coins with one stamp they all resemble one another, but the Almighty coins each person with the stamp of Adam and not one person resembles another. For this reason every individual must say: 'The world has been created for my sake.'"[49]

The practical application of this principle is that each child has the right to be accepted for what he is and should be accorded love, respect, and care as an individual. Every child is unique in his innate temperamental qualities, as has been stressed in recent research findings.[50] This factor must be taken into account in our relationship with the child in the fields of discipline, learning, and socialization.

A basic principle closely related to the importance of the individual is the value Judaism places on human life: "For this reason, man was created solitarily—to teach you that he who destroys one human life is compared to one who destroys the entire world, and he who sustains one human life from the people of Israel—it is considered as if he has sustained the entire world."[51]

The task of child-rearing is considered in the same light in Jewish thought. Anyone who is involved in the care and development of a child sustains a life and thus is compared to one who sustains the whole world.

2
"Be Fruitful and Multiply"

CONCEPTION

The relevant commandment given in the Torah is stated in the form of a blessing: "And God blessed them and said, 'Be fruitful and multiply.'"[1] This is a most important commandment; because of it all other commandments in the world are fulfilled. In light of its nature, it was given to human beings and not to the angels of God.[2]

Rabbi Yochanan ben Beroka points out that the commandment "be fruitful and multiply" (*peru u're'vu*) was directed to both man and woman,[3] but the sages in the Talmud maintain that it is the man and not the woman who is responsible for carrying out the commandment.[4] The latter viewpoint is stipulated as Halakhah in the Code of Jewish Law (145a).

From the beginning of Jewish history to this day, women who did not conceive suffered great mental anguish as a result of their infertility. Our ancestors Sarah, Rebecca and Rachel exemplify the desperation of women who were infertile and were redeemed when God blessed them with a child. Failure to bear children involves more than just personal frustration; indeed, a person who chooses not to have children diminishes the image of God. The sages taught that when even one person in the nation chose not to fulfill the *mitzvah* of procreation, this was reason enough for the Shekhinah to remove itself from the people of Israel.[5]

In Judaism, the very purpose of marriage is to fulfill the commandment *peru u'revu*.[6] Indeed, the Code of Jewish Law states that "marital relations should not be carried out with the object of satisfying one's animal passions, but with the idea of establishing a family which should serve God and be useful to mankind."[7]

According to Rashi, one should have as many children as possible, for it is written, "Be fruitful and *multiply*" (Genesis 1:22). The word "multiply" indicates that one should have many children (Gen. 1:22). Indeed, in the ideal society, women will give birth to children every day.[8] In reality, the sages stipulate that the commandment is fulfilled when one has a boy and a girl (according to the school of Hillel) or two boys (according to the school of Shammai).[9]

Judaism places such a great emphasis on building a family that if a man died before he had a son, his widow was to marry his brother so that her firstborn would carry the name of the deceased and thus ensure that his name not be "put out of Israel" (Deut. 25:5-6). The alternative ceremony of *chalitzah* has superseded the levirate marriage, but the principle is maintained.

Sterility, whether due to the woman or the man,[10] is considered a great curse, for a "man without children is considered like the blind, the pauper, and the leper—as a dead man."[11] The Talmud notes, however, that one who raises an orphan or who teaches a child Torah, is like a parent (see Chapters 1, 19). The Talmud mentions some natural remedies for the treatment of sterility and impotence, such as Rabbi Yochanan's potion consisting of "three measures of *kartemi* pounded and boiled and mixed with wine," or eating garlic and fish.[12] The Talmud recognized psychological causes of impotence, and on one occasion Rabbi Huna treated such a case by inviting the husband and wife together for a meal in order to get them more used to each other.[13] The Bible mentions the use of the fruit *duda'im* as a love potion which supposedly increased fertility.[14] (Wine was also considered an aphrodisiac.) The sages were aware of a wide spectrum of life situations that could cause impotence, and on one occasion Rabbi Judah diagnosed that the social conditions of hunger and poverty were the cause of the failure to bear children. In treating the men involved, the sage ordered that they be bathed and fed well. This cured them of impotence.[15]

Both the wife's failure to bear children after ten years of marriage and the husband's impotence are possible grounds for divorce (indeed, the latter is a reason to prevent marriage).[16] In light of the grave consequences of infertility, the Responsa literature allows treatment of all types of sterility in women and even examination of the semen after the woman has been thoroughly checked and found fertile.[17] As a result of the many complexities involved a Rabbi must be consulted in all cases of sterility.

ARTIFICIAL INSEMINATION

One of the outstanding characteristics of Jewish law is its pragmatic attitude towards advances in medicine (see Ch. 10). Nevertheless, the new techniques of artificial insemination which have created possibilities for conception in an artificial manner involve many legal and moral complexities.

The subject is discussed in the Responsa of various authorized Rabbis especially in light of the questionable legal status of a child born under such circumstances.[18] Nevertheless, if a couple has been married for ten years and is still childless, or if the doctors conclude without a doubt that there is no other hope, an authorized Rabbi may be consulted concerning a decision about artificial insemination.[19]

Rabbinical rulings are in line with the Jewish moral framework and offer a flexible and pragmatic solution to a powerful dilemma. In any case, the most important cure for infertility in

Judaism is considered to be prayer. According to the Talmud, (Sarah, Rachel, and Hannah) were at first unable to bear children because the Almighty desires the prayers of the pious.[20]

PREGNANCY

> At the beginning of a human being's existence, the Creator appointed the mother's body to serve as a couch for the fetus so that it might abide in a safe place, a strongly guarded fortress, as it were, where no hand can touch it, where it cannot be affected by heat and cold, but it is shielded and sheltered and where its food is ready for it. Here it continues to grow and develop, even becomes capable of moving and turning, and receives its nourishment without any effort or exertion. This nourishment is provided for it in a place where no one else can in any way reach it, and is increased as the fetus develops until a definite period. Then it emerges without any contrivance or help on its part, but solely by the power of the wise, merciful, and gracious One who shows compassion to His creatures.[21]

The author of this passage, Rabbenu Bachya, points out the marvels of human development as a means of increasing our awareness of the Almighty. The beauty of the Judaic conception of child-development is inherent in the fact that every aspect of creation is imbedded in the halakhic framework of life.

In order to comprehend the scope of the life-cycle in the framework of Judaism, we must begin with marital relations. Biblical law, by forbidding marital relations for at least five days after the end of the menstrual period (when the wife immerses in the *mikveh* in order to purify herself),[22] lays the physical and psychological foundations for healthy conception. The Talmud points out that the most favorable time for conception is near the menstrual period (opinions differ as to whether the exact time is before the menses or immediately after immersion).[23] The prescription that the husband is to cohabit with his wife on the night of her immersion resolves the question in practice,[24] for as modern scientific investigation has shown, this is the most favorable time for impregnation.

As a framework for life, Judaism does not depend only on biological factors. It also takes into account the subtle psychological elements in marriage. The Talmud notes that the reason biblical law forbids marital relations for seven days after menstruation is that separation makes the heart grow fonder. When the couple meet again after a minimum of twelve days separation they are like newlyweds.[25] As such, the time is ripe for conception and the development of a healthy new child.[26]

The Code of Jewish Law requires modesty in marital relations, as outlined in *Shulchan Arukh Orach Haim, siman 240.* Adherence to these principles has practical implications for the couple's offspring, as is evident from the following story: A woman was asked why her children were so beautiful. She answered that it was because her husband was very modest in his relations with her, which took place (in accordance with the prescription) in the middle of the night and not at the beginning of the night or in the early morning. Similarly, all sorts of children's handicaps are attributed to immodesty during relations between man and wife.[27]

As a result of the importance assigned to conception and the provisions made for the healthy development of the fetus, pregnant women are pampered in Jewish law as well as in Jewish society.

> A pregnant woman who smells sanctified meat [of the sacrifices] or pork [and desires so intensely that if she does not eat it she and the fetus are in danger], one may dip a piece of bread in the sauce of the meat and bring it to her mouth. If this satisfies her, that is good; if not, then it is permitted to feed her the fat of the meat itself, for there is nothing which stands in the way of saving a life, except idolatry, incest, and murder.[28]

It is also permitted to give a pregnant woman food to eat on the fast of Yom Kippur if her situation warrants it. On one such occasion, when a pregnant woman had a longing for food on Yom Kippur, Rabbi Judah the Prince advised that someone should whisper into her ear that it was Yom Kippur. When this was done, the longing disappeared. The son who was born to her became a great rabbi. As a comment on this incident, the Talmud cites the verse in Jeremiah (1:5) "Before I formed thee in the belly, I knew thee."[29]

In the Bible, special precautions are noted to protect a pregnant woman from physical harm: "If men strive and hurt a woman with child, so that her fruit depart from her, and yet no other mischief follow, he shall be surely punished, according as the woman's husband will lay upon him, and he shall pay as the judges determine."[30]

The Talmud mentions that one of the miracles of the Temple was that no pregnant woman suffered from the scent of the holy flesh. (It was believed that strong odors had a bad effect on pregnant women.)[31] The barking of a dog is mentioned in the Talmud as a possible cause of miscarriage.[32]

As a preventive against miscarriage, pregnant women used to wear a stone around their necks. This stone, called the *even tekoma* ("stone of preservation") was worn at all times, even on the Sabbath. (Although it is forbidden to carry weights outside the home on the Sabbath, special permission was granted in this instance.)[33] In addition, the mystic acronym *k h t* was believed to have healing power and to prevent miscarriages.[34]

A woman suspected that she was pregnant when she missed her menstruation, but the Talmud notes that pregnancy can occur before the onset of the menses, as in the cases of Justinia, who became pregnant at the age of six,[35] and Bathsheba, David's wife, who was a mother at the age of six.[36] Pregnancy can also occur after menopause, as in the cases of Sarah, who was eighty-nine years old,[37] and Jochebed, the mother of Moses, who was said to have given birth at the age of 130.[38] However, these cases are remote, and the Talmud notes that sixty years is the limit for a multipara and forty for a primipara.[39] In addition, pregnancy before the age of twelve was prevented.[40]

During pregnancy a woman's limbs become heavier. Diagnosis of pregnancy is certain only after the first three months. (The diagnosis probably involved examination of the breasts or abdomen, for Rav Safra says that a married woman must not be examined, because this would profane her in the eyes of her husband.)[41] Thus, a widow or divorcee was not permitted to remarry until three months after the date of her husband's death or the divorce, so that the paternity of the next child would not be a matter of doubt.[42] Diagnosis of pregnancy in later months is no problem, for as the rabbis state, it is quite evident.[43] One talmudist notes the theory that it is possible to know the sex of the fetus during pregnancy, for the quickening is felt earlier if the child is a boy.[44]

According to the Jewish tradition, the sex of the fetus is determined at the moment of conception. If the man gives forth his seed first, the child will be a girl; if the woman gives forth her seed first, the child will be a male. This is ascertained from the statement, "If a woman gives forth her seed and bears a male child" [Lev. 12:2]. For this reason, it is of no avail to pray that the child will be either male or female once the woman is pregnant. However, in the first three days after conception, it is advisable to pray for a successful fertilization. From the third to the fortieth day of pregnancy prayers should be said for the child to be a male; from the fortieth day to the third month, one should pray that the fetus will develop normally (and not handicapped or malformed as a flat fish); from the third to the sixth month, one should pray that the child will not be lost through miscarriage; and from the sixth to the ninth month, prayers should request that the delivery will be safe. The practice of praying for the child to be male up to the fortieth day of conception would seem to be in contradiction to the tradition that the sex of the child is determined at the moment of conception. However, Rabbi Isaac explains that the prayers are valid if both the father and the mother brought forth seed at the same time, in which case the sex has not yet been determined.[45] More practical measures to assure that the child would be male include giving money to the poor; placing the bed between north and south; abstinence before the approach of menstruation; and drinking wine of the Havdalah service.[46] The varied means of determining the sex of the child share the view that sex is associated with the chromosomes and is already determined at fertilization.

Modern science has determined that normal pregnancy lasts 280 days, or nine months and seven days from the beginning date of the woman's last menstrual period.[47] This is an average figure, and actual delivery may vary a few days before or after this date. The Jewish sages who calculated the duration of pregnancy in the first century arrived at a similar conclusion, with the additional period of seven days following the menstrual period up to the woman's immersion in the *mikveh*.

> Samuel said: A woman becomes pregnant and gives birth after 271 days to 273 days; for this reason, the Chasidim were known to have marital relations only on Wednesday, so that their wives would not give birth on the Sabbath and cause a desecration of the day of rest. [According to the calculation that menses last from five to seven days and that 271 days from that day falls on Sunday, 272 days on Monday, and 273 days on Tuesday; in fact, marital relations among the ultra-Orthodox took place from Wednesday on.] Mar Zutra points out that the numerical equivalent of the word *herayon* [Hebrew for "pregnancy"] is 271.[48]

The question of the duration of pregnancy is associated with the legal problem of legitimacy. Rabbah Tosfa'ah ruled that a child born twelve months after the departure of the husband abroad is legitimate.[49] On the other hand, the minimum period of pregnancy is given by Mar Samuel as 212 days—the numerical equivalent of *harbe,* a word appearing in a biblical passage in connection with the trouble of pregnancy.[50] Various cases in the Responsa literature deal with this question as well.[51]

The specifications in Jewish law and custom concerning diet

and hygiene during pregnancy anticipated modern prescriptions in assuring the healthy development of the fetus. Proper diet is one of the first things an obstetrician discusses with a pregnant patient. Centuries before modern science realized that good nutrition is the most important ingredient in producing healthy children, we find that alcoholic beverages were forbidden to Manoah's wife when she was pregnant with Samson because of the deleterious effect they would have on the child.[52] Indeed, in the Talmud we find the warning that children "begotten during a state of inebriety develop mental deficiency."[53] It is interesting to note that the child's healthy development is directly attributed by the sages to a good diet. If the expectant mother ate fine peeled barley, she would contribute to the good growth of the child. A diet of meat, fish, parsley, paradise apples, and coriander was recommended to assure that the child would be strong, healthy, beautiful, and clear-eyed. In addition, it was believed that eating the *ethrog* fruit would cause the child to have a fragrant odor.[54]

The precautions taken for the healthy development of the fetus extend beyond the medical and environmental prescriptions for the expectant mother into the legal framework of Halakhah. The legal status of the pregnant woman is based on principles assuring the maximum possibility of well-being for the fetus and safety for the mother. According to the Code of Jewish law, a pregnant woman (if divorced or widowed) may not remarry until after the newborn is twenty-four months old (so that she may breastfeed him).[55]

ABORTION

As a result of the supreme value it places on life, Judaism offers a pragmatic and flexible solution to the controversial issue of abortion based on Judaic moral principles. The Code of Jewish

Law forbids cessation of pregnancy unless the continuation of pregnancy constitutes a danger to the life of the mother or might endanger her health, physically or mentally.[56] According to the Talmud, "If a woman is in labor [and her life is in danger], one may remove the fetus from her womb . . . for her life takes precedence over his."[57] This is the case only if the fetus is not yet viable. However, "if the head has emerged, it is not permitted to touch him [the fetus], for one life does not have precedence over another."[58]

The law of the pursuer states that one must save a person who is being pursued by another who intends to kill him, even if this means killing the pursuer. However, this does not apply to the fetus, according to Maimonides, for it is not the fetus that is trying to kill the mother; rather, it is the natural course of childbirth that poses a threat and the fetus is only an intermediary.[59] In this case, it is not clear whether the fetus is pursuing the mother or the mother is pursuing the fetus.[60]

In the Responsa literature we find several rulings based on concern for the mother.[61] If the abortion is intended to secure the mother's health—even if she is not in mortal danger—a Rabbi must be consulted along with medical experts concerning the possibility of abortion.[62]

If there is well-established proof that the fetus will be born handicapped and will suffer (as in cases where the expectant mother has German measles during the first three months of pregnancy,[63] or if the fetus is a carrier of Tay-Sachs disease), abortion may be considered, in the earliest stages of pregnancy, although in all cases a Rabbi must be consulted and the father must grant consent for the abortion.[64]

In summarizing the Jewish sources on conception, pregnancy, and abortion, we find that Halakhah regards life as a gift from God which must be cherished and given every possibility for healthy development in accordance with the moral principles of Judaism.[65]

CONTRACEPTION

The Code of Jewish Law permits contraception in some situations.[66] In all cases, an authorized Rabbi must be consulted. Some sources on the subject are the Chazon Ish, Responsa Ahiezer, Responsa Igrot Moshe.

3
The Birth Process

PRENATAL DEVELOPMENT

The mysteries of prenatal development fascinated the Jewish sages, and they succeeded in unraveling many unknown aspects of the creation of a human being long before modern science attempted to do so.

The Midrash states that the embryo is created when fertilization succeeds and the white drop (the ovum) fuses with the semen. The embryo then develops in the uterus, which is full of blood.[1] The ban on destroying seed in Jewish law[2] is based on the knowledge that the male sperm is an essential element in conception. In modern scientific history, the human ovum was discovered by Baer in 1827, while the existence of the spermatozoa was discovered by Hamm and Leeuwenhoek in 1677.[3]

In many cases, statements on embryology in the Talmud are a blend of philosophical speculation with insights that have been restated as scientific facts in our times. Consider, for instance, the following passage:

> Our sages learned: There are three partners in the creation of man: the Almighty, his father, and mother. His father contributes through his seed the white portions: i.e., bones, fibrous tissue [nerves and tendons], nails, brain, and the white portions of the eye [sclerotica and cornea]. His mother contributes through her ovum the pigmented portions: i.e., the skin, the

flesh, blood, hair, and the uveal tract of the eye. The Almighty contributes the spirit, the expression, vision, hearing, movements, and cognition. When the child dies, God takes His portion to Himself and leaves the remainder to the parents. Rav Papa said: This is the meaning of the saying: "Remove the salt and the flesh is fit for the dogs." As Rashi comments, this means that the soul is like salt which preserves the body—when the soul departs, the body decomposes.[4]

The description of the parts of the body attributed to the seed of the mother and father may be considered as an antecedent of the theory of germinal predetermination and the chromosomes, a breakthrough in modern science.

The miracle of fetal development is further described in the following passages:

What is taught in the verse, "I will give thanks unto Thee for I am fearfully and wonderfully made; wonderful are Thy works, and that my soul knows right well"? Take note of the difference between the Almighty and man! A man puts different seeds together in the soil and each grows in the manner of its own species; whereas God places the embryo in the mother's womb, with the result that both the father's seed and the mother's seed grow into one and the same human being.

Compare: the clothes-dyer puts several dyes in the vat and all unite to form one color, whereas God places the embryo in the womb so that each element of the parent's seed develops in its own natural way.[5]

The wonder of the metamorphoses by which these "elements of the parent's seed" develop into a human being is further unraveled when we note Rabbi Eliezer's statement that "a fetus inside the womb is like a nut placed inside a bladder of water. If you press your finger on the bladder, the nut recedes."[6] This is an obvious reference to the amniotic sac surrounding the baby. Moreover, during the prenatal development period:

> The fetal mouth is closed and its umbilicus is open; it eats and drinks everything that its mother eats and drinks . . . but as soon as it comes into the world, everything which had been closed opens, and that which was open closes, otherwise the child could not exist for a single hour.[7]

> The fetus does not secrete any movements in the mother's womb, for if it did, it would kill its mother.[8]

This is a remarkable description of the life-support system formed by the placenta, to which the baby is connected by the umbilical cord. The baby receives all its nutrients and hormones from the mother by way of the placenta, and also excretes its wastes through the placenta.

Among the Jewish sages were some experienced observers, such as Mar Samuel (a famous embryologist), Abba Saul, and Rav Abbahu. According to some of them, the primary center of formation of the human being was the head, while according to Abba Saul it was the umbilical vesicle, from which the parts of the embryo develop in different directions.[9]

These ancient observers actually examined embryos and based their statements on scientific methods of observation. In the Talmud, we find instructions for examining the embryo—not in water but in oil, and only in the sunlight. Also, the examiner could differentiate the sex of the embryo through a special sound described.[10]

For this reason, we find astonishing descriptions of the developing baby at different stages of prenatal development. The following description of the forty-day embryo by Rav Abbahu is supported by modern scientific findings:

> Its size is that of the locust; its eyes are like two specks at some distance from each other; its two nostrils have the same appearance as the eyes of a fly, and they are very close to each other; its mouth has the same appearance as a strand of hair. Sex can be distinguished, but it is not possible to differentiate between the

upper and lower extremities. The arms and legs are not yet sharply defined. And it is for this stage of development that we find the saying in the Kabbalah: "Hast thou not poured me out as milk, and curdled me like cheese? Thou hast clothed me with skin and flesh, and hast fenced me with bones and sinews. Thou hast granted me life and favor, and Thy visitation hath preserved my spirit."[11]

Thus, we find the distinction between the embryo and the fetus. At a further stage of development, the fetus resembles: "a ledger folded and laid to rest. Its hands rest on its two temples, its two elbows and two legs and two heels against its buttocks; its head lies between its knees; its mouth is closed and its navel is open."[12]

According to the Talmud, no time a person spends is better than the time he spends in the womb,[13] and for good reason. The child in the womb is taught the entire Torah, but when it is time to be born, an angel comes and strikes him on his mouth, causing him to forget what he learned. Moreover, before entering the world, the child must vow to be righteous and not wicked, and even if the entire world may someday proclaim that he is righteous, the child must still consider himself wicked (so that he may still become even better).[14] This beautiful legend, claiming that man attains his highest level of spiritual life while in the womb, may explain the great amount of care and devotion for the unborn child that is evident in the laws regarding the status of the fetus and the Halakhah relating to abortion.

Halakhah stipulates that a fetus disqualifies its mother (if she is a priest's daughter married to an ordinary Israelite) from eating the *terumah* (gifts of food given to the priests), for if the woman is pregnant (even if her husband dies), it is considered as if he has left behind a descendant. On the other hand, if an Israelite woman married to a *kohen* (priest) becomes pregnant, the fact that she is carrying his child does not entitle her to *terumah*.[15] This point is important, for in the former case the fetus is regarded as an individual in its own right, a concept which has great implications in rulings on abortion. In addition, Halakhah stipulates that a fetus inherits from its father (if he dies) but does not cause the first-born to take less of the inheritance than the double portion alloted before the child is born.[16] Again, in the former portion of this law, we find that the fetus is regarded as an individual who attains his rights at the suitable time.

Finally, a very important concept, forming the basis for all rulings in relation to the status of the fetus, is the viewpoint that even during the first forty days after conception, the embryo which becomes a fetus possesses a soul. An authorized Rabbi should be consulted concerning cases of medical emergencies to save the embryo or the mother.[17] This is indeed remarkable, for it raises the status of the unborn child to that of a "life" and thus entitles the developing fetus to maximum care and protection so that it may become a healthy individual.

BIRTH

Nothing in life is more wondrous than the process of birth. The Halakhah concerning women in labor and the historical descriptions of the birth process in Jewish literature determine the special significance of the exciting moment of delivery.

At the very beginning of creation, God ordained to the parturient woman, "You will bear children with sorrow."[18] This was the eternal punishment for the sin committed by Eve when she ate a fruit from the tree of knowledge. In essence, it was the most fitting retribution, for it is a constant reminder that all of creation is a blend of pain and ecstasy, just as the life that follows is filled with happiness and sorrow.

In the historical descriptions of birth, there are women who suffered from contractions and those who had painless deliveries. In biblical times, it was thought that labor with a male child was more difficult than with a female, as in the case of Rachel: "And it came to pass, as she was hard in labor, that the midwife told her, 'Fear not; thou shalt have this son also.'"[19] Rachel actually died during or immediately after childbirth. A woman giving birth is described by Isaiah as "bending over with pain, for the contractions have overcome her."[20] In Psalms, we find the association of extreme pain with labor contractions: "they were seized with pain like a woman in labor."[21] The prophet Micah expresses himself in a similar manner: "Be in pain and labor, O daughter of Zion, like a woman during childbirth."[22] The Talmud notes that three voices are heard from one corner of the earth to the other, and one of them is the cry of a woman giving birth to a child.[23] The Talmud also offers an explanation for death during childbirth: "Women die during childbirth for having committed three sins: If they have not been careful to fulfill the *mitzvot* of *niddah* [purification], *challah,* and lighting the Sabbath candles." Rabbah explains that the woman's misconduct is accumulated and she is punished all at once at a time when she is most vulnerable.[24]

On the other hand, we learn that Sarah had no "trouble" during her pregnancy or delivery.[25] The Talmud gives the example of Jochebed, whose pregnancy and labor were painless, and concludes from this that righteous women are exempt from the verdict passed on Eve.[26]

It was known that the primapara had longer and more severe contractions: "For I have heard a voice of a woman in labor, and the anguish of her that bringeth forth her first child."[27] The mechanics of the labor process are explained in the Talmud as follows: "In the first three months, the embryo dwells in the bottom section; in the middle three, it dwells in the middle; and in the last three months, in the top section. When the time comes for him to be born, he turns over and comes out into the world."[28] It is explained that a muscular force dilates the mouth of the uterus so that the baby can pass into the birth canal and finally into the outside world. Labor pains are first felt in the loins.[29] Moreover, a common sign of labor, the "bloody show," is mentioned in the Talmud.[30]

According to the descriptions in the Bible, women in the process of childbirth either kneeled or sat on someone's knees.[31] A woman in labor flexed her thighs against her groin in the effort to expel the baby.[32] An important sign of childbirth is the fact that the woman's groin becomes as cold as stone.[33] This sign is mentioned as critical in the deliveries assisted by the midwife Puah in Egypt. As Puah's role in the process was to "call out" to the mother, this might be a reference to natural-childbirth techniques similar to the modern Lamaze method of breathing exercises, which are known to have a numbing effect on the muscles and the groin (and thus provide evidence that the delivery is progressing well).

In addition to normal deliveries, we find evidence of obstetrical operations such as the Caesarean section carried out in cases of difficult labor.[34] A child born in this manner (*yotze dofan*, "through unnatural conditions") does not render his mother impure. According to Maimonides, a woman who gives birth through Caesarean section cannot have another child,[35] but according to Rabbenu Gershom the Caesarean section does not prevent another pregnancy.[36]

A description of the operation is given by Rabbi Yochanan, who states that the incision was carried out in the "fifth space" on the right side of the abdomen.[37] According to a talmudic commentary, the term Caesarean was applied to the operation because the first Roman emperor was born in that manner.[38] The Caesarean section was most commonly performed in an effort to save the child when a woman died during childbirth. In fact, according to Mar Samuel, it is permitted to perform this operation even on the Sabbath in order to extract the child.[39]

In addition to the Caesarean section, the Talmud knows of breech presentations, regarding them as abnormal.[40]

The version in which the midwife or doctor grasps the child in the uterus and turns it upside down in order to assure a normal delivery (if the baby presents itself abnormally) is mentioned in the biblical account of the delivery of Tamar's twins: "And it came to pass, when she was in labor, that one put out his hand."[41]

Halakhah affords all possible conditions for a delivery that is safe and normal for both mother and child. If a woman begins labor on the Sabbath, it is permitted to desecrate the holy day for her sake by calling for a midwife, and the midwife may cut the navel on the Sabbath. Since a woman in labor (*yoledah*) is considered to have similar but not identical legal status as a sick person in mortal danger, all her needs must be attended to even on the Sabbath. The Talmud states that it is even permitted to light a candle for a blind woman in the process of delivery if this will soothe her (she will be relieved to know that those assisting her have light). However, in all cases, if it is possible, the manner of performing such acts should be changed, in honor of the Sabbath.[42] The parturient woman attains this status as soon as she sits on the birth stool, or when she has a bloody show, or when her friends carry her. If any of these circumstances exists, one may desecrate the Sabbath on her behalf.[43]

A woman who has given birth (a *yoledet*) is considered to have a similar status as a sick person in mortal danger.[44] As long as her womb is open (which is for the first three days after birth), one may desecrate the Sabbath for her sake if she requires something, whether she asks for it or not. Once her womb closes, this no longer applies. From the fourth to the seventh day after birth, one may desecrate the Sabbath for her sake only if she specifically asks for it; if she states that she does not require it, one must not desecrate the Sabbath for her sake. From the eighth day up to the thirtieth day, she is considered as a sick person who is not in mortal danger, and one must not desecrate the Sabbath for her sake.[45]

A woman who gives birth on the seventh day of Tishri (i.e., three days before the fast) may not be compelled to eat on Yom Kippur, for she is then considered to have the status of a sick person who is not in mortal danger. The period during which she is considered to be in mortal danger is three days including the first day of delivery. As far as this ruling is concerned, it is the number of days that is considered and not the exact time of birth,[46] so that most sages rule that she is required to fast.

If a woman had difficult labor, it was the custom to bring a Torah scroll to the doorstep of her home, but bringing the Torah scroll into the house, was not permitted. The Torah's presence was to maintain a watch over her, but this was not to be considered a good-luck symbol.[47]

Certain customs have developed to provide psychological support during childbirth. In some communities, it was the custom to draw a circle of chalk or charcoal on the floor around the bed of the parturient woman, or to hang posters with relevant portions from the Psalms and the names of our forefathers around her bed.[48] Verse 121 of Psalms is considered appropriate for the occasion. Special prayers were recited in the synagogue for a safe delivery and the mother's recovery.[49]

The midwife (called *meyaledet* in the Bible and *chakhamah*, "wise one," in the Talmud) played an important role in childbirth. She carried out medical functions, as we noted in the birth of Benjamin, and even performed obstetrical operations, as in the case of the twins born to Tamar. She also had the function of caring for the child immediately after delivery.[50] The Bible mentions two midwives during the period of bondage in Egypt, Shiphrah and Puah. According to the Talmud and Midrash they assisted in the delivery and cared for the neonates.[51] As we have seen, Puah would call out the mother's name, thus assisting in delivery, while Shiphrah would soothe and cleanse the baby.

The function fulfilled by Shiphrah is especially interesting, for it would seem to imply that special care was taken to spare the newborn child any unnecessary trauma and to make the entrance into the new world as pleasant as possible (perhaps an antecedent to the modern Leboyer method). Another role specific to the midwife was to serve as one of the three persons entitled to decide in cases of doubt concerning the identification of the firstborn, especially when twins were born.[52]

THE NEONATE

The care of the neonate immediately after birth consisted of cutting the umbilical cord, bathing the baby, rubbing it with salt, and swaddling it.[53] The salt was applied to the baby's skin to make it harden.[54] All these actions must be done even on the Sabbath.[55] The baby was swaddled to straighten out its limbs, which had been somewhat deformed during delivery.[56] Similarly, the baby's head was manipulated in order to bring it back to its proper shape following the elongating due to delivery. Hillel comments that the Babylonians had round heads because their midwives were not competent enough to bring the head to its proper shape.

The entrance of a new individual into the world marks a link in the continuing chain of human development, with all the hope and promise accorded by a new life. "Man enters and departs from the world with loud outcries" as if to announce the importance and contribution of each individual in his own right. The cycle of development in the framework of Judaic thought is summed up in the following statement: "Man enters the world with closed hands, as if to say, 'The world is mine.' He leaves it with open hands, as if to say, 'Behold, I take nothing with me'" (*Ecclesiastes Rabbah* 5:21).

NONVIOLENT BIRTH

According to several Jewish sources, the birth process was carried out as smoothly as possible and with the least amount of trauma to the newborn child. The midwives had an important role in the "nonviolent birth," as we note in the Talmud. The famous midwife Shiphrah was given that name (derived from the Hebrew *le-shaper,* "to cleanse and appease") because it was her duty to cleanse, soothe, and appease the neonate immediately after birth. While the Jews were in Egypt, the women gave birth in natural surroundings, under an apple tree (to assure their safety and provide a calm atmosphere for the momentous occasion). Although there were special circumstances during the period of exile in Egypt (*Sotah* 11b), it is quite probable that this principle and the calm treatment of the neonate were similar throughout the biblical period and in later Jewish history, for we find in the *Pesikta de Rav Kahana* (IX, 77b) that everyone kissed and cuddled the neonate even though he was still covered with blood and mucous. This was an antecedent of the modern Leboyer method of nonviolent childbirth. We even find reference in the Bible that the father was present at birth and was presented with the newborn,[57] although the father is not permitted to view the actual birth. An authorized Rabbi should be consulted regarding the halakha concerning the father's presence during the actual birth.

As we have seen, the occasion of childbirth warrants the desecration of the Sabbath if necessary to save the mother or the child. The Responsa literature considers conditions of birth which warrant such an allowance:[58] "If the hair and nails are found as they should be in a full-term baby, then the infant is viable even if born during the eighth month." In fact, the Talmud notes, even a six-and-one-half-month baby can live.[59] This must have entailed sophisticated techniques for the care of a premature child. Nevertheless, Rav Abbahu states that a premature infant cannot be considered viable until it has reached its twentieth year.[60]

It is interesting to note that the Midrash gives the average length of a neonate as a little over an *ammah kedumah,* about 18 inches, corresponding to the average length of the newborn in our times (about 20 inches).[61]

POSTPARTUM CONVALESCENCE

Following delivery, the mother begins her period of recovery, determined by Halakhah as from three to thirty days. As we have seen, the cycle of development is closely linked with the concepts of purity based on the principle of partnership between the Almighty and man in the act of creation. It is fitting, therefore, that the period of recovery is characterized by laws regulating this cycle. The law is stipulated in the Bible as follows: a woman who has given birth to a male child is considered a *niddah* for seven days and she is to count another thirty-three days of purification. A woman who has given birth to a girl is considered a *niddah* for fourteen days and she must count sixty-six days of purification. Following this period of purification, the woman was to bring certain required sacrifices to the Temple.[62] The Talmud explains that the woman is required to bring sacrifices because it is probable that during labor, she vowed never to have relations with her husband again, and since this is a vow she will regret later on, she must bring a sacrifice.[63]

In accordance with the Code of Jewish Law, a woman remains impure as a result of childbirth for seven days after giving birth to a boy and fourteen days after the birth of a girl, assuming there is no blood flow. Following this period, she must count seven days and then immerse herself in the *mikveh*. Some communities follow the more strict formula of waiting forty days following the birth of a boy and eighty days following the birth of a girl before immersion in the *mikveh*. However, one should not follow the more strict version where it is not the custom.[64]

It is interesting to note that according to modern medical knowledge, it takes about six weeks of rest for the reproductive tract to return to its normal state as it was before the pregnancy.[65]

The Halakhah concerning the puerperium (*yoledet*) assures the young mother the maximum conditions for rest after childbirth, thus completing the cycle of development in which man is a partner to the Creator, and allowing for a new cycle to begin.

4
Welcoming the Newborn

BERIT MILAH

"Concerning five things the word "covenant" is written: circumcision, the rainbow, salt, chastisements, and the priesthood."[1] There is no act in the universe more capable of bringing man the secret of the existence in the image of God than the fulfillment of the *mitzvah* of circumcision (Hebrew, *milah*). "Happy are the Children of Israel! They willingly offer their male children as a sacrifice to God on the eighth day of their birth. The circumcision brings them into the good estate of God."[2]

The ceremony of circumcision officially binds the Jewish child to a life in the framework of Judaism, sealing the covenant with God in the flesh of the newborn so that it may never be violated. "God is the Lord of the Covenant, the Torah is the Book of the Covenant, and circumcision is the Son of the Covenant."[3]

When a Jewish child is circumcised on the eighth day of life, he becomes a complete human being. "Rabbi Bar Abba said: The name Avram adds up to 243 in gematria, while the name Abraham adds up to 248. At first God gave Abraham full rein over 243 limbs, and after he was circumcised, he had control over all 248. The additional five are his two eyes, his two ears, and the mind."[4]

In other words, up to that point, Abraham worshipped God with the limbs in his control, for man sees, hears, and thinks things that are beyond his control. When Abraham joined in the covenant of the Almighty and gained complete control over his body, he was free to see, hear, and think by choice in accordance with the will of God. So it is with each newborn child; upon sealing the covenant with God, he becomes master of his own life as an individual created in the image of the Almighty. Judaism envisages this life as a series of stages leading to higher levels of sanctity. The covenant is a sign that the force of the Almighty is active in the body as well as the soul.[5]

Circumcision is such a basic element of Judaism that "the child does not enter into account in his generation unless he is circumcised."[6] Moreover, "The covenant of circumcision is considered as important as all the *mitzvot* in the Torah together."[7]

The fulfillment of the covenant of circumcision is the reason for the survival of the Jews throughout their traumatic history: "Time and Byzantium will become but a memory, but the nation which practices circumcision will endure forever."[8]

The rite of circumcision is the second commandment to appear in the Bible. "Every male among you shall be circumcised. And you shall be circumcised in the flesh of your foreskin, and it shall be a token of a covenant between Me and you, and your children after you; every male shall be circumcised."[9] Later on the commandment appears again: "On the eighth day the flesh of his foreskin shall be circumcised."[10]

Why was this commandment given? If the Almighty had created men circumcised, man would never have the capability to perfect himself. The Berith Milah hints that just as man perfects his own body, he also has the power and possibility of perfecting his soul through his deeds.

Finally, it is said that the root of the commandment of circumcision is the Almighty's wish that there to be a permanent sign among the people He had separated from all nations to be named after Him. Just as the Israelites are separated from others in the form of their soul, so they will be separated in the form of their body—specifically in the limb which is the means of procreation.[11]

The commandment of circumcision applies to all Jews in every corner of the globe at all times. The responsibility of circumcising male children rests on the father and not the mother. If the father neglects this duty, the *bet din* is ordained to fulfill it. If there is no father, the *bet din* has the responsibility of circumcising the child. The circumcision may be performed by any Jew, but it is better if the person who carries out the circumcision (the *mohel*) is a pious Jew. In cases where a male *mohel* is lacking, a woman may perform the circumcision (as in the case of Zipporah, who circumcised Moses' son).[12]

In accordance with the Code of Jewish Law, the *mohel* must know the laws of circumcision specified in the Talmud and by later rabbinic authorities.[13] The *mohel* must also be capable of examining the infant to determine whether he is healthy enough to undergo circumcision (in addition to the required examination by the doctor or midwife who assisted in the delivery).[14]

If the father knows how to perform the circumcision, it is his prime responsibility to do so. If he does not have the knowledge or experience required, he may and usually does relegate his duty to a qualified *mohel*.[15] In the talmudic period the *mohel* was a qualified surgeon and there was a special street where the professional circumcisers lived.[16] Contemporary circumcisers must receive training in asepsis and in the method of circumcision as well as rabbinic recognition.

THE CEREMONY

The festivities accompanying the circumcision ceremony begin on the Friday night after the birth. At this time relatives and friends come to the home of the child's parents to participate in the happy event[17] and also to console the infant for having forgotten everything he had learned while in his mother's womb. The guests recite psalms and biblical passages relevant to the occasion.[18] This happy event is called the *shalom zakhar* because it celebrates the safe birth of the child on the Sabbath, which is called *Shalom*. According to the Code of Jewish Law, it is a *mitzvah* to attend the *shalom zakhar,* and it is customary for all male friends and relatives to attend.[19] Various cakes, fruits, and other delicacies are served, as well as the symbolic lentils to mark the cycle of life.

Following the *shalom zakhar* is another festivity on the eve of the circumcision ceremony. This is the *vachnacht,* or "night of the guard," when the *mohel,* the *sandak,* and close relatives and friends again gather at the home of the proud parents to recite psalms and prayers to ward off Lilith and other demons who are after the souls of infants before they are circumcised, in order to prevent the fulfillment of the *mitzvah.*[20] It is customary for schoolchildren to come and recite the *Shema* and the biblical passage: "The angel which redeemed me from all evil, bless the children. . . ."[21] A Bible is placed under the mattress of the infant while the parents recite the hopeful prayer that their child will perform everything that is written in the Bible. In some communities it is the custom to place a book of a learned sage under the mattress so that the child will grow up to be a wise scholar. It is customary to maintain a watch over the infant until after midnight. On this occasion as well, the parents serve wine and all sorts of delicacies to display their happiness at fulfilling the commandment of *milah.*

On the eve of the *milah,* the *mohel* examines the child to determine whether he is fit for the operation. The actual ceremony takes place on the eighth day after birth. Although, technically, it may take place any time in the day, it is more desirable that it be performed in the morning after prayers, to emulate Abraham's eagerness to carry out the *mitzvah* on the same day that the Lord spoke to him.[22] The performance of *milah* on the eighth day for a healthy child has precedence over the laws determining the sanctity of the Sabbath and other festivals. Nevertheless, all technical preparations, such as bringing the necessary equipment to the place of the circumcision, must be done before the Sabbath.[23] This includes preparing a bowl with earth in which to place the foreskin to commemorate the Lord's promise to multiply the Jewish people like the earth and sand.

As this is such a joyful occasion, marking the birth of the son and the fulfillment of a basic *mitzvah*, it is customary to share the privilege with honored guests. The *shoshbinim* are a couple chosen to assist in bringing the child into the synagogue. The woman brings the infant into the women's section or to the site where the *milah* is to take place, and the man then takes him from her arms and brings him to the place where the *milah* is to be performed. (The *shoshbinim* are also called *kvaterin*.)

As the child is brought into the room, all those present welcome him with the greeting *Barukh ha-ba*. Since the numerical equivalent of the word *ha-ba* is eight, the greeting has a special meaning suitable for the occasion: "blessed is he who is circumcised on the eighth day of life."[24]

According to the Code of Jewish Law, it is desirable for at least ten males to be present at the ceremony, but if this is not possible, the *milah* may be performed with fewer in attendance. The guests remain standing during the actual performance of the circumcision to commemorate the fact that the Jewish nation stood when the covenant with God was sealed.[25]

Before the *mohel* begins the technical surgery, an honored guest takes the child from the arms of the *shoshbin* and places him on a special ornate chair set aside as "Elijah's chair." This symbolic act is a part of each *berit milah* ceremony to honor the prophet Elijah, who is considered the Angel of the Covenant because he fought for the fulfillment of the commandment at a time when the kingdom of Ephraim had neglected it. For this reason, it is said that the Almighty promised Elijah that he would be present at each *milah* performed for a Jewish child. The following blessing is recited: "This chair is devoted to Elijah the prophet, may his remembrance be for the good."

Another honored guest lifts the child from Elijah's chair and places him on the lap of the *sandak* (the Jewish godfather). The *sandak* holds the infant throughout the ceremony. Before the circumcision is performed, the following blessings are recited: If the father himself performs the *milah*, he says: "I am ready and willing to perform the commandment . . . which the Creator, praised be He, commanded me to circumcise my son." If a professional *mohel* is delegated to perform the *milah,* he says: "Praised be Thou, O Lord our God, King of the Universe, who hast sanctified us with Thy commandments, and commanded us concerning the rite of circumcision."

The circumcision is performed, and immediately before *periah* the father (or the *sandak* if there is no father) recites: "Praised be Thou, O Lord our God, King of the Universe, who has sanctified us by Thy commandments, and hast bidden us to make him enter into the covenant of Abraham our father." Those assembled at the *milah* reply: "As he has been entered into the covenant, so may he be introduced to the study of the Torah, to the marriage canopy, and to good deeds."

After *periah* and *metzitzah,* the circumciser takes a goblet of wine and recites: "Praised be Thou, O Lord our God, King of the Universe, who hast created the fruit of the vine." He continues with a blessing for the welfare of the newborn and the naming formality:

> Praised be Thou, O Lord our God, King of the Universe, who hast sanctified the well-beloved (Isaac) from the womb and hast set Thy statute in his flesh, and hast sealed his offspring with the sign of the holy covenant. Therefore, because of this, O living God, our portion and our rock, command that the dearly beloved of our flesh be delivered from destruction for the sake of the covenant Thou has set in our bodies. Praised be Thou, O Lord our God, who hast made the covenant.
>
> Our God and God of our Fathers, preserve this child to his father and to his mother, and let his name be called in Israel ____ son of ____. Let the father rejoice in his offspring, and let the mother be glad with her children; as it is written: "Let thy father and thy mother rejoice, let her that bore thee be glad." And it is said: "And I passed by thee, and I saw thee weltering in thy blood, and I said unto thee: 'In thy blood thou shalt live.' Yea, I said, 'In thy blood thou shalt live.'"

The Foundations of Development

Next the circumciser places a few drops of wine on the lips of the infant and continues:

> And it is said: "He has remembered his covenant forever, the word which He commanded to a thousand generations: which he made with Abraham, and his oath with Isaac, and established it as Law with Jacob to Israel for a lasting covenant." And it is said: "And Abraham circumcised his son Isaac when he was eight days old, as God commanded him." O give thanks to the Lord, for He is good, for his loving-kindness endures forever. This little child—may he become great. As he has been entered into the covenant, so may he be introduced to the study of the Torah, to the nuptial canopy and to good deeds.

This is followed by a solemn prayer recited by the circumciser while standing:

> Creator of the Universe, may it be Thy gracious will to accept this [*milah*] as if I had brought the infant before Thy glorious throne. And Thou, in Thy abundant mercy, send through Thy holy angels a holy and pure heart to ____ son of ____ who was just now circumcised in honor of Thy great name. And may his heart be wide open to accept Thy Torah, that he may learn and teach, keep and carry out Thy laws.

The ceremony is concluded at this point with a special prayer for the infant:

> May He who blessed our fathers, Abraham, Isaac, and Jacob, bless this tender infant who was circumcised and cure him completely; may his parents (or relatives) have the privilege to raise him up to the study of the Torah, to the wedding canopy, and to good deeds, and let us say, Amen.

Those assembled then recite *Aleinu le-shabbe'ach* to conclude the morning prayers—and to include the circumcised infant in the community as a full-fledged Jew.[26]

The *milah* itself involves the amputation of the foreskin with a double-edged knife,[27] thus disclosing the mucous membrane. The *mohel* grasps the edge of the mucous membrane firmly between the thumbnail and the index finger of his hand and tears down swiftly through the center as far as the cornea. This manual technique is called the *periah*. The goal of this surgery, as we have seen, is to complete the form of the human being by removing the foreskin, which is an unnecessary addition. Finally, the *mohel* performs the *metzitzah* (or suction), which is intended to remove the blood from other parts of the wound.[28] *Metzitzah* is considered by some rabbinical authorities not to be part of the actual *mitzvah* but rather for medical reasons, to ensure the safe healing of the wound.[29] Therefore, even though the father may in many instances perform the circumcision, the *metzitzah* is done by someone else.[30] The technical procedure must be carried out in accordance with Jewish Law.

After the circumcision ceremony, the *kvatterin* takes the infant from the *mohel* and hands him back to the mother. The guests then wash their hands and sit down to a festive feast, which according to the Code of Jewish Law should be prepared bountifully in order to commemorate the festive meal prepared by Abraham on the occasion of the circumcision of Isaac.[31] All three ceremonies celebrated in connection with circumcision (*shalom zakhar, vachnacht,* and *milah*) are carried out in a merry spirit, just as the Jewish nation accepted this commandment with joy.[32]

As the *milah* celebration began with honored guests actively participating in the commandment, it is concluded by delegating various passages of the Grace After the Meal to honored guests. At the end of the Grace, the following passages are recited:

> May the All-Merciful bless the father and the mother of the

child: may he be worthy to rear him, to educate him, and grant him wisdom; from this eighth day on, may his blood be accepted and may the Almighty be with him.

May the Almighty bless the godfather who has overseen the circumcision, and has delighted to perform this act of piety; may He reward him for this with a double recompense, and always exalt him more and more.

May the All-Merciful bless the tender infant who has been circumcised on the eighth day of life, and may his hands and heart be firm with the Almighty, and may he be worthy to appear before the Shekhinah [Divine Presence] three times a year.

The *berit milah* ceremony is a most fitting beginning for a Jewish child's life, for it constitutes an induction into the world of Judaism in a spirit of joy through the fulfillment of a basic *mitzvah*.

HALAKHIC RULINGS AND SPECIAL CASES

We have seen that *milah* is a basic commandment in Judaism, equal to all the other *mitzvot* together. Because of its special importance in Jewish life, the Code of Jewish Law stipulates that one must be very, very careful not to circumcise an infant who is ill. The life of the individual has precedence over all other laws; while it is possible to circumcise a child at another time, it is impossible to revive a soul who is lost. Specific laws concerning when it is possible to circumcise a child who is ill during the primary date for *milah* on the eighth day of life and recuperates later on appear in *Yoreh De'ah* 262-263.[33] Technically, one must circumcise the child seven days after he has been determined to be healthy.[34]

The following rulings in such cases have been summarized by one source in the "Laws Concerning Medicine and Medical Practitioners"[35] As there are extensive controversies about jaundice, a Rabbi should be consulted in all these cases:

1. A "yellow baby" who has even the slightest degree of jaundice must not be circumcised as long as jaundice is seen on his body, even if the doctor has determined that it is receding. If the jaundice has receded from most of the infant's body and the color is back to normal, and if the doctor determines that it is possible to perform circumcision, the *milah* may be performed. If the cause of jaundice is physiological and the above conditions exist, it is possible to circumcise immediately without waiting another seven days. If the jaundice was caused by illness, the seven-day recuperating period must be maintained before circumcision.
2. If the infant has received a blood transfusion, a seven-day recuperating period must precede circumcision, even if the doctor determines that the baby is healthy before the end of seven days.
3. If the infant is receiving antibiotics for an infection, he may be circumcised seven days after completion of the treatment. However, if the doctor determines that the child is healthy before the treatment is completed, the seven days may be counted from that time.
4. If an infant has even the slightest fever, he is considered ill and must not be circumcised until seven days after the temperature has completely disappeared. However, if the temperature is caused by an outside factor, such as the high room temperature or the fact that the baby has "dried up" and his temperature will disappear as soon as he drinks water, he is not considered sick and may be circumcised on time.
5. If there is a secretion from the infant's eyes, and it has been determined after medical and laboratory tests to be sterile, circumcision must be postponed until after it stops completely, but the seven-day waiting period is not necessary.
6. An incubator baby must be circumcised seven days after being removed from the incubator even if the doctor determines that he is healthy beforehand. Nevertheless, low

weight is not considered a sickness, and the infant may be circumcised as soon as he attains a weight which in medical opinion is suitable for circumcision.
7. If the baby was born through a forceps delivery and his head is swollen, or if his hands or legs were pulled in the process of delivery, it is possible to circumcise him on time if the doctors determine that he is not ill, and if he will not suffer from this condition. He may be circumcised on time if the operation will not have a deleterious effect on this temporary handicap; otherwise circumcision must be postponed.

It is interesting to note that the talmudic scholars were aware of the consequences of circumcision for a hemophiliac—an infant who has inherited a blood disease from the mother. Accordingly, talmudic law stipulates that if the mother has lost two sons as a result of circumcision, or if two sisters each lose one child after *milah,* subsequent male children born to either of them or to another sister are not to be circumcised until they are determined medically fit for the operation.[36]

Concerning the performance of the circumcision, the "Tzitz Eliezer" rules out the use of the Mogen clamp and the Gumco clamp in the actual surgery.[37] Indeed, it has been found that the traditional manual technique causes the least pain to the infant.

The question of whether anesthesia may be used, so that the infant will not feel any pain during circumcision, is considered in the Responsa literature. We find that partial anesthesia to the area involved may be permitted, however, the use of general anesthesia is controversial because it is like sealing a covenant with a stone, which does not feel anything, and not with a human being. Such a covenant would have no validity. In addition, it is not permitted to perform circumcision on a sleeping baby, for this is considered wounding the child.[38]

If the child was born through Caesarean section and the eighth day of birth falls on the second day of the New Year, circumcision must be postponed to the following day.[39] If the birth was normal and occurred during the twilight hours, rabbinical authorities should be consulted as to the day of circumcision.[40]

The importance that Judaism attaches to circumcision is ingrained in the very essence of the Jewish people. Throughout Jewish history, from the Roman period through the Nazi terror, we find that Jews sacrificed their lives in order to perform this *mitzvah*.

Modern medical research has discovered that when circumcision is performed in infancy, it offers almost complete protection against the development of cancer of the penis in later life (as well as cancer of the cervix in women). Circumcision also provides protection against inflammation of the prepuce and glans. Despite the medical benefits, circumcision is *not performed as a medical operation, but as a basic mitzvah* that opens the gate of Judaism for every newborn Jewish male. In all questions about the timing of the *berit milah* and other problems, a Rabbi must be consulted.

PIDYON HA-BEN

Judaism grants a special status to the firstborn male child. In every home, the birth of the first child is a special occasion preceded by preparations and a sense of excitement. The parents' attitude toward the newborn is usually one of awe mixed with doubt and hope that they are "doing the right thing." With the birth of subsequent children, the feelings are more settled, and preparations become more routine. The special excitement and wonder accompanying the birth of the firstborn male is captured in Judaism in the special ceremony for the redemption of the first son, *pidyon ha-ben*.

One explanation given for this commandment is that it commemorates the great miracle that took place in Egypt when the Almighty killed all the firstborn Egyptian males and spared the Jewish sons.[41]

Furthermore, the firstborn male child has special rights concerning inheritance and a certain religious obligation to fast on the eve of Passover. This stems from the historic fact that the Almighty sanctified the firstborn males of the Jewish people while they were still in bondage in Egypt, so that they would devote their lives as priests in the Tabernacle and the Temple. This is interpreted by Kitov as a reward for the faith and trust in God displayed by the Jewish people, who fulfilled the commandment of circumcision and the Passover sacrifice while in Egypt and under the difficult conditions imposed upon them. As the entire nation proved their loyalty to God by joining the covenant, the Almighty did not isolate the entire nation for the priesthood but only their firstborn, as it is written: "Sanctify each firstborn male child to Me, among the children of Israel."[42]

However, since the firstborn males joined the nation in their act of worshipping the golden calf in the desert, the Almighty replaced them with the Levites, ordaining: "And each firstborn male child shall be redeemed";[43] "And you shall take the Levites for Me, the Almighty, instead of each firstborn male child in Israel."[44]

The sanctity of the firstborn is retained in his birthright and in the religious regulations specific to him, such as the *pidyon ha-ben* ceremony and the obligation to fast on the eve of Passover.[45]

The ceremony for the redemption of the firstborn is a *mitzvah* bound in religious law. The root of this *mitzvah* is that by performing the determined symbolic act of redeeming his firstborn male child from the Almighty, man acknowledges that all belongs to the Creator and that man has only that which God wishes to bestow upon him.

It is the duty of the father to redeem the son, and the mother is not responsible for fulfilling this commandment. If redemption is neglected or omitted for any reason, the *bet din* may compel the father to do so. The responsibility rests on the father forever,[46] but if he does not fulfill this *mitzvah*, the son must redeem himself after he has reached the age of maturity (*bar mitzvah*).

Since an infant is not considered viable until after the thirtieth day of life, the redemption ceremony must take place thirty-one days after birth. If the thirty-first day of life falls on a Sabbath or festival, the ceremony is postponed to the following day. It is desirable for the father to hasten to fulfill the *mitzvah* as soon as it is time to do so.[47]

The father redeems his son by giving a priest the equivalent of five *shekalim*.[48] The exact amount is determined by the rabbinical authorities in each Jewish community. The redemption equivalent may be given in the form of other belongings, except for property and legal notes.[49]

THE CEREMONY

The *pidyon ha-ben* ceremony is a significant event for the parents, relatives, and friends of the male firstborn. The infant is specially dressed for the occasion in his best formal outfit and is bedecked with jewels and ornaments. In some communities, it is customary to lay the child on a special silver platter for the ceremony. The father brings the child before the priest (*kohen*) and places the five *shekalim* before him. The father then declares:

> This, my firstborn son, is the firstborn of his mother, and the Holy One, blessed be He, hath commanded to redeem him, as it is said, "And those that are to be redeemed of them from a month old shalt thou redeem, according to thine estimation, for the money of five shekels, after the shekel of the sanctuary, the shekel being twenty gerahs" [Num. 18:15]. And it is said, "Sanctify unto Me all the firstborn, whatsover openeth the womb among the children of Israel, both of man and of beast; it is Mine" [Exod. 13:2].

The *kohen* then asks the father whether his wife has ever had a miscarriage or given birth to a child. The father replies, "No." The father then lays the child before the *kohen* and the latter

The Foundations of Development

asks him: "Which wouldst thou rather, give me thy firstborn son, the firstborn of the mother, or redeem him for five *shekalim*, which thou are bound to give according to the Torah?" The father replies: "I want to redeem my son, and here is the value of his redemption; which I am obliged to give according to the Torah." The father then holds the redemption money in his hand and before handing it over to the kohen, he recites:

> Blessed art thou, O Lord, our God, King of the Universe, who hast sanctified us by Thy commandments and given us command concerning the redemption of the firstborn son.
> Blessed art thou, O Lord our God, King of the Universe, who hast kept us in life and hast preserved us and enabled us to reach this occasion."

The *kohen* then receives the money and holds it over the head of the child while reciting:

> This is instead of that, this substitutes for that, this in remission of that. May this child enter into life, the Torah, and the fear of heaven. May it be God's will that even as he has been admitted to redemption, so may he enter into the Torah, the nuptial canopy and into good deeds. Amen.

The *kohen* then places his hand on the child's head and recites the following benediction:

> May God make thee as Ephraim and Manasseh. The Lord bless thee and keep thee; the Lord make His face shine upon thee, and be gracious unto thee; the Lord turn His face unto thee, and give thee peace.
> The Lord is thy guardian; the Lord is thy shade upon thy right hand. For length of days, and years of life and peace shall they add to thee. The Lord shall guard thee from all evil; He shall guard thy soul. Amen.

It is customary for the *kohen* to recite the blessings over wine and in some communities over myrtles, immediately following the benedictions.[50]

Following the ceremony, it is customary to invite the guests to a festive dinner which is a *seudat mitzvah*. The usual custom is for the *pidyon ha-ben* ceremony to take place after the guests have washed and recited the blessing over bread, before they actually sit down for the festive meal.[51]

As the status of the firstborn depends upon the mother, it is interesting to note that one source describes a *pidyon ha-ben* ceremony in which the mother participates in her own right. The order of the ceremony is as described above, but the rabbis taught that the following prayer is recited at the beginning of the "negotiation" for redemption: The *kohen* begins by saying:

> Blessed art Thou, O Lord our God, who has sanctified the fetus in his mother's womb, and on the fortieth day from conception divided his limbs into 248 limbs, and then gave him a soul as is written: "And God gave man a soul" [Gen. 2:7]. He dressed him in skin and covered him with bones as is written: "Thou hast clothed me in skin and flesh, and Thou hast covered me with bones and veins" [Job, 10:11]. And the Lord commanded that he be supplied with food and drink, honey and milk for him to enjoy, and ordered two guardian angels to watch over him in his mother's womb, as is written: "Thou hast given me life and goodness . . ." [Job 10:12].

The mother then recites the following declaration: "This is my firstborn son, with whom the Almighty hath opened the doors of my womb." The father follows by pronouncing: "This is my firstborn son, whom I am warned to redeem, as is written: 'And every firstborn male child shall be redeemed' [Exod. 13:13]." The benedictions that follow are those described for the contemporary ceremony.

The occasion of the *pidyon ha-ben* is enhanced by the beautiful prayers composed for the celebration, which takes place one month after birth, when both the parents as well as their friends and relatives can enjoy the festivities.

HALAKHIC RULINGS AND SPECIAL CASES

The father is obliged to redeem his firstborn male son who is the first son to his wife, as it is written: "Every first issue of the mother's womb—among human beings and beasts—is Mine."[52] If the firstborn is born to his mother after a miscarriage, a rabbi should be consulted concerning the requirement for redemption. Usually, if the miscarriage occurred before the fortieth day of pregnancy, the first viable male child must be redeemed. However, if the mother had a miscarriage which rendered her impure according to the Halakhah concerning birth, the firstborn viable male need not be redeemed.[53] A distinction is made on this matter between the firstborn "for the *kohen*" (i.e., who requires redemption) and the firstborn for inheritance privileges, as detailed in tractate *Bechorot*.[54]

A firstborn male child born through Caesarean section is exempt from redemption.

Kohanim and Levites are exempt from redemption. Thus, if a daughter of a *kohen* or a Levite marries an Israelite, her firstborn male child is exempt from the obligation of *pidyon ha-ben*. If she marries a non-Jew, however, her firstborn male child requires redemption, for she has forfeited her sanctity.

Since low weight does not determine the viability of a child if he is not ill, an incubator baby whose low weight has kept him from being circumcised is nevertheless redeemed on time.[55]

The order of the *pidyon ha-ben* ceremony and the halakhic rulings concerning special cases add to the unique quality of this most impressive symbolic act.

THE BLESSING OF THANKS

While the festivities after birth naturally center around the newborn, the mother is never forgotten in Jewish tradition. According to the Code of Jewish Law, women are not exempt from reciting the *birkat ha-gomel* (the blessing of thanks) after being saved from mortal danger or after recuperating from an illness.[56] The occasion of a safe delivery naturally falls into this category. Therefore, it is customary for the mother to come to the synagogue on the Sabbath after she has regained her strength. (In some communities this is done forty days after the birth of a boy and eighty days after the birth of a girl.) At that time, the father rises to read the Torah, and after he recites the second blessing on the Torah, the mother recites the *birkat ha-gomel* from the women's gallery as follows: "Blessed are You, Lord our God, King of the Universe, who does good to the undeserving and who has dealt kindly with me." The other women present answer as follows: "May He who has shown you kindness deal kindly with you forever." (The Hertz prayer book includes a special prayer composed for the occasion.) In many communities only the father recites the blessing.

In other communities, the blessing is recited on the Saturday night after birth, or after the *milah* a *minyan* (ten people) come to pray in the home of the mother, and after the *ma'ariv* prayer the mother recites the blessing and those gathered reply Amen. Yet others maintain that the blessing should be recited during the *milah* ceremony. In this case, it is a unique opportunity for the woman to fulfill the commandment in a *minyan* (a rare occasion), emphasizing the importance of conception in Judaism and the special status awarded to mothers. In some communities the father rises to read the Torah, and the mother answers: "Blessed are Thou, the blessed eternally."

A JEWISH GIRL IS BORN

Although Judaism places great value on the birth of a boy,[57] the arrival of a girl in the family is also celebrated with great joy and love. There are no specific religious rituals as in the case of a boy, however, the birth of a baby girl is marked with a festive naming ceremony which takes place in the synagogue.

It is customary to name the new baby girl on the first Sabbath after birth. The father is given an *aliyah,* and to honor the occasion the cantor recites the benedictions for the mother who has just given birth and for the baby girl "who was born to her with good luck, and whose name shall be in Israel ____." Thus, with the first formal use of her name, the girl's birth is announced to the community in the framework of the synagogue.

In some communities, it is the custom to announce the birth and name the girl in the synagogue on the first Tuesday or Thursday after birth, when the Torah is read in the morning prayers. In yet other communities, the naming ceremony is held thirty days after birth. Following the naming declaration, it is customary to hold a festive Kiddush in the synagogue. Many parents also schedule a special Kiddush on the Sabbath in honor of the occasion.

An interesting statement in the Talmud adds a symbolic note to the fact that the naming ceremony is held at the same time that the father is given an *aliyah*: "Man should be accessible to grant his daughter her needs with kindness."

Despite the fact that a girl's birth does not bring any specific economic benefits for her parents, and does not ensure the continuance of the family name, Judaism attributes great importance to her status as a future "woman of valor"[58] and affords her the same protection and possibilities for development to her maximum capabilities as in the case of boys. Thus, Judaism acknowledges the need for all individuals to receive the care and attention they require according to their needs.[59]

NAMING THE JEWISH CHILD

The name given to a Jewish child is carefully chosen and usually methodically planned. The event of naming is incorporated in the religious ceremonies after birth, and the choice of a name is integrated with Judaic philosophy and the historic or family sentiments of the parents.

The importance attached to names is perhaps best explained by the following passage from the Midrash: "Man has three names: one by which his fond parents call him, another by which he is known to the outside world, and a third, the most important of all, the name which his own deeds have procured for him."[60]

Jewish parents have three main categories of names to choose from. The most common choice is that of a deceased close relative. The custom of naming children after members of the family arose only after the fourteenth century. Often a child is given more than one name so as to commemorate more than one ancestor.

The second category of Jewish names comprises the names of the patriarchs and of prominent historical figures. The Talmud recommends that names be chosen from the list of Jewish patriarchs and prominent personalities[61] but not from the oppressors or enemies of the Jews, as it is stated: "Have you ever seen a person who named his son Pharaoh, Sisera, or Sennacherib? But he calls him Abraham, Isaac, Jacob, Reuben, or Simeon."[62]

Finally, there are foreign names which have been translated into Hebrew throughout the course of history as the Jewish people came in contact with other nations. (Examples of these are Abba (from Aramaic), Alexander (from Greek), Beruria (from Latin), and Shprintze (from French).

Many Hebrew names have some meaning or symbolical significance. The use of a Hebrew name is most important when the person is called to read the Torah in the synagogue or when prayers are recited on his or her behalf, in times of trouble or illness. The Talmud emphasizes that the people of Israel were redeemed from bondage in Egypt as a result of their admirable tenacity in adhering to their Hebrew names even while in exile (as a symbol of their religious identity).[63]

The importance of giving the Jewish child a Hebrew name is also based on the concept that the language of the "celestial court" is Hebrew. This is connected with a custom originating with the kabbalists of the seventeenth century, in which every Jewish child chooses a biblical verse beginning with the first letter of his name and ending with the last letter of his Hebrew name. This verse is recited after the *Shemoneh Esreh* prayer, and it is believed that the soul reports to the celestial angels with this verse in order to advance the processing of its earthly record after death. It is also believed that the Messiah will use the Hebrew names when he calls the dead to arise.

WHEN THE NAME IS GIVEN

The name of a boy is given officially at the *berit milah* after the circumcision. The *mohel* recites the benediction over a cup of wine and stands at the side of the child as he states:[64]

> "Our God, the God of our fathers, preserve this child to his father and mother, and let his name be called in Israel____ the son of ____. Even as he entered into the covenant, so may he enter into the Law, the nuptial canopy, and into good deeds."

A girl's name is given after the infant is three days old when the father is called to read the Torah in the synagogue on the Monday or Thursday following the day of birth. (In some cases, the name is given on the Sabbath when the mother attends the synagogue for the first time after birth.) The Sephardic version of the benediction is as follows:

> May He who blessed Sarah, Rebecca, Rachel, Leah, Miriam the prophetess, Abigail, and Queen Esther, daughter of Abihail, bless this baby girl, and may her name be called ____ the daughter of ____ with a good omen and in a blessed hour.

64   *The Jewish Child: Halakhic Perspectives*

The Ashkenazi version is:

> May He who blessed our fathers, Abraham, Isaac, and Jacob, bless also the mother ____, daughter of ____, and her daughter born with a good omen. May her name in Israel be ____, daughter of ____, and may her parents be privileged to rear her to the marriage canopy, and to a life of good deeds, Amen.

HEBREW NAMES: BOYS

The following list may be helpful to parents who require a guide in choosing a Hebrew name for their newborn child. The names appear in English transliteration in the order of the Hebrew alphabet.

Alef	Isser (Israel)	Oren
Abba	Itzik (Isaac)	Arnon
Avigdor	Itamar	Asher
Aviyah	Eitan	*Bet*
Aviezer	Eldad	Ben Zion
Avimelekh	Elkhanan	Binyamin
Avinoam	Eliyah	Bezalel
Avinadav	Eliyahu	Barukh
Avshalom	Elimelekh	Barak
Avraham	Eliezer	*Gimel*
Avram	Elizur	Givon
Ada	Elyakim	Gavriel
Adam	Alexander*	Gad
Adar	Elazar	Gedaliah
Adir	Elkana	Gedalyahu
Ahuviyah	Elrad	Gideon
Aharon	Amnon	Gil
Uri	Amitai	Gilad
Oren	Assa	Gilon
Oshiyah	Ephraim	Giyora
Ilan	Arieh	Gai

* A name adapted from Greek.

The Foundations of Development

Gamliel	Tivon	Lavi
Gershom	*Yud*	Levi
Gershon	Yoshiyahu	Liron
Daled	Yigal	*Mem*
Dov	Yedidya	Meir
David	Yehoash	Mikhael
Doron	Yehuda	Mikha
Dori	Yehonathan	Melekh
Dan	Yehoshua	Manoah
Daniel	Yoav	Menahem
Hey	Yoel	Menashe
Hod	Yoash	Mordecai
Hoshea	Yokhanan	Moshe
Hillel	Yom-Tov	Meshulam
Harel	Yona	Matanya
Vav	Yonathan	Mati
Volf-Ze'ev	Yotam	Matityahu
Zayin	Yehezkel	*Nun*
Zeev	Tehiel	Nadav
Zevulun	Yaakov	Noah
Zohar	Yiftakh	Noam
Zakai	Yefeth	Nahum
Zekharia	Yitzhak	Nahemia
Zimri	Yekutiel	Nahman
Zerakh	Yarden	Neta
Chet	Yaron	Nimrod
Chizkiyahu	Yakir	Nissim
Chiyya	Yerukham	Nissan
Chayim	Yerakhmiel	Naaman
Chiram	Yirmiyahu	Naftali
Chanan	Yishai	Natan
Chananel	Issachar	Netanya
Chanaya	*Kaf*	Netanel
Chananyahu	Karmi	*Samekh*
Tet	Katriel	Sinai
Tevya	*Lamed*	Saadia
Tuvia	Leor	Sapir

Ayin
Ovadiah
Oded
Ozer
Uzziel
Ezer
Ezra
Azreil
Ezri
Azariah
Eli
Amos
Ami
Amiel
Amihud
Aminadav
Emanuel
Amram
Akiva
Pey
Pinhas
Palti

Paltiel
Pesakh
Peretz
Petahia
Tzadi
Zvi
Tzadok
Tzidkiyahu
Tzidkiahu
Tzuriel
Tzemakh
Tzefania
Kuf
Kadish
Kehath
Kaniel
Karni
Resh
Reuven
Rakhmiel
Rimon
Ran

Rani
Ranon
Raphael
Shin
Saul
Shevakh
Shabtai
Shai
Shalom
Shlomo
Shamai
Shmuel
Simcha
Shimon
Shmaya
Shneyur
Shmaryahu
Shimshon
Shraga
Tav
Tanhum

HEBREW NAMES: GIRLS

Alef
Aviva
Avigayil
Adira
Adiva
Ahuva
Ahuda
Aharona
Ophira

Ora
Orit
Ilana
Iris
Elisheva
Alexandra*
Emuna
Amitza
Osnat

Esther
Ariela
Bet
Bina
Brucha, Bracha
Bruria
Batya
Bat-Ami
Bat-Tzion

* A name adapted from Greek.

The Foundations of Development

Bat-Shua	Chemda	Marganit
Bat-Sheva	Channa	Miriam
Gimel	Chasida	Marnina
Geula	Chasya	Matana
Givra	Cheftzi-Ba	*Nun*
Gavriela	*Tet*	Nediva
Gila	Tova	Nurit
Galit	*Yud*	Nehama
Daled	Yoela	Nili
Dvofa	Yehudit	Nira
Dora	Yochana	Naomi
Dorit	Yochevet	Nitza
Dorona	Yonina	*Samekh*
Dina	Yasmina	Segula
Ditza	Yael	Simona
Dalia	Yaffa	*Ayin*
Daniela	*Lamed*	Adina
Daphna	Leah	Edna
Drorit	Levia	Atara
Hey	Levana	Aliza
Hadas	Lola	Alma
Hadassah	Libi	Amalia
Vav	Liba	Anuga
Vered	Lili	Atalia
Varda	Lirit	*Peh*
Zayin	*Mem*	Penina
Zehava	Meira	*Tzadi*
Zohara	Mazal	Tzivia
Ziva	Maya	Tzipora
Zakka	Michal	Tzefira
Chet	Mina	*Kaf*
Chaviva	Mira	Kalya
Chedva	Malbina	*Resh*
Chava	Menuha	Rivka
Chaya	Margalit	Ronena

Ruth	Shoshana	Tehiya
Ruti	Shira	Telma
Rahel	Shlomit	Temima
Rimona	Shifra	Temira
Rina	Sara	Tamar
Ronia	Sharon	Tirtza
Ranana	Sharona	Tikva
Shin	*Tav*	
Shulamit	Tehila	

Part II
The First Five Years: From Infant to Child

5
Infant and Child Care

The Jewish tradition of infant care is best summarized in the following statement: "A baby should be as well looked after as a king, a high priest, and a learned man."[1]

The Hebrew word for "infant" is *tinok,* which means "suckling." The age span of the term corresponds to the period between eighteen and twenty-four months of life. Modern psychologists note that the period of infancy is at its end when the baby utters a few phrases, while talmudic scholars observed that the child begins to talk at about the time solid food is introduced.[2] Thus, in Judaic literature, the word *tinok* is applied as long as the baby nurses:[3] according to Rabbi Eliezer, the first twenty-four months; and according to Rabbi Joshua, up to five years of age![4] While the recognized period for nursing has diminished since then and most babies receive solid food at the latest by the age of fifteen months, the Hebrew word is still often applied to a child after that period of time to denote a sense of endearment. It thus symbolizes the Judaic philosophy of infant care—a devotion to the newborn based on love and tenderness.

In accordance with Halakhah, the word *tinok* is applied as long as the child still has the same status as a sick person not in mortal danger, allowing certain actions on the Sabbath, otherwise forbidden by rabbinical law, to fulfill his needs. While the Chazon Ish defines this period as the first two or three years of life in normal cases and over that age if the child is still eating baby food,[6] we find that the limit is set at about ten years, depending on the child's state of development and health.[7]

The needs of the infant are aptly summarized in the advice given to Abbaye by his competent and wise nanny: the care and development of the infant requires first that he be bathed and anointed with oil; later, when he grows older, that he be given eggs and dairy products; and when he grows older still, that he be given the freedom to play with toys.[8] This passage includes three principles of infant care as guidelines for the child's healthy development: (1) personal hygiene, (2) adequate nutrition, and (3) developmental play.

PERSONAL CLEANLINESS AND HYGIENE

The emphasis on personal hygiene is better understood if we consider the Judaic viewpoint on the subject. We learn in the Talmud that "cleanliness leads to holiness."[9] Thus, personal hygiene is a religious duty, for it is only logical that the body, which is created in the image of God, must be kept clean.[10] Following are various aspects of hygiene related to children as are noted in the Talmud and other Judaic sources. The laws and comments offer sound advice on child care.

BATHING

Bathing is considered so essential that we find in the *Midrash Mei ha-Shiloach* the statement: "The existence of the world is maintained with six things—and one of these is bathing."

The Talmud stipulates that the hands, legs, and eyes must be washed every day.[11] Maimonides advised that one should bathe before (and after) bedtime, after the dinner is digested, and that anointment with oil should follow the bath.[12] This is excellent advice in the case of infant care and is recommended by many pediatricians. The benefit of such a schedule are

The First Five Years: From Infant to Child

pointed out by Rabbi Chanina, who attributed his vigor in old age to the baths and oil treatments he was given as a child.[13] Bathing facilities are so important that a learned man "may not live in a town in which there is not, among other things, a public bath."[14]

Nevertheless, limits are recognized, for we find in *Avodah Zarah* (28) the warning that if a child has been bitten by a wasp, or has a sting or a wound or a disease such as malaria, it is dangerous for him to be bathed. In all such cases, it is advisable to consult the doctor.

Special regulations are stipulated in Halakhah concerning bathing on Sabbath and holidays, as will be explained later in this chapter.

WASHING THE HANDS AND PERSONAL HYGIENE

The hands must be washed upon rising from the bed in the morning to protect against evil spirits.[15] It is forbidden to touch any part of the body before washing the hands with "nail water." Washing the hands before meals is required by biblical law,[16] and the Talmud states that the hands must be washed before every meal and the mouth rinsed after eating, by drinking water.[17]

It is recommended that children be taught to wash their hands in accordance with the above traditions. Even infants' hands should be routinely washed upon waking and before eating to assure maximum cleanliness, as their hands sometimes touch food even before they are able to feed themselves.[18] Hands must be washed upon leaving the bathroom in accordance with the Code of Jewish Law (2,9).

The warning that an unwashed hand touching the ear may cause deafness exemplifies the harm done when hands remain dirty.[19] On related matters of hygiene, the Talmud notes that coins should not be put in the mouth,[20] a very appropriate warning for infants and toddlers. In considering other elements of hygiene, the Talmud notes that one should not be kissed on the lips—but rather on the back of the hand.[21]

OUTINGS

Jewish sages have always recognized that sunshine and fresh air are essential to health.[22] Mothers may keep in mind the commentary that damp air is harmful to the body.[23]

A regular outing during the day will do wonders to calm even the most fretful infant. Moreover, "When the sun appears, the patient recovers."[24] The sun does wonders with the sniffles and other such ailments. It is, thus, advisable to expose a child with cold symptoms to the sun whenever possible, unless he has fever.

Special regulations are imposed in Halakhah concerning the use of baby-carriages on the Sabbath and holidays.

CLOTHING

Parents and guardians must make sure that children have adequate clothing for their needs and comfort. This is learned from the example set by the Almighty, who provided Adam and Eve with "clothing made of leather" so that they might be dressed properly (Genesis 3:21).

Mothers who are encumbered with piles of washing-machine loads will be comforted to know that they are adhering to a talmudic precept that clothes be washed frequently, for clean changes of clothes are indispensable to health.[25] Rabbinical authorities also point out that it is dangerous to wear damp clothing. All garments must be dried completely to avoid the risk of skin disease.[26]

Thus, mothers must take care that the infant's clothes are kept clean and dry and meet their growing needs. In all cases, however, the law forbidding the mixture of linen and wool in clothing must be obeyed.[27]

Special regulations are determined in Halakhah concerning the care of diapers, rubber pants, and sheets on the Sabbath.

To summarize the importance of hygiene, Samuel said: "A

The First Five Years: From Infant to Child

dirty head causes blindness, dirty clothing brings on boredom, and dirtiness of the body brings on skin eruptions."[28]

CARE OF THE TEETH

It is important to take good care of the teeth, for decayed teeth are a cause of malnutrition.[29] It is advisable to drink water after eating and to gargle with aseptic and salt after meals.[30] Thus, infants may be given a bit of water to drink after meals to rinse out their mouth.

The Code of Jewish Law stipulates that the mouth is to be washed every day upon rising.[31] Children's mouths were cleansed with *asube yanuke,* "children's herbs,"[32] a possible antecedent to children's toothpaste. Special guidelines are determined in Halakhah for the care of the teeth on the Sabbath.

CARE OF THE NAILS

As nails are trimmed periodically, the parings should be disposed of in a manner to assure that they are burnt.[33] It is customary to cut the nails on Friday and not Thursday (so that good grooming becomes a part of the preparations for the Sabbath).[34] The left-hand nails should be cut first, alternating the fingers rather than cutting in a row.[35] The nails of the hands and feet should not be cut on the same day.[36]

CARE OF THE HAIR

Hair should be routinely washed and combed. Not to comb one's hair is bad for the eyes.[37]

According to the Talmud (*Shabbat* 41a), hair was washed with soda and soap and then anointed with oil.

The hair of boys was not cut until they were at least three years old (so that they might grow the traditional side-curls). A feast was held (and is still celebrated today in many Hasidic circles) on the day of cutting the hair to symbolize the child's entry into the world of *mitzvot*.[38] In Israel, the cutting ceremony is traditionally held at the tomb of Rabbenu Simeon bar Yochai.

EXERCISE

The Talmud mentions that children exercised with balls and weights according to the size of each child.[39] Regular exercise is essential for mental health, stimulation of blood circulation, and as an aid to sleep. Doing simple exercises with infants during diaper changes and whenever the baby is at ease serves the same purposes and helps to develop motor coordination.

SLEEP

Sleep is like food and medication for the body; the rest provided by sleep is life-giving.[40]

Drowsiness is brought on by eating. A person who has not eaten or has eaten little has difficulty in falling asleep, while one who has eaten well has a sweet sleep.[41] From the Halakhah stipulated in the Talmud (*Shabbat* 2,5) that a light may be extinguished on the Sabbath to allow a sick person to sleep, we learn of the therapeutic importance attributed to sleep.

Rabbi Levi noted that the first baby to be placed in a crib was Abraham. This was carried out at the time of weaning. At night the child slept with the mother.[42] Cribs in biblical and talmudic times were made of wood[43] or glass.[44] They had short legs to ensure the baby's safety and prevent major injury if the child should fall out.[45] Bells were put on the cradle to help put the baby to sleep.[46] There were also swinging cradles which served the same purpose.[47] A fan was used to keep flies away from the child's crib,[48] and rubber sheets were placed under the child to keep the bedclothes clean.[49] Maimonides advised putting the baby to sleep on his / her side.

Provisions for the infant's sleep in biblical times were essentially the same as those we make for infants today with utmost consideration for baby's comfort. This attests to the importance attached to sleep for healthy development.

NURSING

The primary function which the mother fulfills upon the birth of her child is breastfeeding. According to Halakhah, this is a task she carries out through her role as a wife.[50] By thus ensuring that each newborn is nursed, Halakhah makes provision for the best possible nutrition for the child as well as the opportunity for the mother to express her love for the infant. During the first three months of life, the infant functions mainly on the basis of reflex and stimulation. Physical contact is essential for the child's developing sense of self. As the mother cuddles and fondles the child during nursing, the infant learns the warmth of love and trust, which is the foundation for healthy mental development. Modern psychologists as well, stress the fact that love must be communicated physically, especially in the first few months of life.[51]

If a woman does not have enough milk, this is considered a curse.[52] The infant must not suffer on this account, however, and the mother may hire a wetnurse. The Hebrew word of "wetnurse," *omenet,* is interchanged with the word *em* ("mother"), suggesting that the maternal role may be fulfilled by a woman who is not the natural mother as long as she gives the child the love and warmth necessary for life.[53] Thus, Halakhah stipulates that a woman who is breastfeeding her child (or someone else's child) may not marry until the child is twenty-four months old.[54] This law is very interesting, for beyond ensuring that the child will have the best source of nourishment in infancy, it shows a basic consideration for the emotional development of the child. As we now know, the first two years of life are crucial for the child's development of a sense of trust and a healthy mental state. Judaism makes sure that the child has all the technical opportunities to receive what is naturally due him—the care and attention of his mother (or mother-substitute) for the first two years of life.

NATURAL SPACING

Another vital point inherent in this law is that it allows for natural spacing between children. Modern psychology has pointed out the importance of the first three years of life for the child's developing personality.[55] Children who experience the birth of a baby brother or sister within that period of time are forced to share the attention they received until then with the new arrival. This causes a number of problems, including sibling rivalry, jealousy, and a deep sense of frustration at times when the child feels that he is receiving less attention. By setting the time span for breastfeeding at eighteen to twenty-four months, the rabbinical sages incorporated a built-in mechanism for spacing between children, for it is a law of nature that the lactating mother has slim chances of becoming pregnant (although this possibility is not entirely eliminated). In fact, nursing mothers are one of the three categories of women who may legally practice contraception in accordance with Halakhah.[56] Nevertheless, the question of natural spacing is a complex one in Jewish law, and parents must discuss it with a competent Rabbi before making a decision on the matter.

In practice, the Talmud stipulates that the mother is required to suckle the infant only as long as he wants to nurse.[57] If the infant recognizes his mother and wants to nurse only from her, she is compelled to nurse him—according to Rav, for three months; according to Samuel, for thirty days at least—but no set limit may be determined, for in each case it should be as long as the infant wants to nurse. In modern Responsa, we find

The First Five Years: From Infant to Child 79

the awareness that babies rarely want to nurse after fifteen months.[58] Similarly, if the child is weak, breastfeeding is obligatory.[59]

The emotional and physical benefits of breastfeeding were known to be so important that a mother who refused or neglected to suckle her child was compared to an ostrich, a creature that has no feeling for her offspring.[60] A symbolic representation of such a mother is used by the prophet Jeremiah to represent cruelty.[61] The mother's duty to breastfeed is upheld even if she had vowed not to nurse. According to the school of Hillel, the husband may invalidate his wife's vow and compel her to breastfeed.[62] If the woman is divorced, the husband can compel her to nurse only if the child is over thirty days, in which case he must pay child-support.[63]

Nursing is so basic a need for the infant that even if he nurses all day no harm comes from it.[64] According to a Midrash, although mother's milk is of uniform quality, the baby finds in it various delectable tastes,[65] so that he never tires of it.[65]

On the subject of demand feeding versus scheduled feedings, Judaism takes a clear stand: "The infant must nurse at any hour during the day or night." There is no room for controversy when the infant's well-being is at stake. Until the infant settles into his own routine feeding schedule, he should be fed when he is hungry, even at midnight.[66]

A woman who is nursing a child must not do other work, as is exemplified by Hannah, who put aside all domestic duties in order to suckle her child (Samuel). In this decision, she was wholeheartedly supported by her husband, Elkanah, who said to her: "Do what seems to be good, remain at home until the child is weaned."[67] The same advice is offered today by pediatricians and by the La Leche League,[68] who recognize the importance of the mother's having a relaxed state of mind and freedom from tension if she is to nurse successfully.

A woman must adhere to the laws of modesty during nursing; according to Rabbi Meir, a woman who nurses in the street may be divorced.[69]

WETNURSES

The mother's milk is always preferred to that of the wetnurse.[70] However, if the mother is ill, of if she has died, a wetnurse may be employed to provide the infant with natural mother's milk. The Talmud allows the wetnurse to take over the responsibility of nursing even in cases where the mother's status prevents her from doing so.[71] Halakhah thus makes all allowances to ensure that each child has the possibility to nurse under all circumstances. Special allowances are made for nursing mothers on the Sabbath and holidays.[72] Orphan babies were suckled by neighborhood women in turn or were fed milk and eggs, which were considered the second best nutrition for infants.[73]

The wetnurse must not suckle more than one child if she is given a charge.[74] The wetnurse must be given abundant food.[75]

According to some rabbis, it is permitted for a gentile to suckle a Jewish infant if the infant is in mortal danger and must receive breast milk and if the gentile woman is the only person available.[76] Others cite the case of Moses, who refused to nurse from a gentile woman and accepted nourishment only when given the breast of a Jewish woman.[77] Contemporary rabbis have concluded that although it may be permissible in certain cases for a child to be nursed by a gentile, if this may be prevented all the better.[78]

NURSING ON SABBATH AND HOLIDAYS

Following are guidelines for problems arising concerning nursing on Sabbath and holidays. As the problems are controversial, a Rabbi must be consulted. If an infant requires mother's milk and cannot nurse at the breast for any reason, it is permitted for

The First Five Years: From Infant to Child

the mother to empty her breasts into a container for the child.[79] The mother may empty her breasts to prevent engorgement, although this must be done in such a way as to make sure that the milk is not fit for consumption.[80] A lactating woman may clean her nipples with tap water by hand before nursing, but she is not to use a cotton swab to do so, for this entails squeezing the water absorbed by the cotton, which is forbidden on the Sabbath. Similarly, the mother may spray a few drops of milk into the baby's mouth in order to entice him to nurse if he refuses at first.[81]

If her breasts are infected, a woman may prepare cotton or cloth with medicated cream before the Sabbath to be used on the Sabbath. A nursing mother is permitted to take medicine and shots if necessary to prevent breast infection.[82] Indeed, during the first three days after birth, a lactating mother may even use cotton swabs to apply medication to sore nipples.[83]

A nursing mother is required to fast on the Day of Atonement, but if the infant is dependent on breast milk and will be endangered without it, and the mother risks losing her milk if she does not drink fluids, she is permitted to drink the accepted measure of 40–45 grams of water every nine minutes during the fast (to ensure her supply of milk for the baby).[84] However, it is better for her to try to drink enough fluids before the fast to prevent dehydration.[85] In any case, if attendance at a synagogue may cause her to require water, the nursing woman is forbidden to attend the services.[86]

While the nursing mother is normally required to fast on other required fast-days, she may break the fast if the fasting has affected her milk supply and as a result there is danger to the child.[87]

DIET OF THE NURSING MOTHER

The diet of a nursing mother is of importance for the well-being of the infant as well as the mother, for "all that the mother eats, the infant receives through nursing."[88] This has been confirmed by modern research pointing out the importance of a well-balanced nutritious diet for the lactating mother. Thus, rabbinical sages warned that a woman should not nurse if she must eat certain forbidden foods as a result of illness, for this will transmit a bad habit to the infant.[89]

The following foods were considered bad for nursing women according to Rav Kahana: pubescent cucumbers or melons, young greens, small fish, and clay (moist earth attached to vegetables). Abbaye included the quince fruit. Rav Papa included palm leaves (which were eaten when soft) and unripe dates. Rav Ashi added sauces made from curdled milk and fish hash. All these foods have the effect of stopping the flow of breast milk or altering its composition.[90] Thus, a lactating woman should make sure that she eats fresh dairy products to avoid upsetting her digestive system.[91] It is beneficial for the nursing mother to drink a bit of wine,[92] but no more than one cup was ever offered to a woman.[93]

In considering the principle that the baby is nourished by whatever the lactating mother eats, the following food items are recommended for nursing women, for each has a beneficial effect on the child: old wine and meat will maintain the child's health as well as the mother's; fish eaten during the nursing period will make the child graceful; adding eggs to the diet acts to produce large-eyed children; parsley is especially recommended to produce beautiful children; coriander acts to produce muscular children; and lemons serve to give children a pleasant odor.[94]

A nursing mother who finds that her milk flow has decreased or ceased is advised to eat eggs and milk (*Yevamot* 44).

If a mother wishes to breastfeed successfully, she will do well to follow a well-balanced nutritious diet in accordance with the recommendations of the pediatrician. This will help her bestow upon the child a great gift with which to begin life: "the blessing of the breast" (Gen. 49:25).

PLAY

In order to demonstrate the importance of play in a child's development, Rav Abbaye notes that Rabbah used to buy broken crocks at the market and bring them to his son so that he could play with them and break them if he wished to let off energy.[95]

The following anecdote points out the importance of play for the infant: A man left a clause in his will stipulating that none of his belongings should be given to his son until the latter made a fool of himself. Rabbi Yose went to consult Rabbi Joshua ben Karcha about this case. When approaching his home, he saw the sage through the window as the latter was crawling on all fours with a piece of grass in his mouth, playing horses with his baby. Upon entering the house, he asked Rabbi Joshua about the case. Rabbi Joshua laughed and answered: "Why, the exact thing which you have asked me about has just occurred here. For when a man has children, he often makes himself look like a fool to amuse them."[96]

Throughout the Talmud, we find references to children's toys, such as a toy horse,[97] the eternal ball,[98] toy hats,[99] and various fruits and vegetables used for play.[100] It is customary not to give children toys with images of people or forbidden animals to play with.

It is evident that the principle of play as an important element in learning and motor development and as a pleasant pastime is recognized in Judaism. In light of the ever-increasing sophistication of children's toys, a number of guidelines have been established in the Code of Jewish Law Responsa so that parents may select the proper toys for use on the Sabbath by preschoolers.

The following toys and games are permitted on the Sabbath:[101]

1. Rattles (although the baby need not be stopped from playing with rattles, the adult may not touch it or shake it to produce a sound).

2. Marbles (children may play with them on a table or on the carpet but not on the floor).
3. Balls may be used indoors and outdoors where there is an *eruv*; if the ball becomes stuck in a tree, it is not permitted to remove it on the Sabbath. Inflated Balls are prohibited.
4. Sandbox (if the sand is prepared before the Sabbath; it is not permitted for children to mix the sand with water, for this constitutes kneading, which is forbidden)
5. Wind-up toys (if they do not make musical sounds). Battery operated toys are prohibited.
6. Blocks (if they do not attach permanently to each other).
7. Beads and strings (as long as no tie is knotted to make a permanent necklace or bracelet).
8. Outdoor games not involving carrying.
9. Jungle gym made of iron or wood. Exercising on Sabbath is not permitted.
10. Swings (unless attached to a tree which would shake when the swing is in motion).
11. Tricycles (indoors and outdoors where there is an *eruv*, but the bell must be removed before the Sabbath; if it is not the custom to allow children to ride tricycles in one's community, the custom should be followed). The same applies to skates.
12. Running and jumping games; e.g., hide and seek.
13. Soap bubbles (children must not be stopped if they play with soap bubbles, but adults may not make soap bubbles on the Sabbath).
14. Snapping one's fingers to amuse a child.

The following toys and games are not permitted on the Sabbath:

1. Clay, play-dough, wax

2. Bicycles (for older children)
3. Magic boards
4. Stickers which stick when moistened or when the protective layer is removed
5. Drawing of all sorts, such as making forms on the ground or the street
6. Swimming, boating, and playing with sand on the beach
7. Sand (outside a sandbox)
8. Football
9. Making snowballs or snowmen
10. Games that usually require writing for recording scores.
11. Sticks and stones or pits unfit for animal consumption if found outside on the Sabbath (unless the child is used to playing with these items daily); it is forbidden to remove the pit of any fruit or vegetable on the Sabbath if it is intended for play.
12. Climbing trees or a ladder attached to a tree

Thus, modern Responsa have provided the necessary guidelines to assure a wide spectrum of playthings for infants, toddlers, and preschoolers on the Sabbath within the framework of Halakhah. (Play on the Sabbath for older children is considered in another chapter.)

If a question arises concerning the suitability of toys or games not listed here, an authorized rabbi should be consulted.

As the child learns the restrictions governing the toys and games he plays with on the Sabbath, he begins to realize the uniqueness of the day of rest, which is set apart from other days.

INFANT CARE ON SABBATH AND HOLIDAYS

It is said that the steadfast fulfillment of the commandments to observe the Sabbath and to circumcise newborn male children, even in the most difficult and hazardous situations, has assured the preservation of the Jews as a unique and chosen people.[102]

The two commandments are singled out as a "unique sign," for wherever the Jewish people fulfill these two *mitzvot* it is assured that they too will continue to exist.[103]

The observance of the Sabbath as a day of rest is the most concrete expression of the recognition of the Almighty in the Jewish home. By refraining from all worldly, routine daily activities and dedicating the day to rest and Torah learning, the Jew reaffirms his faith in God, who created the universe in six days and rested on the seventh day. Thus, all activities that were carried out in biblical times in the Tabernacle are forbidden.[104] According to Rabbi Samson Raphael Hirsch, one must regard the Sabbath as if it were the afterworld, where all is prepared for man in advance; therefore all activities which cause a change in that which exists are forbidden.[105] On the other hand, since the holidays were given to the Jewish people for rejoicing,[106] it is permitted to do that which is necessary to prepare food which is part of the festivities.

The laws for observing the Sabbath and holidays pertain to women as well as men, and this inlcudes mothers who must care for their infants and children on these special days. Halakhah takes into consideration the special needs of the infant and child and at the same time assures the mother the possibility of maintaining the observance of the day of rest. Thus, the guidelines concerning infant care on the Sabbath (and the holidays) balance the fulfillment of the child's needs with the required observance of the *mitzvot*. As many of the examples given in this section indicate, modern Responsa have made it possible for infants and children to receive all they care they require for healthy development within the framework of Sabbath observance.

All babies up to the age of two or three, and over that age if they still eat baby food, are considered to have the same status as a sick person not in mortal danger, and it is permitted to ask a non-Jew in order to prepare the food or milk they require to prevent an upset stomach. (Of course, one must try to prepare suitable food before the Sabbath.)[107]

In addition, the non-Jew may be requested to fulfill a

child's needs other than nutrition if the child (up to the age of nine or ten) is weak and requires special treatment.[108]

If the doctor prescribes vitamins or cod liver oil daily, it is permitted to administer these on the Sabbath as well.[109]

The child may be anointed with a small amount of oil even in the area of a diaper rash. Scales on the head may be anointed with oil. The oil must be liquid, and the application should be by hand and not with the use of cotton, which absorbs the oil. It is not permitted to smear creams of any sort on the baby on the Sabbath.[110]

(Special guidelines for the care of a sick child on the Sabbath appear in Chapter 10.)

BATHING ON THE SABBATH

Children must not be bathed on the Sabbath, but it is permitted to wash each limb separately with water heated before the Sabbath. The baby may be dried as long as this activity does not entail absorption of water. It is forbidden to use baby cream on the Sabbath. Cotton swabs required for baby care must be prepared before the Sabbath. It is permitted to powder the child even in sensitive areas, even though this is considered medication.[111]

In all cases, one must use liquid soap and refrain from using sponges or washcloths which absorb and squeeze water.[112] Some Rabbis do not permit the use of liquid soap on the Sabbath.

Although the same applies to holidays, if the child is routinely washed daily, it is permitted to bathe him on holidays. The water used must not be heated especially for the bath; instead, one must use water already heated. If the child is bathed, it is permitted to put a clean towel in the bathtub to prevent him from slipping.[113] It is forbidden to wring out the child's hair when drying.

It is permitted to wipe a child's mouth and remove food stains from his face with a paper towel. However, care should be taken to rinse the stains by hand before wiping.[114]

The teeth should not be brushed on the Sabbath, but it is

permitted to use mouthwash to rinse the mouth (it is preferable to prepare the mouthwash solution in water before the Sabbath).[115]

DIAPER CARE

It is forbidden to soak diapers in water on the Sabbath, but removal of feces from the diapers without the use of water is permitted. The diapers may be kept in a special closed container and deoderized with Lysol to prevent flies and roaches from approaching. If infection is feared, it is permitted to soak diapers in Lysol but not in bleach.[116] In any case, it is advisable to use disposable diapers on the Sabbath although care must be taken not to tape or fasten the diapers.

Rubber pants which are not made of cloth, as well as rubber sheets or clothes made of pure synthetic fibers, may be soaked on the Sabbath for further use on that day, but one must take care not to squeeze water in the process.[117]

The above-mentioned articles may also be hung to dry for use on the Sabbath, but they must not be placed near a furnace.[118]

Although in general, it is not permitted to hang clothes out to dry on the Sabbath, the mother may remove dry diapers and baby clothes from the line if the items are needed for that day.[119]

OUTINGS ON THE SABBATH

It is permitted to take the baby for a stroll in the carriage in areas where there is an *eruv*. A child's seat may be propped on the carriage with the use of valves, but not by using screws. A carriage may not be converted into a stroller, and vice versa. No repairs may be made on carriages or carriage wheels during the Sabbath.[120]

In areas where there is no *eruv*, it is not permitted to carry the child in one's arms or to stroll with a carriage.[121]

It is not permitted to spread a net on the carriage, crib, or playpen unless it has been spread before Sabbath to cover the span of a hand-breadth.[122]

FAST-DAYS

It is permitted to feed a child on a fast-day if needed and to wash one's hands before preparing or serving the food if the child is not required to fast.[123] (The age when a child is to begin fasting is discussed in Chapter 8.)

BABYSITTERS

It is permitted to hire a babysitter to care for the child if the person is hired before the Sabbath and is paid for the service rendered on a weekday in addition to regular wages.[124]

In all cases, a gentile may be asked to carry out an act that would consist of desecrating the Sabbath in order to fulfill the needs of a child up to ten years of age who is considered the same as a sick person not in mortal danger. Thus, the gentile may be asked to put out a light so that the child can sleep or to light a room for the child if he is afraid of the dark.[125]

SUMMARY

There is no specific commandment in the Bible concerning daily child care, apart from the Halakhah concerning the obligation of the father to feed and educate his children for a required number of years and the laws concerning the child's status in the family and society.[126] The daily care of infants and children as discussed in this chapter is left to nature, for it is the motherly instinct to provide for her child's needs during the most vulnerable period of life. Nevertheless, this natural instinct is implicit in the very essence of Judaism, as we learn from the example set by the Almighty and imprinted as part of creation and human development. The fact that the Almighty created man after the universe was completed is attributed to the care He took to ensure in advance that all the necessities of life would be prepared for man's needs.[127] Likewise, the Talmud notes that man was created at the end of the creation of the universe so that he would be able to eat and nourish himself immediately.[128] The Almighty also provided man with leather clothing and all his other needs for survival and development.[129] Man, who is created in the image of God, must learn from this example and provide for the needs of his offspring upon birth,[130] together with the additional element of the love and tenderness fundamental for healthy development.

The natural mother is the person most suited for this task. Her love for the child is natural. When the prophet Isaiah speaks of the comfort to be offered by the Almighty to the people of Israel, he uses the example of a mother comforting and caring for her child.[131] The fact that each child is naturally considered fragile and unique by his mother makes her the one most able to fulfill his physical needs.[132]

Attention to the spiritual and emotional needs of the child, in contrast, is a responsibility of both parents. The importance of providing for the emotional and spiritual needs of children should also be learned from the example set by the Almighty, who bestowed commandments for spiritual and emotional development to man immediately after his creation.[133] This model dramatizes the view that man's most important task in life is to instruct his children in the way of the Lord, the way of life that assures a healthy spiritual and emotional development.[134]

If the parents are unable for any reason to fulfill their role as caretakers and teachers, Judaism allows for substitutes to carry out the important tasks. Thus, a governess may be appointed to assume responsibility for the child's physical and emotional needs in infancy.[135] (Sometimes, it was the grandmother who assumed this role.)[136] In other cases, the *bet din* is responsible for appointing a parent-substitute or for making sure that the child's physical and spiritual needs are met in other ways.[137] Under no circumstances is any child to be neglected or denied his basic physical, emotional, spiritual, social, and intellectual needs. Provisions for fulfilling these needs are woven into the fabric of Judaism, as is evident from the references in the Bible to motherly love and the father's responsibilities to his children, as well as the numerous discussions in the Talmud concerning the child's needs, legal status, characteristics, and rights to a healthy life in accordance with the principles of Halakhah.

6
Nutrition

THE LAWS OF KASHRUT

The child's rate of growth and development depend to a great extent on nutrition. The younger the child, the greater are his nutritional needs during the stage of rapidly building cells, tissues, and organs in the process of growth. Recent research has revealed that in addition to its effects on physical growth, nutrition is also connected with mental development. The importance of proper nutrition is a basic element in Judaism, for it is known to "promote health and prevent disease."[1] The role of nutrition in building and sustaining life is marked in Judaism with the laws of Kashrut, halakhic regulations on preparing and selecting food.

The laws of Kashrut are based on the commandments concerning the types of animals and fish permitted for human consumption according to Torah law (Lev. 11:1-47) and the commandment "Thou shalt not seethe a kid in its mother's milk" (Deut. 14:21). Meat and poultry chosen for the kosher kitchen must be ritually clean, and must be slaughtered and prepared according to ritual laws. "Kashering" meat and poultry involves drawing out the blood before cooking. Separate dishes, cutlery, and cooking utensils are required for meat and dairy dishes in the kosher home. (Separate meat and dairy dishes are also required for Passover.) It is customary to wait six hours after a meat meal before eating dairy, whereas) after eating

The First Five Years: From Infant to Child

dairy, one must only rinse the mouth and clean one's hands before eating meat or poultry, (after eating yellow cheese one must wait six hours before eating meat). Although fish need not be kashered, one must take care to serve only those fish which have fins and scales according to Torah law. Fish as well as other foods, such as grains, eggs, and beans, are *parve* (neither dairy nor meat) and may be eaten with either. Care must be taken to discard any eggs in which blood is found on the yolk.

The goal of these laws is to unite the Jewish people in their eating habits by adhering to a diet based on cleanliness and purity. By abstaining from nonkosher food and eating habits, the Jewish people are singled out to achieve a level of holiness exemplified by the Almighty.[2] Yet the laws of Kashrut are based not only on spiritual elements but also on considerations of human physical and mental development. Jewish sages note that an improper diet—in this case, eating meat which is not ritually clean—causes man himself to become ritually unclean and makes him "dull."[3] In addition to the spiritual and physical effects of nutrition, improper eating habits may bring about a deficiency in intellectual functioning.

For complete details on the laws of Kashrut, consult the Code of Jewish Law: section A, chapters 35-47.

RECOMMENDED EATING HABITS

Members of the medical profession today recognize that the individual's health depends on nutritional foundations initiated during prenatal life.[4] The same conclusion was reached thousands of years ago by the talmudic sages, who laid down guidelines for the diet of the pregnant and lactating mother, on the theory that the mother's eating habits would affect the child's physical and emotional development.[5]

According to some sources, the baby's first source of nutrition after birth should be mother's milk, for artificial milk is not considered good for the average infant.[6] The benefits of mother's milk over goat's milk or cow's milk are so important that Halakhah makes all the required provisions to assure that the infant receives what is actually best for him. Thus, the law that a widow who is nursing may not marry until the child is weaned is specific in its purpose. The Talmud states that although it is technically possible for the mother to wean the child earlier and feed him eggs and milk, this should not be done and the proper time limit must be adhered to.[7]

WEANING

The term "weaning" designates the period during which the mother begins giving the baby other foods in addition to breast milk and finally ceases nursing altogether. The normal age for weaning was set by some sages as twenty-four months,[8] but others maintained that the infant was ready for solid foods at fifteen months.[9] As such long periods of nursing are not practiced in modern times, (since it is considered dangerous for the baby to go without solid foods for so long, a fact confirmed by Rabbi Feinstein), it is the practice for mothers to follow the advice given by the talmudic sage Samuel: the baby should nurse as long as he wants to.[10] If the child becomes ill at any point after weaning, it is the mother's responsibility to continue nursing if this will help relieve the baby's illness.[11]

In biblical times, it was the custom to make a joyous feast on the occasion of weaning the child to give thanks to the Almighty that the child had survived the most perilous stage of infancy. This is learned from the feast prepared by Abraham on the occasion of his son's weaning.[12] In talmudic times, it was the custom to celebrate the child's weaning any time from eighteen months to five years. (According to the school of Hillel, the child is weaned at eighteen months; according to Rabbi Eliezer, the child may nurse up to twenty-four months; according to Rabbi Joshua, a child should be allowed to drink breast milk up to five years!)[13] Accordingly, we note that Samuel was weaned at the age of three, after which he was admitted into the services of the Temple.[14]

SOLID FOODS

The first solid food given to a baby is milk and eggs.[15] The milk was usually goat's or sheep's milk.[16] Milk (as well as all liquids) must be covered at night to prevent contamination.[17] Milk is recognized as a basic nutrient required for sustenance.[18] Drinking milk assures that the teeth will be white and healthy.[19] The benefit of milk and dairy products for healthy development and beauty is acknowledged, so that if a parent wished his daughter to develop as a fair maiden, he was advised to feed her milk (and young birds) in her childhood.[20] Milk was considered to have a rather bland taste and the addition of honey rendered it more tasty.[21]

Honey was thought by some to be good for babies,[22] but Maimonides maintained that it was not.[23] The controversy continues today as well. Nevertheless, children themselves were known to show a preference for honey and butter, as was pointed out by Isaiah.[24] In fact, it is said that the manna tasted like honey to little children.[25]

The second nutrient group given to children was grains. It is noted that a child does not know how to call out "mother" or "father" until he tastes grain.[26] This observation implies that by the time the child was given cereal and other grains to eat, he was at the stage of primary language development. In biblical times this would correspond to about two years of age, while today a child often begins to utter his first words at the age of eleven to thirteen months—just about the time he begins to receive solid foods. Maimonides recommends whole grains rather than refined flour.[27]

The third group of nutrients important for development is

made up of fruits and vegetables. Vegetables are considered an essential addition to meals throughout the year, while fruits are known to be essential for healthy development.[28] The Talmud warns that one should not live in a town in which there are no vegetable gardens and orchards (or an insufficient water supply).[29] Rav Chisda notes that vegetables arouse the appetite, while fruit brighten the eyes.[30] Maimonides especially recommends eating figs, grapes, and almonds.[31] Squash is good for the digestion.[32]

The fourth essential nutrient group consists of meat, fish, and eggs (which supply protein). The talmudic sages noted that meat and eggs are the most nutritious foods. Fish is easily digested and nutritious; the meat of an ox, roasted meat, fat, fried eggs, nuts, cheese, and liver are digested less easily.[33] Meat and eggs are known to have the same nutritive value, and both have six times the nutritive value of flour.[34] Meat provides three times as much energy as pearl barley.[35]

Water is the most beneficial beverage for bodily functions. Although it does not build any body tissue, the body requires it for sustenance.[36] It is beneficial to drink water after every meal.[37] (It is known today that a growing child requires 100–135 grams of water per kilogram of weight.)[38]

The amount of food eaten is an important factor in healthy development. Each person should eat the amount of food required for his size. This is learned from the manna, which was supplied according to each person's size; thus, for an infant a suitable portion was added to the mother's measure, and as the child grew, his portion was increased accordingly.[39] Talmudic scholars add that a person should eat the amount of food warranted by climate, season, occupation, age, sex, body weight, and state of health.[40]

The amount one eats is important; the talmudic scholars warned against overeating, because more people die from eating too much than from eating too little.[41] They note especially that eating too much meat is unhealthy.[42] Maimonides declares that overeating and eating the wrong foods are like poisoning the body and are the main cause of illness.[43] This declaration is based on the verse "He who guards his mouth guards his soul against troubles," which is defined by Maimonides as meaning that he who guards against eating bad foods and overeating prevents illness.[44]

It is recommended that one eat plain foods[45] and that one should eat slowly and chew the food well, for this prolongs life.[46] This is excellent advice for young children, who should be taught the proper eating habits from the very beginning.

It is recommended that the type of food served vary with the season. Thus, certain foods, such as garlic, radish, and cabbage, should be eaten during the rainy winter season, while other foods, such as pumpkin, are more suitable for the warm season. In addition, the amount eaten during the warm season should be two-thirds of that served during the winter season.[47] Thus, in spring and summer children should be offered light foods with smaller portions, while in autumn and winter, heavier meals may be served with larger portions for each child.

The rabbis provided general guidelines for hygiene in the preparation and serving of food: In accordance with the principles of hygiene and Kashrut, food should be fresh and stored in a proper and sanitary way.[48] Food must be kept in clean dishes and covered to prevent foreign matter from spoiling it.[49] Food which is old and not stored properly and unripe food may cause illness.[50] Smoked and salted fish, cheese, and old meat, as well as mushrooms and any food which has a bad odor, are considered to be very bad for human consumption at all times.[51] Beef must be thoroughly cooked to kill the parasites it may contain.[52] Finally, a person should not eat food which his system cannot digest.[53] This is a basic guideline for mothers of young children, for care must be taken to suit foods served to the digestive ability of the child.

HALAKHAH CONCERNING NUTRITION

A child must be fed any food he requires for his health, even if the food is forbidden by the sages (but a child may not be given food forbidden by Torah law).[54] As this applies to any food necessary for health, it is permitted to feed a child milk from an animal which is not kosher if no other is available.[55] In all such cases a Rabbi should be consulted.

Children may be fed before prayers and before hearing the Kiddush on the Sabbath, if this is necessary for their well-being. This regulation applies even though it is necessary to wait until after prayers and Kiddush for meals.[56]

If a young child requires milk for his well-being, he may be given milk one hour after eating meat, even though the adult is required to wait a period of six hours. A child who is old enough to say the blessing after the meal should do so and later be given milk. A younger child should have his hands washed of the meat and the meat dishes removed from the table.[57]

FEEDING CHILDREN ON THE SABBATH

Although it is not permitted to mash uncooked fruit and vegetables on the Sabbath, these may be chopped finely for older children and mashed for young babies if necessary for health. This must be done immediately before the meal.[58] Other foods, such as cooked eggs, fish, or meat, may be mashed even with a fork.[59] (On holidays, it is permitted to mash fruit and vegetables in any case.)

It is permitted to squeeze lemon, orange or grapefruit juice onto solid foods and to blend them for the baby, if this is done in a different manner than regularly (i.e., the lemon should be squeezed on the side and blended differently than on weekdays). This is the case for all dry foods which are prepared for the baby by adding a liquid.[60] The same applies to crumbling biscuits and mixing the crumbs with white cheese or adding juice to such a mixture.[61]

It is forbidden to squeeze the juice of any fruit into an empty container or into another liquid, whether this is done by hand or in a utensil. However, the juice may be squeezed by hand into a solid food, if this is done to improve the taste of a dish such as salad. It is forbidden to liquefy grapes even onto a solid, but if this is for the sake of a baby it is permitted. (On holidays, it is permitted in any case.)[62]

As children are considered to have the same status as a sick person not in mortal danger, it is permitted to measure food to be prepared for the baby (but if possible, estimate the amount). Similarly, a child may be weighed before or after meals if this is necessary for his health.[63]

WARMING FOOD FOR A CHILD ON THE SABBATH

Food for a child may be placed near a fire or on a warming tray or a gentile may be asked to cook or warm food for the baby if necessary. The Jew must not do anything to help him and is not allowed to eat what has been warmed for the baby.[64]

It is permitted to use a food-warming plate in which boiling water is placed under the food to warm it up. Boiling water may be poured over a bottle in a dish to warm the milk as long as the water does not cover the bottle. The use of an electric warming apparatus for milk bottles is not permitted on the Sabbath.[65]

STERILIZING AND CLEANING BOTTLES ON THE SABBATH

Sterilizing is forbidden on the Sabbath (so that all bottles must be prepared before the Sabbath) unless it is a matter of *pikuach nefesh*—saving a child's life. (On holidays, bottles may be sterilized with water prepared in advance.)[66] Bottles may be washed on the Sabbath and on holidays treated with antiseptic.[67] The same applies to nipples, but it is not permitted to enlarge or create a hole in the nipple on the Sabbath.[68]

PASSOVER

Children are not permitted to eat *chametz* (leavened foods) during Passover. While it is the Ashkenazi custom to refrain from cornflour and rice during Passover, these food items are permitted in the Sephardic tradition, and they may be cooked for babies in an Ashkenazi household during Passover if necessary. In such cases, the water should be boiled first and special utensils should be set aside for these items.[69]

FEEDING CHILDREN ON FAST-DAYS

Boys under twelve years are not permitted to fast an entire day (at the age of twelve they may do so if they are robust and healthy). It is permitted for a child to carry food on Yom Kippur, to feed a child and to wash one's hands when serving the food. (It is said that Shammai did not wish to wash his hands when feeding a child on Yom Kippur, but the talmudic sages concluded that both hands must be washed to feed the child.) It is advisable to prepare a holiday meal for the child in celebration of the holiday.[70]

CONDUCTING THE MEALS

Jewish law acknowledges the relevance of medically approved methods for healthy digestion of food as most important for good health.[71] Thus, it is advised to walk or work to build up an appetite (as stated in the psalm: "Thou shalt eat bread with the sweat of thy palms").[72] During meals, one should sit upright or lean to the left. After meals it is advised not to move around much or to take a walk, not to sleep for two hours, and not to take a bath immediately, for this hampers proper digestion.[73]

One should eat only when hungry and drink only when thirsty.[74]

Breakfast is considered a most important meal.[75]

Thirteen things were said concerning bread eaten in the morning: it is an antidote against the heat, cold, winds, and demons; it makes the simple wise, and it causes one to win in a lawsuit; it aids one in learning and teaching Torah; it causes one's words to be heeded and helps maintain the scholar's excellence; it helps one to love his wife and not lust after another; it destroys tapeworms and, some say, it drives away envy and causes love to enter.[76]

When serving various types of food, care should be taken to serve the lighter foods first (such as chicken before beef) and leave foods which are more difficult to digest for last.[77]

One must take care to chew food properly, for this is the beginning of digestion (a most important bit of advice for children).[78]

One should not drink before meals, and very little during meals, in order not to hamper digestion. The proper time to drink is after meals, when the digestive process has begun.[79]

FOODS TO AVOID

For the sake of proper digestion and good health, Maimonides advised that the following food items should be avoided: old smoked fish and old salted cheese, mushrooms, old salted meat, wine made from unripe grapes, cooked food which has spoiled, any food with a bad odor or a bitter taste.[80] (This passage may be a reference to food treated with nitrites and food spoiled by bacteria.)

Certain food items should be eaten only rarely, such as large fish, dairy products which were left to stand one day after milking, meat of large oxen and goats, certain beans and lentils, chickpeas and barley bread, matzot, cabbage, leeks and onions, garlic, mustard, and radishes. Such foods should be eaten mostly during the rainy season and not at all on hot days.[81]

Other food items, such as ducklings, pigeons, dates, bread

kneaded with oil, and refined semolina should be eaten only in small quantities. Fish should not be served with meat. A piece of bread should be eaten or a beverage served between the two if one follows the other in a meal.[82]

Unripe fruits are very bad for the digestive system. Carobs are considered hard to digest. Sour fruit should be eaten sparingly on hot days.[83]

As a general rule, one should eat foods suited to one's temperament.[84] Thus, an overactive child should not be given spices and sugar, but rather foods which are cool and sour; a withdrawn child should be given foods with some spices; an average child should be given foods which are neutral in this sense. In all cases, the foods served should suit the climate and season. On hot days, one should eat cool and refreshing foods, such as young chickens and some sour foods, and on wintry days, hot, robust foods.[85]

SUMMARY

From biblical times through the talmudic era to the contemporary responsa, we find that Judaism assigns an important role to proper nutrition as an essential factor in promoting health and preventing disease. Indeed, it appears that Judaism is a forerunner of natural medicine and the prevention of disease through the proper diet.[86] The laws of Kashrut with their emphasis on cleanliness and purity in preparing and selecting foods are intended to help man fulfill his role as a Jew. By maintaining a healthy body, one is enabled to learn the ways of the Lord and to function accordingly.[87]

The foods served to a growing child must be chosen with care, for his nutritional needs are greater than those of an adult. This is a basic fact recognized by Jewish law.[88] The foods served to children should be selected in accordance with their temperament and size, and also should be suited to the season (portions should be smaller in the summer). Feeding a child the wrong food and overfeeding are dangerous for health. Children should not be forced to eat food they dislike; in fact, Jewish law forbids eating food that one considers distasteful.[89] It is advisable for children to build up an appetite by playing or taking a walk before meals. Children should not be fed when they are nervous or upset.[90] A child should be trained to eat a nutritious breakfast every day.[91]

The Judaic prescriptions for proper nutrition are all-encompassing. Although they precede modern science by hundreds of years, they are in perfect accord with the advice given by pediatricians and nutritionists today.

7
Child Behavior

As the very essence of Judaism is based on a divine moral code, the Judaic attitude toward child behavior has much to offer those who are committed to providing their children with a sound moral and ethical upbringing. One of the fundamental principles of Judaism is that children are not responsible for fulfilling the commandments. Boys undertake this responsibility when they reach the age of thirteen, and girls when they reach the age of twelve. From then on they are regarded as adults insofar as observing the *mitzvot* is concerned.[1]

Why is this so? Are we to conclude that children are not intelligent enough to fulfill the commandments? Certainly not, for many children of ten or eleven are brighter than adults much older than they. Moreover, there is no overwhelming change in the child's mental capacities the day he becomes thirteen (or twelve if a girl), the age of assuming responsibility for the *mitzvot*.

Our sages explain that the obligation of fulfilling the commandments depends on the acquisition of morality.[2] In Judaic terms, this means the development of the spiritual elements of the soul—or in scientific terms, the "morality of self-accepted moral principles."[3] The commandments were given to enable man to amend his soul and rise to the level of sanctity exemplified by the Almighty. According to the Kabbalah, the spiritual element does not develop in the human being until the the age of thirteen.[4]

This philosophy of human development is a fundamental principle engraved in Judaism. Through this viewpoint the most subtle concepts of modern child psychology are interwoven into the fabric of Judaism.

THE SOURCES OF BEHAVIOR

Behavior constitutes the individual's unique pattern of responses to the environment. A state of equilibrium between the individual's inner drives and the external demands of society and environment constitutes mental health. The highest order of mental health exists when the equilibrium is based on a value system.

Judaism envisages the sources of behavior in the human mind as governed by the *yetzer ha-tov* (the good spirit) and the *yetzer ha-ra* (the evil spirit). One or the other of these forces determines all of our responses to the environment. Life is a constant struggle between the two.

The cornerstone of this philosophy is that the evil spirit is created at birth, as declared in the Torah: "the spirit of man's heart is evil from the days of his youth!"[5] Furthermore, on the basis of the passage "For sin lieth at the door," the talmudic sages concluded that the evil spirit is present in the child at birth.[6] Discussing whether the evil spirit enters man at the time of conception or the time of birth, Rabbi Judah the Prince maintained that it was present at conception. Antoninus, citing the preceding passage as support, pointed out that if this were so, the child would kick in his mother's womb and emerge. Therefore, one must conclude that it enters man only at the time of birth.[7]

How is the evil spirit manifested in the newborn? A famous Jewish sage presents the following example to demonstrate the nature of the child:

> Come and look at a kid or lamb. When it sees a well it retreats

[and saves itself from a dangerous fall], for it has no evil spirit; but the infant is overcome by the evil spirit [his pleasure-seeking instinct], so that he places his hands on a snake or a scorpion and is bitten, he places his hand on coals and is burnt.[8]

Every parent knows this to be true from personal experience, since all children begin life with "egocentric pleasure-seeking drives."[9] In fact, modern child psychology agrees with the theory that the child at birth and in the first few months of life seeks pleasure exclusively, through the demand for food and comfort. As the baby develops, he seeks satisfaction for emotional as well as biological needs.

The task of child-rearing involves the establishment of a harmony between the child's drives and conscience.[10] This is accomplished by maintaining the moral law in everything concerning the child, so that he can internalize it in the process of growth.[11]

Judaism and modern child psychology agree that the child must be taught to modify or renounce his egocentric needs for the demands of the outer world through the integration of a solid value system.[12] The study of children in different cultures has shown that what is considered typical behavior or the norm for children of certain ages in one culture may not be true of another culture. The demands of the Jewish moral code embodied in Halakhah fulfill the requirements of child-rearing by necessitating that the child curb his egocentric drives in subordination to the commandments of a higher authority. By learning to fulfill the *mitzvot*, the child learns to distinguish between good and evil and to perfect his behavior.[13]

THE CHILD'S BASIC NATURE

Before considering how this should be done, we must base our child-rearing techniques on a basic perspective of the child. How should we regard the tiny, egocentric newborn? Is the child born evil, so that we must discipline him to be good, or is he born a *tabula rasa,* with no characteristics or will of his own, so that we must educate him from scratch?

In contrast with other historic conceptions of childhood, Judaism does not envisage the child as being born evil or as a *tabula rasa.*[14] It sees the child as an innocent creature guided by natural impulses.[15] At this point in the child's life, the "evil spirit" serves to arouse egocentric demands for biological satisfaction (and later for emotional satisfaction), but these are carried out without evil intent, for man is born with a pure soul.

> When the soul is given to the embryo, the Almighty says to the latter: "This soul which I have given thee is pure. If thou wilt return it to Me the same as it comes to you, well and good; if not, I will burn it before thee."[16]

The sages have composed a prayer to this effect, including the pronouncement recited daily: "Thou hast given unto me a pure soul."[17] The paradox is made clear by the following talmudic explanation: "Rabbi Meir used to say: Man comes into this world with closed hands, as if he were claiming ownership of everything; yet he leaves it with his hands open and limp, as if to say that he takes nothing with him."[18]

Every child is born with a treasure of varying characteristics, talents, drives, tendencies, and aspirations unique to him.[19] According to the reknowned Jewish educator, Rabbi Samson Raphael Hirsch, Judaism teaches us that these innate characteristics are neither good nor evil but have the possibility of becoming either in the course of the individual's life. The critical question for effective child-rearing is, "What factor will tip the scales either way"?

DEVELOPMENTAL STAGES AND MORAL EDUCATION

Child-development theory holds that "in searching for the

origins of early developmental phases of behavior, we must start with the fetus and not the neonate."[20] Judaism goes further, explaining that the source of motivations is rooted in the soul,[21] which according to the talmudic sages enters man at the time of conception.[22]

> Antoninus said to Rabbi [i.e., Rabbi Judah the Prince]: "At what stage is the soul given to man? At the time of insemination or impregnation?" He answered: "At the time of impregnation." He [Antoninus] said: "Is it possible for a piece of flesh to remain three days without salt without decomposing? Rather, it is given during insemination." Rabbi acknowledged this and brought the following passage for support: "And Thy visitation has guarded my soul" [Job 10].[23]

The faculties of the soul according to Judaism include thought, recollection, the power to forget, feel shame, and understand, and the power of speech.[24] During childhood, these faculties are in the formative stage. The single most impressive function they fulfill at this stage is that of free choice.

> The angel appointed over pregnancy is called Lilah. And he takes a drop and places it before the Almighty and says: "Lord of the Universe, what is to be the fate of this drop? Will it be strong or weak, wise or foolish, rich or poor?" And why does he not ask whether he will be evil or a saint? The answer is as Rabbi Chanina said: "Everything is in the hands of God except for the fear of God."[25]

Immediately after birth, the infant expresses his will by demanding food and comfort. As he grows, his desires increase and encompass varied material needs in accordance with his egocentric nature.

Eventually, the child is forced to choose between his inner demands and the requirements of the outer world. As "the child is not a thinker and cannot distinguish between good and evil,"[26] childhood is the period of life in which he learns the basis of morality. If child-rearing succeeds, then at the end of this period, by the time the child is about thirteen, he will have the capacity to behave in accordance with internalized moral principles. If we follow the sequence of stages determined by scientific theory, the development of moral judgment in the child begins with the premoral stage, in which his behavior is the result of fear of punishment or in obedience to his parents; in the second stage of development, his behavior is based to a large extent on morality and is determined by his need for approval by others or by role conformity. Finally, in the last stage, the child internalizes the moral values of his society and acts accordingly. All children pass through these stages, though not all at the same rate.[27]

Jewish sages have determined that the child reared in accordance with the principles of Judaism arrives at the third stage at the age of thirteen (if a boy or twelve if a girl). It is at this point that the good spirit (*yetzer ha-tov*) enters the individual, for only then are the spiritual elements of the soul developed sufficiently to enable the child to fulfill *mitzvot* with the goal of perfecting his acts.[28]

The fact that the "evil spirit is thirteen years older than the good spirit"[29] explains the exemption of children from the requirement of fulfilling *mitzvot* until that age and must at the same time affect our attitude toward the child at all times. When a child misbehaves or does something we consider bad, we must shape our reaction to his behavior in accordance with the knowledge that he is acting out of the natural impulse to satisfy his own needs at a time when he has not yet given thought to other forms of behavior. This awareness will prevent much of the parental frustration and anger, and the concomitant unnecessary fighting and emotional damage, that may otherwise result in such cases.

If there is one esential factor to keep in mind in our dealings with children, it is the observation made by Maimonides on the biblical passage: "and you shall be as God, knowing good and evil."[30]

"Mankind," said Maimonides, is unique among God's creatures, for the knowledge of good and evil arises within himself and his soul, and accordingly he chooses his actions."[31] However, this knowledge is not entirely innate. The child is not aware of all this knowledge, and it is up to his parents and society to teach him the distinction by instilling in him the values which will lead him to choose either.[32] The *mitzvot* are the actions which the individual chooses to fulfill or not. His choice will determine the extent to which his soul has acquired the fear of God. Yet this choice can be made only when the individual attains the spiritual capacity to restrain his strengths, talents, characteristics, aspirations, tendencies, desires, and impulses.[33] In accordance with the Judaic philosophy of child-rearing, this occurs when the child reaches the age of thirteen and has acquired the *yetzer ha-tov*.

What must be done during the first thirteen years of life to make sure that the process of moral development succeeds and the child internalizes the values of Judaism so that he freely chooses the good? Judaism offers a number of prescriptions based on Halakhah and the subtleties of child psychology.

PARENT-CHILD RELATIONS

It is an acknowledged fact in Judaism that the ability to control impulses is dependent on ties to a stable and loving parent or parent-substitute. The capacity of the individual to adapt and find solutions to balance his inner needs and the outer reality depends to a great extent on his primary human ties.[34] According to Rabbi Samson Raphael Hirsch: "Concerning education for moral perfection, there is no substitute for the care given by the mother."[35] The Rabbi of Belz declared that the mother has the main role in educating children, for she has the capacity to

The First Five Years: From Infant to Child 111

rear them in the ways of the Amighty.[36] This view is traced back to the Talmud, where we find the observation that the reward promised to women is greater than that awarded to men, for the main responsibility for educating the child belongs to the mother.[37] Indeed, the Bible makes it clear that both women and men are to be taught the ways of the Lord so they may teach them to their offspring.[38] While the father is responsible for certain aspects of the child's education,[39] the mother, who has the most contact with the child at this point in his life, has responsibility for the child's primary spiritual and moral learning.[40] Accordingly, it is prescribed in Halakhah that the mother should pray, when she lights the Sabbath candles, that her children will develop in the light of the Torah and grow to accept the values of Judaism.[41] According to the Code of Jewish Law, fathers are required to educate their small children to fulfill all the *mitzvot,* both Torah law and rabbinical law, each *mitzvah* in accordance with the child's intellectual ability at each stage of development.[42] In all cases, education must be based on a relationship of trust between the child and the educator.

A basic rule to be followed in all parent-child relationships is embodied in the following talmudic statement: "In dealing with a child, let the left hand repel, while the right hand draws near."[43] In any situation which involves educating or disciplining the child, the (parent) educator must first repel the child by restraining him. This is to be accompanied by the most important function of the educator—to draw the child to him in the bond of mutual love and trust that is the basis for healthy mental development and learning.

The first two years of life are crucial for building this foundation of trust; the third and fourth years of life are the basis for the developing sense of autonomy.[44] This theory, now widely accepted in child psychology, was expressed in Jewish sources as a fact of nature:

Which is the child to be fondled? the two- and three-year-old.

Rav Aha, in the name of Rav Levi bar Yossi, said: the four- and five-year-old.[45]

Which child no longer requires his mother's [fondling]? The child who is already four or five years old.[46]

Thus, the first five years of life, during which the child is afforded love, warmth, comfort, and care, serve as the basis for the child's developing sense of identity and independence.

During the first five years of life and up to ten years, the child is not considered a sinner. After ten years of age he develops the evil spirit.[47] If the child is to counter this evil spirit and develop a healthy *yetzer tov* that will emerge as part of his identity during the period of adolescence, the parent-educator must instill a sound sense of values in the child. This is done by fulfilling the halakhic requirement of teaching the child each *mitzvah* that he or she will be responsible for fulfilling as an adult.[48] (The details of early childhood education are discussed in Chapter 8.)

Education is deemed so important in Judaism that every effort must be made to assure its success. The recommended measures are based on sophisticated techniques of educational psychology, as is evident from the emphasis on moderate discipline,[49] tolerance and respect for the child,[50] and knowledge of his temperament and personality.[51]

The talmudists lay down as a general rule that one must teach one's child patiently, avoiding anger in carrying out this holy task.[52] Discipline must begin at the very onset of life, so that the child learns to restrain himself from an early age, but this too must be done calmly and with moderation. The aim of Jewish education is to train the whole child, influencing his character, values, and life-style in accordance with the morals and values of the Jewish heritage. This can only be achieved if the child trusts his teacher and accepts him as an authority to be listened to and heeded; if the child fears his teacher, he will build up hostile feelings and, consequently, will reject what he is taught.[53]

Parallel to the role of discipline in building the child's character, Judaism stresses the importance of respect for the child as an individual. Judaism teaches us that each individual has the right to feel that the world was created for his sake.[54] The Midrash points out that just as people do not resemble each other in appearance, they have individual thoughts and opinions.[55]

As a result, the general rule recognized by Jewish sages is that man is more strongly motivated by the desire for honor than by any other desire.[56] Even the youngest child feels hurt when he is not respected as an individual. Judaism recognizes that in addition to the emotional harm which may result, the child's emerging personality may suffer if his feelings are disregarded and his opinions and need for attention are neglected.

Finally, a most practical technique in child-rearing is prescribed by Solomon: "Teach each lad in accordance with his ways, then he will not forsake your instruction even in his old age."[57] A very sophisticated psychological observation to this effect is made by Maimonides, who stated:

> It is impossible that man is born with a certain virtue or deficiency, just as it is absurd to consider that he is born with a specific profession. However, it is possible that he is born with a nature predisposed to a certain virtue or deficiency—and certain functions are easier for him than others.[58]

This theory has recently been validated by scientific research on the subject of temperament and individuality.[59]

The first step in building a relationship with a child and in ultimately educating and developing his character is to "know him," to be aware of his unique temperament and predispositions. On that basis it is possible to anticipate his reactions to certain teachings and disciplinary methods and to employ techniques suited to his temperament and unique personality.

One of the most powerful forces which shape the child's behavior patterns is the example set by parents in their own behavior (see pg. 129).

DEVIANT BEHAVIOR

In cases where the process of building the child's moral character seems to be failing and the child displays deviant behavior by defying his parents or resorting to delinquency, Judaism prescribes strong measures to curb this behavior before it becomes acute. When routine disciplinary measures have no effect on the child, it is up to the parents to punish him so that he does not accustom himself to delinquency. If the child steals or causes damage to property, it is incumbent upon the *bet din* to punish him in order to deter him from repeating his delinquent act.[60] If the child steals something, the object must be returned if he is found with it. If the article is not found, there is no obligation for the child to repay its worth, but when he grows up he should do so. This applies to other sins committed in childhood as well: when he is sufficiently mature it is worthy for him to repent in some way.[61]

In cases when the child eats a forbidden food or commits a prohibited act there is a question whether the *bet din* is not responsible for punishing him or preventing his act, but it is worthy for the father to scold him and educate him toward sanctity.[62]

Finally, if the child's behavior is unmanageable and deviant to the extent that even these procedures are not effective, a competent authorized rabbi should be consulted. If the child shows evidence of mental disorder, a competent professional must be consulted to help the child.[63]

SUMMARY

Judaic law and philosophy have a great deal to offer in understanding and coping with the child's behavior patterns. Under-

The First Five Years: From Infant to Child

lying the Judaic philosophy of child behavior is the view that all human action is governed by the *yetzer ha-ra* and the *yetzer ha-tov*, the evil inclination and the good inclination, which are in a constant struggle. "During his lifetime, man is a constant slave to his inclination and his Creator. When he fulfills the wishes of his inclination, he angers his Creator, and vice versa."[64]

While the *yetzer ha-ra* is present in the child at birth and manifests itself through his egocentric drives for biological and emotional satisfaction, the *yetzer ha-tov* develops as the child matures and is present in his soul by his thirteenth year. The child is born with the freedom to choose his course of action in accordance with the good inclination or the evil inclination.

Early childhood is the period set aside for the individual to learn the foundations of Jewish values and morality which should affect his choice of the good or evil during the course of his life.

"Man is born wild like a young ass" (Job 11:12). Rashi comments that in the course of human development, man changes from his wild nature, which resembles that of a young ass, and becomes a civilized human being. To this Meiri adds:

> Man should always be kind and considerate about his children's affairs and consistent in disciplining them, the younger and the older children alike. In any case, the worthwhile time to make efforts in disciplining them toward the ultimate goal of Judaism is from the time that knowledge begins to sprout until it ripens.[65]

The primary responsibility for setting children on the right road toward a moral life belongs to the parents. During the formative early years, they must guide their offspring in the spirit of Jewish values. The parents' relations with their children must be based on respect for them and knowledge of their unique personalities. This will prevent the parents from having exaggerated expectations and from making overwhelming demands on their children. At the same time, through Torah education and relevant disciplinary practices, the parents will be channeling the developing behavior patterns of their children toward the Jewish way of life.

The ultimate remedy for the power of the evil inclination is Torah study and good deeds, as expressed in the following talmudic statement: "Happy is Israel, for when the people are involved in the Torah and good deeds, their inclination is in their hands and they are not in the hands of the inclination."[66] This too is the ultimate aim of Jewish child-rearing.

8
Early Childhood Education

LEARNING READINESS

The subject of learning readiness is treated in Judaism within the framework of Halakhah and relevant considerations of child psychology. In the Bible, we find specific references to the age at which a child should begin his education:

Whom shall one teach knowledge?
And whom shall one make understand the message?
Them that are weaned from the milk,
Them that are drawn from the breasts.[1]

This is a clear indication of the significance attributed to early childhood education in Judaism. The child is compared to the fruit of trees in the first three years, which according to Halakhah is forbidden for consumption. During the fourth year, the fruit is consecrated to the Almighty. Similarly, the child in his first three years of life is considered to be under the age of initial education; and in his fourth year, he is consecrated to the study of the Torah.[2]

In essence, however, Judaism believes that "kindergarten is too late,"[3] as is shown by the following statement: "Education begins with life itself, for the impressions of the environment are internalized by the infant and become more concrete to him each day. Therefore, the caretaker's relationship with the child must be based on careful thought and action."[4]

Talmudic commentators, too, felt that early childhood is the decisive age in education. Thus, Meiri comments that Torah learning in the earliest years of life is beneficial, for it is imprinted forever.[5] This is further explained in *Avot de-Rabbi Nathan*, which notes that what is learned in early childhood is absorbed in the blood.[6]

When is the child considered ready for learning? On one hand, we find: "Out of the mouths of babes and sucklings has Thou founded strength."[7] The biblical theory that the child learns at the very beginning of life is supported throughout Jewish law and literature. The noted educator Rabbi Samson Raphael Hirsch taught that the most important and decisive age in education is early childhood, "the age of the suckling," during which the child must be prepared to accept the noble foundations for a moral life.[8]

On the other hand, we find the talmudic precept that a child under the age of six should not be submitted to the yoke of the Torah if he is weak. However, if he is strong and healthy, he may be admitted to study earlier, and the rate of his progress is according to his strength, his language ability, and his intelligence.[9]

While these somewhat different views would seem to present a contradiction concerning the actual age for the beginning of *chinnukh* (education), the Halakhah on this subject resolves the matter in the best practice of child psychology:

(a) Each father is obliged to educate his small children in all the *mitzvot*, whether *mitzvot* originating in the Torah or rabbinical law, each *mitzvah* according to the intelligence of the child, and to remove them from all forbidden items, as the source states: "Educate each lad in accordance with his ways."[10]

(b) Each father is obliged to teach his sons the Torah, as it is written: "And you shall teach them to your sons." As soon as the baby begins to talk, he is to be taught the verses from the Torah "Moses taught us the Torah" . . . and "Hear, O Israel."[11]

In prescribing the Jewish curriculum for early childhood

education, Halakhah incorporates the subtleties of educational psychology to ensure the maximum measure of success in the goal of raising the children as good Jews. The Torah imposes upon each father two duties in relation to the education of his offspring: (1) that he teach his children the Torah, according to the verse: "And you will teach them to your children; [12] (2) that he recount the tale of the redemption from Egypt to his children on Passover, as it is written: "And you will tell your son on that day."[13]

In order to ensure that the child indeed learns the Torah, the curriculum is divided into two spheres: (1) knowledge of ethics and the fear of God—*chinnukh* in Torah with the goal of teaching the child the difference between good and evil; (2) actual practice in fulfilling the *mitzvot* through the child's active participation in those *mitzvot* which he is capable of executing.

In the first case, learning begins as early as possible. It is related that the mother of Rabbi Joshua ben Chananya carried him to the rabbinical academy in his cradle so that his ears might grow accustomed to the sound of the words of the Torah.[14] From this we learn that in the earliest stage, care should be taken to introduce sanctity into the life of the newborn. Thus, the parent must make sure that the baby does not eat any forbidden food item, in accordance with Halakhah.[15] The Book of Ethics teaches us that man must try to teach his child the Torah from the earliest days of life, in accordance with the child's strength and age. Thus, before the child begins to speak one should show him the holy books and teach him to kiss them, so that they will be endeared to the child. When the child learns to speak, he is to be taught "Moses commanded us the Torah" and "Hear, O Israel." When the child grows older, the father buys him books and hires a teacher for him.[16] In fact, Maimonides specifically states that the obligation to teach children the Torah begins as soon as the baby starts to speak (as above mentioned).[17] The emphasis on early education is explained by Meiri: "for the baby in his first years of life is molded in accordance with the habits and customs he is taught at the very beginning."[18]

PARENTAL EDUCATIONAL OBLIGATIONS

The father's responsibility for teaching his sons Torah stems from the Torah law "And you shall teach them to your children," which appears in the Pentateuch in several places.[19] After the child learns the first two verses prescribed, the father should continue to teach him a new verse each day, in accordance with his ability to learn, until the child is six years old. When the child reaches the age of six, the father is obliged to provide him with the necessary schooling.[20]

In addition to teaching his sons the Torah, the father is responsible for teaching his daughters whatever they must know in order to fulfill the *mitzvot* relevant to women.[21]

The father is also obliged to teach both his sons and his daughters the written Torah and rabbinical statements and commentaries, with the goal of causing them to revere and love the Almighty.[22] In this case, the obligation toward the children of both sexes is equal, for the parent's responsibility is to educate his offspring to know the difference between good and evil and develop as good Jews.[23]

It is worth noting that while the obligation to teach one's sons the Torah is based on the *mitzvah* of learning Torah per se, as well as the ultimate goal enabling them to fulfill the *mitzvot*, the requirement concerning one's daughters is to teach them as a means of enabling them to be capable of executing the *mitzvot* relevant to women in a knowledgeable manner. In both cases, the father is obliged to learn with his children, with the goal of imparting Jewish values to them, and in both cases, parents should remove their children from forbidden items so that they may develop pure in spirit. Indeed, it is said that the Chatam Sofer himself studied rabbinical legends with his daughters so as to impart Jewish values to them.[24]

In addition to this, the father is obliged by Torah law to tell his children the story of Israel's exodus from Egypt on the eve of Passover.[25] The *mitzvah* of relating the story to children is repeated four times in the Pentateuch, to point out the importance of telling the tale to each child according to his capacity for understanding.[26] The Passover Seder is conducted in such a manner as to arouse the child's curiosity and entice him to ask questions about the novelty of the procedures. In replying to the child's questions, the father recounts the story of Israel's exodus from Egypt, which is a basis for the Jewish faith. Children are included in the reciting of the Hagaddah and the conduct of the Seder as soon as they are able to speak.

TORAH EDUCATION AND REVERENCE FOR GOD

In order for education to succeed, the child must be reared at the most tender age to revere the Almighty and strive for holiness. In accordance with Jewish educational philosophy, this has precedence over education toward the active aspects of *mitzvot*[27] for it applies even to the infant. While the Jewish values of revering the Almighty and striving for holiness form the element of behavior referred to in Judaism as the soul, primary integration of these values occurs in the memory. As memory involves the retention of a learned response from a brief sensory register to an extended period of time, it is in keeping with the most sophisticated principles of educational psychology to begin this *chinnukh* from the first day of life.

Thus, although the parent is not obligated to restrain his child from observing prohibitions until his second or third year, he will do justice by removing his child from forbidden foods as soon as he is born, so that he may grow to be just.[28] Similarly, the parent should take care not to play profane music in the child's room, and not to sing songs that entice the evil inclination.[29]

This psychological principle of imprinting in the child the

aim for holiness and Torah through impressions instilled in early life is instituted in the Bible itself. The commandment to gather the entire nation to hear the words of the Almighty, including men, women, and young children—and even babies who are not yet capable of understanding—sets the precedent for *chinnukh* in early childhood.[30]

It is considered a good practice for parents to take their children to the synagogue and to teach them to remain still and in awe during the services. The father may teach his child when to pronounce "Amen." In fact, Jewish sages maintain that a child is eligible for the afterworld as soon as he pronounces "Amen" for a blessing he hears.[31] Similarly, children are brought to kiss the Torah scroll on Sabbath and holidays. It is customary to gather all children under the *talit* on Simchat Torah while reading a portion of the Torah. These symbolic acts endear the Torah and *mitzvot* to the child while he is touching and actually feeling the scroll.

Parents should take care to wash the child's hands upon rising and should train him to wash three times consecutively in accordance with Halakhah (to remove the evil spirits present during sleep).[32]

EDUCATION IN MITZVOT

In contrast to and parallel with *chinnukh* to Torah, which begins with life itself, *chinnukh* to *mitzvot* requires learning, which involves the changing of behavior as a result of practice and experience. Judaism acknowledges the difference between *chinnukh* to Torah, based on the development of memory and cognition, and learning, which requires concrete experience. According to modern psychological theories, such as Piaget's stages of cognitive development, such learning becomes possible as the child adapts to the environment and his structures of thinking become organized. This principle is instituted in

Judaism by the Halakhah that children should be taught *mitzvot* in accordance with their level of maturation and their attention span.[33] A third requirement for learning, reinforcement, should arise from the Jewish values instilled in the child at the most tender age.

In accordance with this principle, the child should be taught to recite the blessings that are said before performing a *mitzvah* and the blessings recited to the Almighty before and after partaking of various kinds of pleasure, such as eating.[34] When teaching the child to recite the blessings, it is permitted for the adult to pronounce the holy names, but one should not say "Amen" after the child's blessing until he is six years of age. The child should also be taught gradually to recite the blessing after meals until he knows it entirely.[35]

As soon as the child is able to chew solid foods such as bread, he should be taught to perform the *mitzvot*. Accordingly, the parent should offer the child the required minimal portion (*kezayit*) of *matzah* and bitter herbs during the Passover Seder.[36] The child should also be taught to drink the four cups of wine during the Passover Seder.[37]

As soon as the child is capable of dressing himself with the *tzitzit* and of holding it in his hands while reciting the *Shema*, his father is obliged to buy him *tzitzit*. It is customary to begin *chinnukh* to *tzitzit* at the age of three, at which time the father should explain the importance of the *mitzvah* to endear it to the child.[38] The father should train his son to look at the *tzitzit* every morning while reciting the blessing and to consider it a symbol of all the *mitzvot* and good deeds.

The same holds for all the positive *mitzvot*. As soon as the child has reached the necessary level of maturation, in accordance with his ability and intelligence, he should be trained in observing that particular *mitzvah*. Thus, as soon as the child understands the sanctity of Shabbat, he is to hear the Kiddush and Havdalah recitations, and so on for all the *mitzvot*.[39]

As *chinnukh* to positive *mitzvot* includes *mitzvot* from the

Torah and rabbinical laws, the father must train his son to recite the blessings over the *lulav* and *etrog* on Sukkot, to hear the reading of Megillat Esther on Purim, to recite the *Shema* in the morning prayers and at night, and the like.[40] Although the father must buy the child a set of *lulav* and *etrog* if he is capable of shaking it as required, the set need not be especially choice grade. On the first day of Succoth, the child may recite the blessings over his father's set, only after the father has recited the blessings.[41] Moreover, the child should be taught the Shema at the obligatory times in the morning and evening, although he is not required to recite the prayer.[42]

It is customary to allow young children to light Chanukah candles even though they are not obligated to do so.[43]

The principle of *chinnukh* in early childhood is deemed so important that some sages permitted the exemption of children from certain prohibitions in order to train them in the *mitzvot*. For example, a young child may practice blowing the *shofar* on Rosh Hashanah after the services, although an adult is prohibited from doing so.[44]

Finally, when the child is four years old and considered to be ready to learn, he is to be taught the letters of the alefbet as a major step in *chinnukh* to Torah and *mitzvot*.[45]

Halakhah is even more perceptive concerning *chinnukh* involving prohibitions. While the child is in the sensorimotor (infant-toddler) stage of development the parents should train him / her to refrain from prohibited acts, although there is a legal dispute whether the parent must stop his child from performing a prohibited act.[46] However, a parent or any adult may not cause a child to eat a forbidden food or execute a prohibited act in Torah law.[47] (If the child is ill and must be given medication prohibited by law, it is permitted only if the prohibition is from rabbinical law and it is administered by a gentile.)[48] A Rabbi should be consulted if Torah law need be violated to save the child in special cases.

When the child reaches the pre-operational stage of development (at the age of two and a half to three years and on), his parents must see to it that he does not eat any forbidden food or carry out a prohibited action. At this stage, the child is capable of understanding when told that something is not allowed; therefore, his parents have the responsibility to begin training him to refrain from prohibited acts (though this responsibility is not extended to others dealing with children).[49]

In practical terms, the parent must train his child not to use bad language and not to curse or lie. The child must be trained to refrain from fighting and swearing. According to the Code of Jewish Law, this obligation rests upon parents and also upon nursery-school teachers.[50]

On Yom Kippur, children up to the age of six may wear shoes made of leather and must not be allowed to fast. However, it is good to train them to fast for a little while by serving their meals a bit later than usual. (It is not permitted to bathe children on Yom Kippur.)[51]

PARENTS AS EDUCATORS

Basically, Judaism recognizes that the home is the educational foundation for the moral development of the child. It is a well-known fact that "what the child speaks in the marketplace, he has heard at home from his mother or father."[52] Indeed, the family is the major educational institution mentioned in the Bible. Based on the commandment "and you shall teach them diligently to your children,"[53] the mother and father were totally responsible for teaching the child the ways of the Almighty so that he might develop as a good Jew. As society progressed, schools were instituted to teach children Torah and *derech eretz* ("the way of the world"). (See Chapter 18.) Nevertheless, the realm of early childhood education has remained in the sphere of the home as the basis for the child's emerging conception of the world around him.

Although the father is delegated the primary role in ensuring the child's formal Jewish education, the mother fulfills a significant function in her own right. The Bible commands, "Listen my son to the instruction of your father, and do not forsake the teaching of your mother."[54] What aspects of *chinnukh* are delegated to the father, and what is the role played by the mother in educating her young child?

According to Halakhah, the father has the primary responsibility of teaching his children Torah.[55] In teaching his children Torah, the father fulfills a positive commandment, and it is considered as if he had received the Torah from Mount Horeb.[56] In fact, it is specifically stated in the Talmud that the father has the responsibility of teaching his children Torah and that women are exempt from this task.[57]

Similarly, according to Maimonides and Rashi, the obligation of *chinnukh* toward one's children is delegated to the father and not the mother.[58] Indeed, in all instances in Halakhah concerning the *chinnukh* of children for mitzvoth, the Code of Jewish Law specifically mentions the father's responsibility—as in the case of *tzitzit* and the Megillah. In the Talmud, we find the instruction that the father must teach his son the *Shema*, Torah, and the Hebrew language. The father should begin educating his son at the age of three by teaching him the letters of the Torah.[59]

Nevertheless, Halakhah does not neglect the mother's contribution to the child's *chinnukh*. On the contrary, her role as primary educator of her children is inscribed in the Jewish tradition. According to various talmudic sources, the mother also has responsibility for her children's *chinnukh*. Rashi specifically states that the responsibility for *chinnukh* toward one's children is delegated to the mother and the father.[60] This view is based on the biblical passage: "And so shall you say to the House of Jacob [referring to the women] and to the children of Israel [implying the men]." The women are mentioned first because the primary role of educating children to the values of the

Torah, *mitzvot,* and good and honest deeds lies with the mother, who has the power to rear children in the ways of the Almighty.[61] This view is also held by the Chatam Sofer.[62] A primary function to be fulfilled by the mother is language development, which she can teach in her daily contacts with the child.[63] Language, as the basis for more sophisticated thinking, is the cornerstone of *chinnukh.*[64] Furthermore, it is the mother who brings her child to (nursery) school and then to *cheder* to learn Torah. (For this, the mother gains the right to the afterworld.)[65]

In summary, while the father has the specific responsibility of teaching his children Torah, both parents share the function of *chinnukh* to Torah, *mitzvot,* and good deeds. Both parents are rewarded for their share in educating the young child, by seeing him follow their ways in continuing the Jewish heritage.

TECHNIQUES OF EARLY CHILDHOOD EDUCATION

In introducing the subject of *chinnukh* of young children, Halakhah offers sound advice on teaching methods: If the child is not disciplined while learning, the educator may use physical means to make sure that he learns, but he should not be cruel in disciplining the child. In all instances, the educator must administer punishment immediately after the child commits a bad deed or refuses to learn. If not, then the educator should refrain from punishing him later, to prevent the child from becoming tense and depressed. It is likewise forbidden to frighten or threaten a child by saying something profane, such as "The dog or the cat will come and bite you."[66] The child should never be harshly beaten. In fact, the Code of Jewish Law specifies that the educator may not use a stick or whip to administer punishment. Rather, the instrument used should be a shoestring.[67] The Talmud goes further, warning that a person may not impose great fear in his home,[68] for this ruins the relationship between parents and children and removes the basis for trust and love which are the foundations of education. The sages advised that since children will not readily accept something said in anger or by shouting, the labor of the Almighty—the task of *chinnukh*—should be carried out with patience and quiet.[69]

The guiding principle in all matters of *chinnukh* should be the rabbinical saying, "In dealing with a child . . . let the left hand repel while the right hand draws near."[70] All admonishments should be followed by a show of love for the child. This builds the child's self-esteem and at the same time teaches him that the punishment is directed at his wrongdoing and not at himself.

HONOR THE CHILD

In order to succeed, the educator must respect the child as an individual. The sages wisely pointed out that man is motivated more by his own honor than by all other desires in the world.[71] Care must be taken to respect the child's opinions and individuality.

A second guiding principle in educational methods is implicit in the biblical saying, "Guide each lad in accordance with his ways."[72] In teaching the values of Judaism, the educator must keep in mind the child's unique personality and temperament. By suiting the pace of *chinnukh* to the child's needs, the parent is assured that the child will accept what is being taught with love and devotion. By understanding the child's weaknesses and strengths, the parent can help the child develop to his fullest capabilities as a good Jew.[73]

Consideration for the child's integrity and individuality is such an important element in *chinnukh* that it is incorporated in Halakhah. Thus, *chinnukh* to *mitzvot* must be based on the child's personal level of maturation and ability to comprehend each *mitzvah*. The parent must also show respect for the child's dignity by allowing room for independence, which is vital for the growth of personality.[74]

SETTING AN EXAMPLE

The most effective educational technique in *chinnukh* to Torah and Jewish values is the personal example set by the parents in their daily behavior and relationships. The noted Jewish educator, Rabbi Samson Raphael Hirsch, notes unequivocally that parents must keep in mind that there is no substitute for the educational influence of their own example.[75] The first step in educating the child to Jewish values is to look at one's own conduct and try to improve one's own characteristics in order to serve as a model for the child, for "the child sees in the picture of his parents' life, the shape of his life in the future, and as he desires to be like them, he will do as they do."[76]

SUMMARY

The obligation of each parent to teach his child Torah and *mitzvot* forms the basis for early childhood education in the Jewish home. The Jewish philosophy of education is implied in the word *chinnukh*, based on the root "to inaugurate." The child must be taught Jewish values at the very beginning of life so that he may assume the framework of life prescribed by the Torah. The basic Jewish values of reverence for the Almighty, striving for holiness, justice, kindness, love for fellow man, and good manners are to be impressed upon the child from the first day of life through the example set by the parents and the home environment. This introduction to Torah, impressed upon the youngest infant, forms the root of the child's cognitive development.

The Hebrew word for "learning," *limud*, is related to the word *lomud*, which means "is accustomed to." Here, too, the

Jewish philosophy of learning is implied in the word itself. In learning the *mitzvot,* the child is introduced in practice to the actual fulfillment of positive commandments in accordance with his capabilities to do so. Judaism acknowledges that the individual cannot be expected to fulfill the moral code until he is spiritually and intellectually ripe. For this reason, children under the age of thirteen are exempt from the requirement of fulfilling the *mitzvot* and must be taught to practice them in accordance with their level of maturation until they reach the stage when they are accustomed to the acts and may freely choose to perform them.

The parental role in education is very great—so much so, in fact, that parents are required by law to pray for the Almighty's compassionate assistance in facilitating their children's growth in the path of Torah and *mitzvot* and their acquisition of good characteristics.[77] When lighting the candles on Sabbath eve, the mother should pray that her children will grow in the light of the Torah.[78]

Early childhood education is deemed so important that the Almighty Himself, it is said, sits with young children at the fourth hour of the day and teaches them, as it is written: "To whom shall I teach knowledge . . . to those that are weaned from the breast."[79]

The education of young children toward the Judaic framework of life must be based on respect for the child, knowledge of his unique personality, discipline with moderation, and above all, the element of "love and the close relationship between parent and child" that nurtures trust.[80] This basis of trust is the foundation for the success of early childhood education and the healthy development of the child within the framework of Judaism.

9
Discipline

THE CONCEPT OF DISCIPLINE

Parental discipline seeks to limit and restrict the influence of factors in the environment, and is intended to teach children responsibility, self-control, and the ability to defer the need for self-satisfaction. In this sense it has a dual role in Judaism. On one hand, it is a means of instruction; on the other, it is punishment for wrongdoing. Judaism provides humanistic guidelines for both of these applications of discipline. It emphasizes that disciplinary measures should always be carried out in such a manner as to convey the message that the agent (whether parent or teacher) has the child's welfare and well-being in mind.

Jewish law and literature insist that disciplinary measures must be accompanied by expressions of warmth and love, as is shown by the following passage from the Talmud: "A child, discipline him with the left hand and draw him closer with the right hand."[1] The same concept applies in the relationship between God and man; "For he whom the Lord loves, He admonishes like a father who appeases his son."[2] Rashi comments on the second part of this verse that the Lord is likened to a father who strikes his son with a rod in order to correct his misbehavior, then soothes and appeases him by speaking words of affection.

Although God punishes disloyalty to divine teachings, it is always made clear that Israel is as precious to Him as a child to a father and that He will never abandon His people. The following passage aptly points out this parallel:

Is not Ephraim a dear son unto Me? or a child that I dandle? For whenever I speak of him, I do earnestly remember him again; therefore are My inward parts moved for him; I will surely have mercy upon him, saith the Lord.[3]

Israel is likened to a dear son of the Lord. Although this son is being disciplined for wrongdoing, the fatherly love brings with it feelings of compassion and mercy.

THE ROLE OF DISCIPLINE IN CHILD-REARING

The crucial role of discipline in child-rearing is brought to light in the story of David and Absalom. "Because David did not rebuke his son Absalom, and did not chastise him, Absalom turned to an evil culture . . . causing him no end of severe troubles."[4] Furthermore, Adonijah initiated a rebellion against David, his father, and wanted to reign in his place, because his father had never stopped him to say, "Why did you do such a thing?"[5] Similarly, Eli the priest did not discipline his sons and thus brought about a tragedy for himself and his family.[6]

In light of all this, the parent is advised: "Chastise thy son, for there is hope; and let not thy soul spare him for his crying."[7] Furthermore: "Correct thy son and he will procure thee rest; yea, he will give delight unto thy soul."[8] Another passage in Proverbs adds an additional dimension to this advice: "A wise son [becometh so] by the correction of his father; but a scorner hearkeneth not to rebuke."[9]

Thus, discipline, when applied in the spirit of Judaism, benefits both the parent and the child. The father will delight in his offspring and the child will grow to be wise and learned. The benefit to the child is further stressed in this passage: "The rod and reproof impart wisdom; but a lad abandoned to himself bringeth shame on his mother."[10] Rashi comments on this verse that it refers to the case of Ishmael, who brought about his mother's banishment from her home as a result of his misbehavior.

From Ben Sira we learn: "He who loves his son will consistently use his rod, so that he may rejoice in the end."[11] Although the phrase "to use the rod" appears often in statements on parental and classroom discipline, it is not to be applied literally. (see pg. 137). Before considering the methods of discipline according to Judaism, it is necessary to stipulate when a child should be disciplined according to Halakhah and by whom.

WHEN TO DISCIPLINE

The first biblical reference to parental discipline appears in the Book of Deuteronomy.

> If a man have a stubborn and rebellious son, who hearkeneth not to the voice of his mother, and they chastise him, and he will not hearken unto them; then shall his father and his mother lay hold on him and bring him out unto the elders of his city, and unto the gate of his place; and they shall say unto the elders of the city, "This our son is stubborn and rebellious, he will not hearken to our voice; he is a glutton, and a drunkard." And all the men of his city shall stone him with stones, that he die; and thou shalt put away the evil from the midst of thee; and all Israel shall hear, and be afraid.[12]

According to his passage, parents are authorized to punish their child for wrongdoing. As we see, it is the parents who must bring their son to the elders and state that he is rebellious and stubborn, thus bringing about his punishment. Since the law of the rebellious son was hedged with so many conditions that there never was and never will be an actual case of stoning a rebellious son, the passage has been cited by talmudic jurists for its educational and deterrent purposes.

Nachmanides comments on this text that according to the

opinion of the rabbis, the passage regarding the rebellious son does not apply to young children, because they are exempt from all punishments in the Torah and from fulfillment of the *mitzvot*. However, as soon as a youngster has two hairs (i.e., matures), he is liable to punishment for two sins (shaming his parents and rebellion).

The Ralbag, commenting on the verse, "Correct thy son and he will provide thee rest,"[13] says that the advice is directed to the parent of a young child. Ben Sira states: "Bend his head in his youth and strike his buttocks when he is young."[14] Maimonides stipulates that "It is worthy for the *bet din* to strike the children according to a child's strength—as punishment for theft, so that they do not accustom themselves to it."[15] This is an extraordinary case in which the *bet din* carries out punishment against a young child with the aim of preventing further delinquency. Maimonides teaches us here that in cases of delinquency, it is the *bet din* which executes punishment against children—even young children.

Thus, Judaism attributes great importance to preventative discipline, which should begin at an early age. As the child matures, the parent must suit disciplinary measures to his or her needs and stage of development. This is implied in the biblical passage: "You shall not place a stumbling-block before the blind."[16] We find in the Responsa literature that this passage concerns one who strikes a grown child. Rashi explains that an older child who is hit may strike back and is thus incited to violate the injunction against striking a parent. Because of this, Jewish law forbids administering physical punishment to a grown child (a girl over twelve or a boy over thirteen) or to a younger child who is mature (shows two hairs).[17] In the Responsa of Benjamin Ze'ev, the author cites Rabbenu Jonah as explaining that one should not strike a grown child, for this causes the youngster to sin with his tongue and curse his father.[18] Similarly, Maimonides states that the courts ban a father who strikes a mature child. (Hilchot Teshuva)

The First Five Years: From Infant to Child

In the talmudic period, it was considered the father's duty or *mitzvah* (not prerogative) to discipline his child. Similarly, it is a *mitzvah* for a teacher to discipline his pupil. Rabbah, one of the greatest sages in Babylon, who was active in the field of education, expresses the opinion that the father must relate to his son with a strong hand even if the son wants to learn—for it is written in Proverbs: "Correct thy son and he will procure thee rest; yea, he will give delight unto thy soul."[19]

It seems from the commentators that this is intended more as an argumentative point than actual instruction for application. Indeed, we find that Rabbi Judah and Rav warn: "Parents should not impose too much fright in the home, for in the end the parent is led to commit three sins: adultery, murder, or desecration of the Sabbath."[20]

In any case, we find that even in the study of the Torah it was required to adhere to disciplinary measures: "When a person teaches his son Torah, he must do so with trepidation."[21]

In the halakhic literature, these viewpoints are expressed explicitly. In the *Laws of Murder,* Maimonides states that since a father who strikes his son and a rabbi who hits his pupil are performing a *mitzvah,* there is no liability for punishment if death unintentionally results.[22] Similarly, in the Responsa of the Rashba, we find: "The father who strikes his son and the teacher who hits his pupil are exempt from punishment, for they are performing a *mitzvah.*"[23]

In the Responsa of Rabbi Jacob ben Joseph Reischer, we find the question: "A teacher who strikes his pupil in anger because he did not learn and wounds him—is he liable to punishment or not?" The reply is that the father who strikes his son and the rabbi who hits his pupil are not liable to punishment, because they are performing a *mitzvah.* The author adds that although we have learned that a pupil must be hit only with a shoestring and not with cruelty, nevertheless, the teacher should not be fined for his action. However, in order that the teacher should not make a habit of displaying anger—since a hothead should not be a teacher—and in order not to violate the teaching of the sages that a pupil should be hit only with a shoestring, the teacher must pay the medical expenses.[24]

Rabbi Moses Feinstein lists tractate *Makkot* 8 as the source for the conclusion that the father who hits his son and the rabbi who whips his pupil are exempt from punishment.[25] Rabbi Feinstein notes that students may be punished for specific acts of wrongdoing but not for something which is suspected. The statement in *Makkot* that it is permissible to punish a student even though he is perfect (i.e., knows how to learn and does learn) applies to a student who has the ability to learn more but does not do so because he is lazy. Thus, if a student who learns well misses something in his studies, this is considered laziness and is worthy of punishment. It is up to the teacher to decide when to punish him, for he is the expert and may judge. If a teacher suspects one of his students of misbehavior, he must chastise him, saying things that bring him closer to the Torah; when the teacher knows without a doubt that the pupil has misbehaved, he is permitted to punish him calmly and without anger.

From Rabbi Moses Feinstein we also learn more details about the case in which a father strikes his child and kills him accidentally. According to the Talmud, (Makkot 8) the father is not liable to punishment. Rabbi Feinstein notes that a father must discipline even a weak child, but he must be careful to do so in accordance with the child's strength. We find in this case, that the father fulfilled the *mitzvah* of punishing his child for wrongdoing, but did not exercise sufficient caution and did not do it well.[26]

METHODS OF DISCIPLINE

The question of methods of discipline has always been controversial. Indeed, we find many references to using the "rod" with children, as in the following passage: "Withhold not from a lad correction, for if thou beat him with the rod he will not die. Thou wilt indeed beat him with the rod, but thou wilt deliver his soul from perdition."[27]

We know that in some cases this was taken literally, with occasional dire consequences, as in the story of the son of Georgias of Lod, who threw himself into a well out of fright when his father threatened to punish him for running away from school. A similar story is told of a boy in Bnei-Brak who broke the Sabbath goblet.[28] It seems, however, that "use the rod" is meant to be figurative and demonstrative rather than literal. Again in Proverbs, we find the advice: "Chasten your son, for there is hope, but set not your heart on his destruction."[29] A clear statement in the Talmud serves as the basis for the means of discipline (punishment) according to Judaism: "Rav said to Rav Samuel bar Shilat: If you hit a child, strike him only with a shoestring."[30] Rashi comments that this means the child should be punished with a light stroke which does not harm him. Thus, Judaism advocates restrained physical punishment. Maimonides concludes that a teacher should hit a pupil in order to discipline him, but he should not strike him harshly as he would an enemy. Therefore, the teacher should not strike pupils with a stick or a whip but with a small string.[31]

Another fundamental principle in the Judaic conception of discipline is that punishment must be immediate in order to be effective: "Do not threaten a child that he will be hit later; if you see him doing a wrong deed, strike him immediately or be completely silent."[32]

In this manner, the punishment is clearly linked to the child's misbehavior. This method also prevents the child from developing anxiety as a result of fearing the punishment over a period of time. As such, it also maintains the child's sense of dignity and self-respect. Thus, it corresponds to the principle stated above that discipline should be followed by a show of love and warmth, enabling the child to understand that the punishment is not directed against him but rather at his wrongdoing.

In all cases, discipline must be followed by a communication of love for the child according to the passage: "Be it ever your way to thrust off with your left hand and draw to you with the right hand" (Sotah 47a).

The Judaic conception of discipline is humanistic and advocates individualized means of action to instill obedience and prevent delinquency. We have seen in the Responsa of Rabbi Moses Feinstein, that teachers and fathers are advised to discipline children in accordance with their individual temperaments and strength. This view originates in the following passage: "Teach each lad in accordance with his course."[33]

Another method of educational discipline described in the Talmud fits the modern concept of reinforcement. An interesting anecdote on this aspect of discipline is related as follows:

> Rav came to a place and decreed a fast-day [because of drought]. The rains did not come. A public servant came before him and said, "Let the wind blow," and the wind blew. He said, "Let the rain fall," and the rain fell. Rav said to him, "What is your profession?" The man answered, "I teach young children, and I teach the poor as well as the rich; and whoever cannot pay tuition—I do not take anything from him. And I have a pool of fish, and whoever does not wish to learn, I 'bribe' him with fish, and I entice and appease him, until he comes to learn."[34]

The method of positive reinforcement—or training by reward—was utilized in the period of the Talmud. Indeed, this method is highly recommended, as is evident from the preceding tale, which relates the teacher's special attributes in practicing educational discipline through positive reinforcement.

We have seen that the methods utilized to discipline young children include restrained physical punishment and positive or negative reinforcement. We have also seen that it is forbidden to adminisiter physical punishment to a grown child. What method, then, should be used to discipline adolescents, who are in the prime stage of rebellion and restlessness? The following passage offers wise advice on this matter: "A rebuke enters deeper into a person of understanding than a hundred stripes a fool."[35]

In addition, a clear strategy is indicated in the Responsa of Rabbi Yechiel Jacob Weinberg. Rabbi Weinberg was asked about a sixteen-year-old yeshiva student who was enthralled with gambling and had become friendly with a group of hoodlums. Despite his bad tendencies, the boy continued to adhere to the *mitzvot*. The worried parents wanted to know whether it was worthwhile for the father to forbid the son to use the equipment he had purchased in order to gamble by compelling him not to do so. Rabbi Weinberg replied that for educational reasons it is necessary to abstain from using forceful measures against a son who has veered from the righteous path. The prohibition on using physical punishment on a grown son does not apply only to the use of force; it relates to any forceful means used to bring about the opposite results. Therefore, he advised the parents to find another pastime for the boy or to send him to Israel to learn in a yeshiva, suggesting that upon his return the boy might no longer be interested in gambling.[36]

SUMMARY

Discipline occupies a central role in Jewish childrearing. It is a means of education and a source of authority to provide punishment for wrongdoing. The classic biblical case of the rebellious son illustrates the parent's duty to punish his child for wrongdoing. In the talmudic period, it was considered a *mitzvah* for a parent to discipline his child and for a teacher to discipline his student. The many references to discipline through the use of the "rod" are not to be taken literally, for the rabbis instructed that a child should be hit only with a shoestring (i.e., restrained physical punishment).

Punishment for wrongdoing should be immediate if it is to be effective, and the parents should not threaten the child if they do not intend to carry out the punishment immediately, as this may cause the child anxiety.

Methods of punishment should not be arbitrary, each parent and teacher must suit his disciplinary measures to the nature and strength of the individual child. Punishment should always be followed by a demonstration of warmth and acceptance.

Wherever possible, preventative discipline and enticements should be utilized as a means of reinforcement to educate children and ward off misbehavior. Behavior modification and rebuke should be used in disciplining adolescents, for it is forbidden to use physical punishment with an older child.

10
Health and Disease

The talmudic scholars coined the term *tza'ar giddul banim* ("the difficulties of rearing children") to designate all the ailments accompanying child development.[1] The fact that these ailments are pervasive and sometimes debilitating is evident from the declaration that "it is easier to see a whole forest of young olive trees grow than to rear one child in Palestine."[2] Illness is certainly the most difficult trouble of infancy and childhood. Nothing causes more anxiety and frustration than the sight of a child who is suffering pain from disease.

While mothers spend a great deal of time and energy caring for the health and safety of their children, it is surprising that we find no description or example of this in the Torah. It would seem that child care in biblical times was relatively simple, limited to providing for the child's basic needs, such as food and clothing. Indeed, it is very likely that mothers in those days did not have to deal with colds, measles, mumps, or other childhood diseases, for the Talmud states that man was not afflicted with illness until the generation of Jacob and that medical treatment for disease originated in the period of Elijah's prophecy.[3] Another source says that weakness descended on mankind with the death of Rabbi Gamliel.[4] As one might expect from these statements, we find references to childhood diseases in the Prophets and more detailed descriptions of symptoms and diagnosis as well as prevention and treatment in the Talmud.

The obligation to take care of one's health is incorporated

into Judaism as a fundamental halakhic principle based on Torah law. Each person is responsible for safeguarding his body and maintaining his health, based on the biblical verse: "Take heed and take care of yourselves."[5] Jewish scholars quoted in the Talmud and the Responsa interpret this passage as a halakhic rule stemming directly from the Torah.[6] Each individual must strive to be fit in accordance with contemporary medical knowledge.[7]

This responsibility is extended to include the parent's obligation to safeguard his child. "A man must honor his wife and his sons by dressing and feeding them more than himself, for they are dependent on him and he is dependent on the Almighty, who created the universe."[8] In case of danger the father must defend his family, as exemplified by Jacob, who placed his life in jeopardy to save his family.[9]

Another example of parental responsibility for children's well-being is given by Rabbi Abraham Mordecai of Gur. When a woman complained to him that her husband was neglecting the family, he cited the passage in the Torah where Moses complained to the Almighty, "Have I given birth to this nation? Where am I to take meat to feed them?"[10] It would seem unnecessary for him to ask: "Have I given birth to this nation?" However, said Rabbi Abraham Mordecai, this teaches us that a parent who gives birth to a child is responsible for his child's needs and well-being, for the Almighty has granted him the privilege of rearing children.[11]

Moreover, Maimonides points out that if a person only takes care of himself and keeps fit so as to make himself able to have children who will then do his work for him and labor on his behalf, this is not the right thing to do. Each man must take care of himself in order to be capable of leading a life in the framework of Judaism, for it is impossible to learn knowledge and the wisdom of the Almighty if one is hungry or ill. In caring for one's children, each parent must consider that his child will grow up to be a scholar and must afford him all necessities to make sure that he is healthy and safe during his period of development. A man who acts accordingly is fulfilling the role assigned to him by the Almighty.[12]

Maimonides elaborates by detailing the means to be taken in order to maintain a healthy body (which is the way of the Almighty).[13] The guidelines set by Maimonides are incorporated into Halakhah along with prescriptions by other rabbinical medical experts.[14] In order to fulfill the goal of Judaism to strive toward knowledge of the Almighty, man must withdraw from whatever causes him harm and must conduct himself in accordance with what is healthy and good for him. The essence of physiological health in Halakhah (based on scientific principles of physiology) is the maintenance of homeostasis, the process by which the internal environment of the individual is maintained relatively constant in the face of changes in the external environment.[15] The main influences on man's health related to homeostatis and the adaptative capability of his body are nutrition, physical environment, psychosocial stress, and the immune defenses of the body.[16] In order to maintain his health, man must, according to Halakhah, take care to receive proper nutrition, remove damaging elements from his physical environment, relieve himself of psychosocial stress, and provide for all medical treatment necessary in case of illness. In the case of parents, this responsibility is extended to include any offspring who are dependent on them for healthy development.

GUIDELINES FOR HEALTH AND THE PREVENTION OF DISEASE

What must a parent do in order to afford his child the maximum possibility of healthy development? Above all, Halakhah recognizes the importance of proper nutrition for health and the prevention of disease. On the basis of medical facts, Halakhah attributes physical health to proper digestion.[17] It is accepted that proper digestion takes place if one does not eat too much and the food is easily absorbed.[18] In order for a person to be nourished according to these specifications, the choice of foods must take into consideration the age and temperament of the person involved, and the climate. Young children require food more often than older people, while elderly people require that their food be light for digestion. In the summer portions should be smaller than in winter (some doctors suggest serving two-thirds of the winter meal during the summer).[19] Children should be served food which agrees with their temperament and metabolism; an active child should be given food that will moderate his nature while a bashful child should receive nourishment intended to induce activity, all in accordance with environmental conditions and the season.[20] Children should not be forced to eat if they are not hungry and must be taught to chew properly for good digestion.[21] Children should not be overfed, for too much food is like poison. It is of the utmost importance to choose the proper foods for the child's meals, for "most of people's ailments occur as a result of eating bad food."[22]

The framework for natural and pure nourishment as the basis for promoting health and preventing disease is provided by the laws of Kashrut, which regulate the Jewish diet, and by the recommendations of the Jewish sages, which emphasize the necessary nutrients. Adherence to this framework in the early years of life, when the growing organ systems require the most and best nutrients available, is crucial for the developing child. Improper or deficient nutrition during the critical stages of life may result in disease, stunted growth, or mental deficiency, as has been highlighted by recent research findings.[23] With these facts in mind, it becomes clear that the Judaic legal and philosophical principles concerning proper nutrition for health have the interest of the child at stake. According to the sages, a person who does not eat the proper nutritious food required for health commits a prohibition rooted in the Torah: "Thou shalt not destroy thy body."[24] This is reinforced by the father's legal obligation to feed his young children and provide for their care.[25]

As a consequence of this legal philosophy, a parent must feed his children the best available food to provide the nutrients necessary for good health.[26] Care must be taken to maintain proper sanitary conditions and to avoid food which has a bad odor (i.e., is spoiled by bacteria) or liquid which has been exposed.[27] Everyone's diet must be chosen according to medical specifications in order to receive the nutrients suitable for one's temperament, the climate, and the season.[28] Care should be taken to choose food which is not constipating. If constipation occurs a doctor should be consulted.[29] Proper nourishment and digestion are the primary means of assuring homeostasis and a balanced metabolism.[30]

EXERCISE AND SLEEP

In order to fulfill the requirement of guarding one's body against illness, one must exercise moderately in accordance with the season, time, and body size. It is advisable to exercise by working or walking before a meal to build up an appetite and assure proper digestion.[31] One should not overdo exercising, nor should one rest too much; both rest and exercise must be carried out with moderation. One should exercise less in hot weather and more in cold weather.[32] Children should be instructed to rest during the day, especially after meals in order to assure good digestion. Rigorous exercise and bathing are not advisable until digestion is completed.[33]

Children should sleep for the average time required by their age. Sleep is important for health; while the senses rest, the body digests the nutrients necessary for growth.[34]

FRESH AIR AND SUNSHINE

One simple precaution to take in warding off illness is to maintain the proper temperature in the home. Overheating in winter may be the cause of cold symptoms and many other ailments.[35] Children should be kept out of drafts and not overheated. Parents must take care to live in an area where there is clean unpolluted air, preferably at a high altitude.[36] Mountain air is especially recommended to cure various illnesses.[37] Parents should make sure that their home is free of mold and mildew. The rooms or apartment must be aired frequently and deodorized to provide maximum comfort and health.

Daily outings for children are recommended, as discussed in Chapter 5.

PSYCHOSOCIAL STRESS

In normal human development, man must cope with dangers of all kinds. According to Jewish philosophy, the various functions of the soul, such as worry, anxiety, anger, and fear, must be understood.[38] Worry, anxiety, and fear may cause illness.[39] It is man's responsibility to be content with what he has and to attempt to be in good spirits at all times. Children should be guided toward acquiring a cheerful disposition in accordance with this philosophy as a means of affording them happiness in life. The most effective way to accomplish this is to make the child feel loved and wanted from his very first day of life. The high mortality rates in the foundling homes of the eighteenth and nineteenth centuries, as well as the psychic and psychosomatic disturbances in hospitalized children[40] and in children separated from their parents during World War II,[41] point out the importance of a loving relationship between parent and child for both physical and emotional health. Bowlby's research on the importance of the mother-child interaction,[42] and Gardner's observation that children who were emotionally deprived when raised in institutions developed hormonal imbalances, such as a decrease in the growth hormone, further attests to the importance of a warm parent-child relationship to healthy child development.

An awareness of this phenomenon is instituted in Judaic philosophy with the warning that in dealing with the child the parent should "repel with the left hand [discipline as necessary] and draw forth with the right hand [show love and warmth for the child as an individual]."[43] Moreover, according to Halakhah, the parent must not threaten a child with punishment and execute it later on. The parent should either punish the child immediately or keep still. (An example is given of a child who ran away from school. His father threatened to punish him, but as he did not do so immediately, the child was overcome with anxiety and killed himself.)[44] In addition, it is forbidden to frighten a child by threatening that a dog or boogie-man will come and eat him up, or the like.[45] In all instances, the parent must deal with the child with understanding and must avoid inducing undue anxiety which may cause mental or physical illness.

CHILDHOOD DISEASES

Before discussing the references to various childhood diseases in Jewish literature, it is important to note that the talmudic medical analysis and treatment for diseases were quite sophisticated for their time; the pragmatic nature of Halakha ensures that modern medical knowledge and techniques override outdated treatments (see Kitzur Shulkhan Arukh 32a). Numerous childhood diseases are described in Jewish sources. Although the biblical references pertain mostly to the birth process, care of the newborn, and the pathology of neonates, later talmudic sources deal in more detail with pediatrics in general. The talmudic sages advise, among other things, on nursing, nutrition, and various ailments, often discussing both their medical and their legal aspects.[46] The childhood diseases mentioned in the Talmud are: neonatal jaundice, discussed in relation to the execution of the *berit milah*;[47] hemophilia as a blood disease transmitted by females to males (also discussed in connection with *berit milah*);[48] and diphtheria as the most dangerous and fatal childhood disease.[49] As diptheria was such a deadly disease, Wednesday was declared a weekly fast-day for praying that it would not befall little children.[50] It was believed that diphtheria occurred as a punishment for the sin of slander.[51] In order to prevent the disease, talmudic sages recommended (in addition to fulfilling the *mitzvot*) eating lentils once a month, drinking water after any other beverage, and adding salt to the diet.[52] If diphtheria does attack, it usually begins at night.[53] The symptoms are vomiting, pain in the throat, and finally, suffocation.[54]

The Talmud also mentions tonsillitis and ways to treat it.[55] Intestinal worms were recognized as a childhood ailment.[56] Various treatments suggested include the use of garlic[57] and several potions made especially to ward off the worms.[58] Measles was treated by making sure the child's room was properly aired and the temperature moderate. The child was to adhere to a simple diet.[59] Teething was known to cause pain for the baby. In order to soothe the pain, applications of butter or chicken fat to the gums, neck, and throat were recommended.[60] An effective treatment for diarrhea occurring in children was the administering of a solution with carob syrup.[61] While this remedy is employed even in our times, the medical sources of *Toledot Adam* list another remedy for diarrhea: rubbing the stomach with a solution of anise and vinegar.[62]

Coughing spells and asthma were relieved by rubbing the chest with unsalted butter mixed with chamomile oil and almond oil or by inhaling sweet and bitter almond oil.[63] The remedy mentioned for whooping cough was to drink a broth of beets and cane sugar or warm milk and to eat sweet and fatty foods.[64] If the child had an earache, it was treated by applying drops of the juice of roasted goat kidneys.[65] Tonsillitis was treated by having the child suck a medication prepared from pyrethrum wood and vegetables, or a mixture of bran, linseed, and hops.[66]

The First Five Years: From Infant to Child

Children under the age of one were especially susceptible to the fatal effects of a hornet sting. As a remedy, the sting was treated with palm tree moss ground with water, or with bruised flies or the urine of an infant.[67]

Following the talmudic era, there arose a chain of Jewish pediatricians whose practices and insights closely resemble those of contemporary medical practitioners. Among the most noted were Dr. Tobias Ben Moses Cohn (Tuviyyah Katz); (1652–1729) and Dr. M. Studentzki (1809–1883).[68] Medical practice and knowledge are considered so important in Judaism that some sages declared it to be a legal responsibility for each person to set aside time to learn about medicine and health.[69]

Maimonides notes that every illness must be treated in accordance with the procedures required to restore health.[70] Since a doctor must be consulted for physical and mental illness,[71] one was not permitted to live in a town in which there was no doctor.[72]

Halakhah mentions special means of safeguarding one's eyesight. Parents should take care not to place a baby's crib near a window or a source of bright light, for this will cause the child to look constantly in that direction and his vision will be damaged.[73] One should accustom his eyes gradually to a change from darkness to bright light, and vice versa. Reading at twilight and at midday is bad for the eyes. It is bad for the eyesight to live in a dwelling in which the windows face north.[74]

Afflictions such as blindness, deafness, and epilepsy were believed to be punishments for some transgression as well as the result of negligence of basic sanitary measures.[75] Although the legal status of those who are blind or deaf, is inferior to that of normal children, Judaism strictly guards their rights as individuals. The statement that it is prohibited to place a stumbling-block before a blind person includes many rulings for this and other cases.[76] Someone who caused a blind person to wander out of his way was cursed.[77] Judaism recognizes the importance of special education for afflicted children, for "wisdom opens the mouth of the dumb."[78] The Talmud notes that deaf-mutes are capable of being instructed and should not be considered idiots. To support this statement it tells how Rabbi Judah the Prince noticed that two dumb boys attending his lectures were moving their heads and lips as if repeating his words. Rabbi Judah prayed for their recovery, and when they were cured it was found that they had indeed absorbed all his teachings during the period of their affliction.[79]

THE TREATMENT OF DISEASE

The treatment of childhood diseases is a legal responsibility mandated in the Torah (as is medical practice in general).[80] The Talmud notes that a child has more chance of surviving disease than an older person.[81]

The general halakhic rule is that no treatment that may cure or relieve an illness may be prohibited, besides idolatry.[82] This is a broad opening for the use of all relevant medical treatments in curing and relieving illness. As the Judaic perspective on medicine is a pragmatic one, it is in keeping with the modern advances in medicine. While the Bible mentions isolation and disinfection in treating certain diseases,[83] the Talmud includes the use of various drugs and even lists categories of pharmaceuticals available in those days.[84] The practice of surgery is a recognized medical treatment in the Talmud[85] and there are references to the acceptability of vaccination in preventing and treating disease.[86]

The practice of visiting the sick is important for the good deed itself and because it cheers the patient. Rav Acha bar Chanina maintains that caring visitors help the patient to recover.[87]

In time of illness it is beneficial to pray for the recovery of the patient in the synagogue during the reading of the Torah and for the patient himself to pray for his own recovery.[88] In fact, the Talmud declares that repentance has the power of curing any

The First Five Years: From Infant to Child 151

illness, based on the passage: "All diseases which I brought upon Egypt, I will not bring upon you, for I am the Lord your healer." That is to say, "If you follow the Torah, I will not bring upon you the afflictions; however, if you do not heed the words of the Lord and commit sins, I will bring them upon you. Then if you repent I will heal you."[89] Thus, although Judaism acknowledges the need for scientific knowledge and treatment of disease, it also sees health and illness as originating in man's actions and his choosing either to follow or to violate the commandments. Indeed, the Talmud explains that disobedience to the Almighty causes the death of young and innocent children so that they may plead the cause of their parents before the Lord. In cases of severe or complex illness, a Rabbi should be consulted.

MEDICAL CARE ON THE SABBATH

Since Judaism places the value of life above all else (for the Torah was given for the living), it is a general rule that the Sabbath must be desecrated in order to save a life, even of a one-day-old infant[89] or a fetus less than forty days old[90] (although a Rabbi must be consulted, as this is a complex legal matter). Indeed, it is even permitted to desecrate the Sabbath to fulfill the needs of a newborn child if he has the chance of living only for one hour.[91] The sages permitted the desecration of the Sabbath to fulfill the needs of any child up to the age of nine or ten if he weak and requires special treatment.[92] Such a child is considered to have the same status as a sick person who is not in mortal danger, and the same halakhic regulations apply to his care on the Sabbath.[93]

When life is endangered, it is a *mitzvah* for the parent himself or another Jew to desecrate the Sabbath in the attempt to save the child. If a child is ill but not in mortal danger, the parent or another Jew must not desecrate the Sabbath by violating a Torah prohibition. In this case, a non-Jew is requested to fulfill the child's needs.[94]

The following guidelines have been stipulated by some

authorities: If the doctor has instructed that the child must be given codliver oil or vitamins daily, it is permitted to administer this on the Sabbath.[95] It is also permitted to weigh the child's food or the child himself after a meal if this is necessary for medical purposes.[96] One may treat diaper rash or cradle cap on Sabbath by pouring some oil on the baby's skin and applying it by hand (but not with cotton).[97] In the same manner, it is permitted to apply gentian violet to a child's bruise to avoid infection and heal the wound.[98] The wound may be washed and bandaged to prevent infection. One may apply dermatol to stop bleeding, but no cream may be applied. It is also permitted to remove a splinter from the child's body.[99]

The child may be given any medication, including eye drops, nose drops, syrups, and tablets, required for his health. It is also permitted to crush a tablet and dissolve it in water for the child.[100]

If the child is in deep pain from a digestive disturbance or diarrhea, a doctor must be called immediately.[101] If the child is suffering from an earache or the like, the doctor may light a flashlight to examine him.[102] If the child has difficulty breathing, it is permitted to operate a vaporizer to ease his condition (although it is better to prepare the instrument before the Sabbath and to use water which has been boiled and placed on the fire before the Sabbath in the machine).[103]

If the child is afraid of the dark or may be overcome with anxiety as a result of being in the dark, a non-Jew may be asked to switch the light on for the child and to switch it off when the child falls asleep.[104] As a child is considered to be like someone who is ill but not in mortal danger, a gentile may be asked to cook food for him on the Sabbath if necessary for his health; in such cases, it is better for the non-Jew to feed the child, for the dish is *muktzeh* (i.e., it may not be handled on the Sabbath).[105]

A non-Jew may be asked to carry the child if there is no *eruv* or to drive him to the doctor if necessary.[106] If the child's life is in danger, a Jewish parent or another Jew is permitted to drive him to the doctor or hospital or to drive the doctor to the patient's home, or to bring medicine.[107] However, the driver must avoid any unnecessary desecration of the Sabbath during the drive.[108] It is also permitted for a member of the family or any person trusted by the patient to accompany him to the doctor or hospital in order to prevent unnecessary anxiety for the child.[109]

A child's temperature and blood pressure may be measured on the Sabbath if necessary,[110] but instead of smearing the tip of the thermometer with petroleum jelly, it should be dipped in oil; if no oil is available, it may be dipped in a cream. The thermometer may be washed with alcohol (but one should not dip cotton into the alcohol for this purpose), and the thermometer may be shaken down if one intends to use it again on the Sabbath.[111] The use of a digital thermometer is permitted if the temperature is marked only through a change of color (and the numerals or letters indicating fever are visible beforehand).

If it is necessary to record the child's temperature or weight, this may be done by preparing signs before Sabbath and inserting them in the proper place when necessary.[112]

If the child shows symptoms of a simple ailment, such as a sore throat or hoarseness, he may be given any food which may alleviate his discomfort, such as honey, candies, lemon squeezed on a sugar cube, and the like.[113] Medications should be prepared before the Sabbath (if it is necessary to dilute them).[114]

SUMMARY

The halakhic regulations concerning health and disease provide the most concrete evidence that the Torah was given to the Jewish people for the enhancement of life. The sacred value of human life embodied in Judaism applies to the individual as soon as he is born: "One desecrates the Sabbath for the sake of a day-old infant, but not for the dead body of David, King of Israel."[115]

Although the sages explain that weakness was not brought upon man until after the death of Rabbi Gamliel, the responsibility of each Jew to safeguard his health is rooted in Torah law, as is the parent's obligation to care for his child so that he may develop into a healthy adult and a good Jew. Parents must grant each of their children the maximum care for health, for it is possible that the child may grow up to be a scholar. In any case, the obligation to maintain one's health is linked with the goal of Judaism, which is to learn the wisdom of the Almighty. This can only be accomplished if one is healthy in mind and spirit.

The causes of disease and childhood ailments are numerous. Judaism recognizes that a child may become ill as a result of unsanitary environmental conditions—especially polluted water,[116] and excessive heat, cold, or draft[117]—infection from afflicted people,[118] heredity,[119] inability of the body's immune defenses to ward off disease,[120] God's punishment for sin,[121] or the evil eye.[122]

Although we do not find many references to childhood diseases and the treatment of illness in the Torah, the talmudic sages recorded many of the diseases prevalent in their time and the accepted treatments, which in most cases are valid to this day.

In order to prevent disease and maintain health, Judaism prescribes that each child be given proper nutrition, live in a sanitary and safe environment, develop in an affectionate, trusting atmosphere, avoid unnecessary psychosocial stress, and receive the best possible medical care promptly (even on the Sabbath) in case of illness.

The act of saving a child's life (even a day-old infant or a fetus) is considered so essential in Judaism that it is a *mitzvah* for the parent or any other Jew to desecrate the Sabbath so that a child in mortal danger may have the chance to live and develop as a good Jew. The Halakhah permitting the desecration of the Sabbath to perform surgery to save a fetus and the postponement of *berit milah* if the infant shows signs of illness are clear indications of this philosophy, which maintains that it is better to desecrate one Sabbath for the sake of the child so that he may fulfill the *mitzvah* of Sabbath many times.[123] (See Chapters 3 and 4.) If a child's life is in danger, the parent or another adult Jew must hasten to do whatever is necessary to save his life and must not try to postpone any act until after the Sabbath, thus endangering the child further. The Sabbath may be desecrated to save the life of a child even if his life may be prolonged by the action for only a short while. In doubtful cases, the parent must consult a rabbinical authority to determine what is permitted on the Sabbath for a sick child.[124] Excellent guides on the Halakhah concerning medical treatment on the Sabbath appears in *Shemirat Shabbat KeHilkhato* (by Y. Y. Neubirt) and *Care of Children on Shabbos and Yom Tov* (by Rabbi S. Wagschal).

The maintenance of health occupies a central role in Judaism, for a healthy child can more readily learn the wisdom of the Almighty and fulfill the commandments. From the halakhic standpoint, medical treatment of illness is a *mitzvah*. The Torah commands us to treat a child who is afflicted, as it is written: "And thou shalt return his body to him." If one sees that a person is in danger, one must attempt to restore his health by helping him physically, financially, or through the means of medical knowledge.[125]

Part III
The Dimensions of Development

Introduction

Child development is a complex process involving interrelated dimensions of growth. Each dimension—physical, intellectual (or cognitive), emotional, and social—has its own distinct process of development, yet all are intertwined. This view is embodied in the Halakhah in various rules related to the aspects of development, such as the guidelines on the behavioral characteristics the individual must follow or avoid, the laws for maintaining physical and emotional health, and the rules indicating what must be avoided in order to prevent danger to the natural course of human development. As Maimonides points out, an individual who neglects his physical well-being cannot relate intellectually and emotionally to the goals of life envisaged by Judaism. Cognitive development presupposes mental health, while emotional development depends on the formation of perception.

Judaism views all facets of development as a totality, in accordance with the basic tenet that "the Torah of the Almighty is all-encompassing" (Psalms 19:8). Accordingly, Jewish values based on Torah law and rabbinical rulings form the basis for halakhic guidelines encompassing all elements of development. The parent, the educator, and the Jewish environment (relatives, friends, and neighbors; i.e., the community) guide, supplement, and regulate the course of the child's development in accordance with Jewish values. The principle means of guiding development is *chinnukh*—education involving every dimension of development in harmonious and thoughtful coordination. The child's journey through the process of development within the framework of Judaism should lead to a life of peace and integrity based on the capacity to deal with conflict and frustration. The aim of Jewish child-rearing is to enable the child to create an equilibrium between his inner needs and the requirements of society, and to correct and perfect human development. "And your children shall be taught of the Lord: and great shall be the peace of your children" (Isaiah 54:13).

How are children to be "taught of the Lord"? The basic guiding principle in Judaism is that "each child be reared in accordance with his ways" (Proverbs 22:10). This implies the necessity of knowledge about the dimensions of child-development. The parent, teacher, or social worker who understands the varied and interrelated nature of the child's physical, intellectual, emotional, and social development has a better chance to relate to each child most effectively and thus to ensure the successful integration of Jewish values.

What is the child's nature? Does the child develop according to a genetic code or does he learn his way through life? According to rabbinic law (*Verdicts*, pt. II, sec. 119), on every halakhic issue dealing with blood ties, the child is linked with the mother, whereas the root of his genealogy is tied to the father. Thus, the child has natural endowments from both parents. Yet the essence of Judaism lies in the view that all of creation must be perfected by man himself: "Everything which was created in the first six days of creation requires correction . . . even man must perfect himself" (*Genesis Rabbah* 11).

The Almighty in His wisdom gave the Torah and *mitzvot* as tools to purify man (*Tanchuma*, Tazria). Halakhah, the body of laws emanating from the Torah and forming a framework for life, embodies a detailed evaluation of the physical, cognitive, emotional, and social *middot*, or characteristics, which the child should acquire in the proper proportions in order to ensure harmonious development of all dimensions of growth.

11
Physical Development

The child's development is a complex process involving the interaction of all dimensions of growth. In this process, the child's physical development is crucial in determining his uniqueness and human characteristics. All parents marvel at the miracle that unfolds as their child learns to use his limbs, progressing from turning over to sitting in the crib to crawling on the floor and finally to walking, jumping, and running. The members of the family, friends, and neighbors all delight in noticing the child's growth and healthy development. As Jewish parents, we must view this miraculous process within the framework of Judaism. The question which arises in this context is the nature of the relation between genic endowment and environmental influences on growth according to Jewish philosophy. Finally, how can the Jewish perspective on physical development enrich our capacity to guide the child's growth to its maximum potential?

THE PURPOSE OF PHYSICAL HEALTH

Physical fitness and health are regarded as the cornerstone of the spiritual faculties enhanced by Judaism. Rabbi Abraham Isaac Kook states: "The body needs to be healthy and whole for the purpose of spiritual rejuvenation. The more strength the body achieves the more it enhances its spiritual power."[1]

This view is incorporated in Halakhah as specified in the Abridged Code of Jewish Law:

> Our rabbis, may their memory be blessed, stated: "Which is the small portion of the Scripture upon which all elements of the Torah depend?" ..."Thou shalt know Him in all thy ways" [Proverbs 3:6], which means even in your physical activities, such as eating, drinking, walking, sitting, lying, rising.... indeed, all bodily requirements should be aimed toward the purpose of worshipping the Almighty, or toward something which brings about worship of God.[2]

In the perspective of Judaism, the body is given to man as a tool for worshipping the Almighty and not for self-benefit. The body is considered a sanctified casing or tool for the soul. Indeed, the Torah and the *mitzvot* were given to us with the purpose of sanctifying the body and raising it to a level of eternity. As the sages state, "He who honors the Torah honors his body."[3]

This philosophy is realized immediately after birth with the fulfillment of the *berit milah,* which, as we have seen was given to man in order that he may purify himself.[4] The Almighty has endowed each individual with physical and spiritual capacities, with the intent that man himself perfect them through the fulfillment of the *mitzvot.*[5]

Another beautiful tradition which realizes this philosophy is embodied in a joyous childhood ceremony enjoined by Halakhah. As noted in Chapter 5, it is traditional not to cut the hair of boys until they reach the age of three. On the festival of Lag ba-Omer, those families fortunate enough to be living in the Land of Israel bring their three-year-old sons to the tomb of Rabbi Simeon bar Yochai in Miron. There, amidst joyous singing and dancing, the child's hair is cut for the first time in the area of the forehead, where he will lay the phylacteries when he reaches the age of thirteen. The explanation for this custom is rooted in the Kabbalah, according to which various parts of the body are identified with the realm of judgment or charity and kindness. The hair falls in the category of judgment, but by virtue of his great work in laying the foundations of the Kabbalah, Rabbi Simeon bar Yochai removed it from the realm of judgment to that of charity and kindness. By cutting the boy's hair for the first time at the age of three when he enters the world of the Torah, the parent gives a tangible meaning to this symbol of consecrating the physical characteristics of the child to the Almighty.

Yet another materialization of this philosophy is to be found in the laws concerning modesty of dress. Based on the verse "**And** thou shalt walk in modesty before the Lord,"[6] all Jewish **men**, women, and children are obliged to dress modestly and conduct themselves with honesty, integrity and simplicity.

Finally, the *mitzvah* of wearing *tzitzit* is directly related to this view, as its purpose is to remind the individual of all the *mitzvot* and to divert him from worldly desires. As soon as the young child is capable of dressing himself with the *tzitzit*, he is taught to recite the blessing and wear it daily. This usually begins at the age of three when the child symbolically enters the world of the Torah. At this stage, the child's attention may be brought to the fact that this garment represents the *mitzvot* as a symbol of the sanctity of the Torah, which envelops his body.

Along the same trend of thought, the phylacteries, which are worn on the forehead and bound on the arm (from the age of thirteen on), represent Judaism's aim of consecrating the physical attributes of man to the worship of the Almighty.[7]

Despite this perspective, Judaism in no way advocates that we neglect our physical needs or sensual requirements. On the contrary, as we have seen, the Bible ordains us to "guard our lives,"[8] with all the implications for the halakhic requirement to conduct ourselves in such a manner as to strengthen our bodies and maintain our health.[9]

This seeming contradiction is resolved in the following Midrash, which explains why the Torah was given to man and not to the angels:

Rabbi Nechuniah said in the name of Rabbi Judah: This is comparable to a man who had a child, and this child was missing one finger on his hands. The man sent his child to learn a trade, and for this purpose it was necessary to use all five fingers. The father came to visit the son and discovered that he had not learned the trade. He asked his teacher: "Did you not teach my son this trade?" The teacher replied: "the trade required the functioning of all five fingers. As your son lacks one finger, he cannot learn this trade." Thus, the Almighty said to the angels: "You cannot fulfill the Torah. Why? Because you do not procreate, there is no death or defilement or disease among you—you are already holy."[10]

Our sages recognized that the study of man's physiology itself is a source of worshipping the Almighty, for the realization that all bodily faculties "have definite functions, whose purpose is to promote physical well-being," will stir man "to thank his Creator and praise Him for them, as David said: 'All my bones shall say: 'Lord, who is like unto Thee.' [Ps. 35:10]."[11]

HEREDITY AND ENVIRONMENT

In order to fully comprehend the Judaic perspective on physical development, it is necessary to understand the relationship between genic endowment and environmental influences on growth according to Jewish philosophy.

Child psychologists use the term "genotype" to refer to the "totality of inherited elements—the potentialities inherent in the twenty-three chromosomes inherited from each parent and represented in every somatic cell of his body."[12] The person's "phenotype" describes him "in terms of observable qualities" which consist of the interaction of his genic endowment with the environment.[13]

HEREDITARY INFLUENCES

The Mishnah refers to genotypes in a passage conceding that "the father endows his child with beauty, strength, riches, intelligence, and life."[14] Indeed, the Bible mentions several cases in which the individual's constitution is attributed to genic endowment. For example, according to the Talmud, Isaac's countenance was like that of his father, Abraham;[15] the Midrash adds that Isaac resembled Abraham in everything: beauty, strength, etc.[16] The same is said of Joseph, who resembled his father, Jacob, in everything.[17] Genic endowment is especially considered concerning intellectual qualities.[18] The Talmud notes that if three successive generations in one family are learned, it is certain that knowledge will never die out from among the descendents of the family, for "the Torah will always return to its own residence."[19] Furthermore, if one sees that knowledge dies out in his offspring, one should marry his son to the daughter of a learned man. This is learned from the observation in Job (14, 7-9) that if a tree is cut down, there is hope that it will sprout again . . . .[20]

The talmudic sages knew that hemophilia and certain mental diseases were inherited, and considered the possibilities of hereditary constitution.[21] In the case of hemophilia, Judaism recognized the element of genic endowment to the extent that if two sons died as a result of *milah* (due to the inability of the blood to clot), it was forbidden to circumcise the third child (at least until he grew strong enough, in the doctor's opinion, to live through the operation). Halakhah incorporates a knowledge of genotype in the laws concerning the right match: "A man should always attempt to marry the daughter of a scholar."[22] One should always try to marry a person from a good family; for example, "Moses married the daughter of Jethro and from them descended Jonathan; Aaron married the daughter of Amminadab—from this union was born Phinehas."[23] Finally, genic endowment is the reason for the strict law forbidding one to marry a woman in whose family there is a history of epilepsy or leprosy if there are three recorded cases of death due to the illness.[24] Maimonides explains that in addition to genic endowment of physical appearance and other bio-physical qualities, "when a person has a certain defect, he usually endows his child with this defect."[25] In many cases, biological research has found this theory to be true.[26] Again, on the basis of this knowledge, the sages advised that "a tall man should not marry a tall girl, so that they do not beget a giant; a midget should not marry a midget, so that they do not have tiny children; a person with very fair skin should not marry one with the same fair skin, so their children shall not be extremely fair; a man with a dark complexion should not marry a woman with a dark complexion, so that their children shall not be black."[27]

ENVIRONMENTAL INFLUENCES

How does life history contribute to development? The Talmud raises the question by inquiring: Why are the children of scholars not necessarily scholars themselves? The answer to this dilemma resolves the controversy of nature versus nurture, indicating how Judaism requires that each person work for himself to learn the Torah, so that no one may claim that he inherited it.[28] Man's task on earth is to utilize his physical, intellectual, and emotional endowments to their fullest potentail by fulfilling the *mitzvot*. By creating an environment based on Torah values, each parent may enhance his child's sphere of learning and experience. As the child integrates various elements of Judaism in his daily life, these become as much a part of him as his genetic predispositions. The external influences of the Torah values materialized in his daily environment, become bound up with the inherited genic material to form the child's unique contribution to development.

By applying the Judaic principle of physical development, in which all bodily functions should be aimed at worshipping the Lord as well as fulfilling corporeal needs, we find that the individual's genotype and phenotype are combined in a harmonious synthesis. As a result, the child's constitution is determined by the interaction of both forces toward the ultimate goal of developing as a good Jew. The Torah and halakhic law incorporate detailed rules governing hygiene, nutrition, and proper practices for physical well-being and health. Some of these regulations (which are detailed in the Code of Jewish Law, secs. 32–33, and Maimonides, *Hilkhot De'ot*) are outlined in Chapter 5.

Rabbi Samson Raphael Hirsch maintains that training the child's physical faculties is a parental responsibility with implications for the child's physical and spiritual development.[29] For the first three to five years of the child's life, this responsibility requires that the parent choose the right type and amount of nutrients for the child, plan a moderate schedule of rest, sleep, and play, and arrange for outings and exercise. The parent, as we have seen, should begin to teach his child basic routines of hygiene, such as washing the hands upon rising, before meals, and after excreting wastes, very early in life. The child should be bathed regularly and taught the fundamentals of personal cleanliness, all in accordance with the regulations in the Code of Jewish Law (sec. 33).

Later on, as the child matures, the parent should guide him to become independent in personal care in order that he may fulfill the commandment, "You shall guard your lives."[30] The child should be taught that in all matters concerning his physical well-being, he must be strong enough and healthy enough to worship the Almighty and learn the values of Judaism. For example, the child should be made aware that his nourishment, sleep, and rest are to be carried out for the purpose of gaining strength to learn Torah and fulfill the commandments. If the child understands this and acts accordingly, these acts will become second nature to him. He will eat the proper foods in the correct amount, and he will plan to sleep and rest as much as required for him to be alert and wide awake during learning hours. Finally, these habits will have implications in all the child's activities, such as speech and socialization, and later on in his professional life.[31]

12
Cognitive Development

How do children function? What is the basis for the child's actions and reactions? When and what does the child conceive of himself and others? How does the child develop the tools for intellectual development: language, thought, memory, creative skills, and identity? How do all the facets of cognitive development relate to the child's growth as a Jew? The first four questions, which have been explored by modern child psychologists, have formed the basis of *chinnukh* in Judaism for over five thousand years. Indeed, Jewish sages recognize that *"chinnukh* begins at the very moment of birth, for the infant aptly absorbs the impressions of his surroundings, and these [impressions] become more meaningful each day; therefore, our contact with the child must be well thought out and planned."[1] Accordingly, the rabbis determined guidelines based on biblical philosophy to assist the Jewish parent in creating the right atmosphere for the child to develop his cognitive abilities to their fullest potentiality. Judaism acknowledges that its strength comes from the potential of the young—or in the words of the psalmist: "From the mouths of babes and sucklings hast Thou ordained strength."[2]

DEVELOPING THE CHILD'S COGNITIVE POTENTIAL

The child's cognitive potential may flourish from the moment of birth with the help and encouragement of the parents, who provide the necessary environment for learning. The essence of this principle is woven into the very fabric of Judaism, as is evident from the following biblical passage: "Thou shalt assemble the nation, the men, women, and little children, as well as the gentiles who renounce idolatry and live among you, so that they may hear and learn and see the Almighty and fulfill all the commandments of this Torah."[3]

The commentators naturally ask why parents must bring along the young children who do not yet understand speech. The answer teaches us the importance of setting the stage for learning immediately upon birth and offers the first guideline for cognitive development.

The parents' initiative in bringing young children to the scene of Torah learning is considered good grounds for rewarding the parents themselves. The next verse elaborates on this theme: "And their sons who did not know [the Almighty] will hear and learn to revere the Almighty, for all the days in which you live on the land to which you are crossing the Jordan to inherit."[4]

The *Or ha-Chayyim* comments that even the youngest child who has not yet learned Torah will acquire reverence for the Almighty if exposed to the atmosphere of Torah learning, for "when young children are taught from the very beginning of life to revere the Almighty, this reverence is established for life."[5]

The atmosphere of Torah learning must exist not only on special occasions—it must be a part of each day in the child's life. The parents, by conducting their home and family life in accordance with Jewish values, play a crucial role in ensuring that the Torah spirit penetrates to the senses of even the youngest child. The young child absorbs these values instinctively if he thrives in an environment of love and stimulation, the first requisites for cognitive development.

This, then, is the psychological and educational principle emanating from the biblical ordinance cited above. Children must be included in the assembly to provide stimulation for their developing cognitive abilities within the framework and spirit of Judaism. Yet all learning must take place in the context of the young child's daily life, which at this stage is dominated by the family routine. Within this sphere of learning "A most important factor, and perhaps the decisive one, is that of the love and endearment between parent and child."[6]

THE JUDAIC PHILOSOPHY OF COGNITION

How these two elements merge in the process of cognitive development is explained by the Judaic philosophy of cognition, or *chokhmah*, the faculty of the soul which acquires and maintains theoretical knowledge of the Torah and the arts. According to the Midrash, the individual acquires knowledge of the Torah as soon as his soul is created. At the moment of birth the angel appointed for this function strikes the child and wipes away the memory of all that he has learned.[7] When the child is born, he must learn on his own with the capacities endowed upon him by the Almighty. Child-development researchers define this capacity as "cognition," a term designating the mental abilities through which knowledge is acquired and maintained.[8] The cognitive processes include memory, problem-solving, sensation, perception, thinking and speech.[9] A similar explanation is outlined by Rabbenu Bachya, who categorizes the soul's faculties of thought and recollection, forgetting, shame, understanding, and speech as the prime advantage bestowed upon man, endowing him with the excellencies of a human being.[10] The cognitive activities carried out by these physical senses and mental abilities form the basis of all human functioning from the very first day of life.

The basis for the child's actions and reactions is his individual level of cognitive ability, which begins to function instinctively at birth: "When the infant has emerged into the world, all his senses, except those of touch and taste, are weak."[11] As each day passes, the child's capacities develop more fully. The parents are charged with the task of guiding this development. They are well suited to this crucial role, because "God inspires the parents' hearts with kindness, love, and compassion for their offspring, so that rearing is not a burden to them. . . . His parents do not tire of him nor become angry at his multitudinous wants and slight recognition of the burden which they bear in caring and providing for him." On this basis, the "infant's physical faculties grow stronger, so that it is able to distinguish sights and sounds." The parents continue to provide the background environment necessary for cognitive development, and "the solicitude they feel on his behalf increases till he reaches adolescence," when his "physical senses and mental faculties have become strong enough to acquire wisdom and knowledge."[12]

THE STAGES OF COGNITIVE DEVELOPMENT

Judaism recognizes that cognitive development progresses through an orderly series of stages, as is evident from the recommendation made by Judah ben Tema regarding the ages most suitable for teaching Judaism to the developing child: "At five years the child should study scripture; at ten, Mishnah; at thirteen he must fulfill the commandments; at fifteen he should study the Talmud; and at eighteen he should marry."[13] Since the stages of development are universal, it is impossible to skip any of the child's stages of development . . . for any demand which is not in accordance with the child's age (or developmental) level might cause great damage to the young child's emotional and cognitive progress."[14] The sages considered these to be normative guidelines, while in practice one must consider each child's level of learning readiness.

The first stage of development, as described by Rabbenu Bachya, involves the progression from instinctive-reflexive action at birth to symbolic activities. Halakhah sets the period of this first stage at about two or three years,[15] corresponding to the sensorimotor stage of cognitive development described by the renowned psychologist Piaget. In both cases this is the period in which the child develops the ability to coordinate sensations and perceptions with physical action. It is also the crucial stage in which the child begins to develop his self-concept, "the differentiation between self and environment, and the emergence of differentiated emotions and notions of executive dependence and volitional omnipotence."[16] In terms of Judaic philosophy, the child begins to respond to the environment with the innate egocentric drives governed by the evil spirit; the good spirit develops within the cognitive process that culminates during adolescence, when the sense of identity is firmly established in a healthy child. Both the good spirit and the evil spirit emanate from the human mind, the source of cognition.

During this period in the child's life, learning takes place as a result of biological pressures to adapt to the environment. As this miraculous process of learning unfolds, we may apply the talmudic observation that "he who learns by himself is superior to he who learns from a teacher."[17] The parental teaching role in this stage of cognitive development is to stimulate and build the foundation of love and trust that is the basic building block of learning throughout life. The guidelines emanating from the biblical passages quoted above, are recommended by such noted child-development experts as Piaget, Erikson, and Spock.

When we study the complete range of cognitive-development stages outlined by Jewish sages throughout Judaic literature, we find that they are roughly equivalent to Piaget's theory. The second stage, termed the "pre-operational period" by Piaget, extends from two years to seven years according to Piaget, and from three to six or seven according to the Jewish sages. The Midrash in *Yalkut Shimoni* maintains that the passage "And you shall plant each fruit tree and consecrate its fruit" (Lev. 19:23-24) refers to child-rearing. Prior to this stage, a child is like the fruit of a newly planted tree; just as a tree's produce may not be eaten until after the fourth year, the child, in the first three years of life, is not capable of reasoning and thus is not ready to partake of the practical aspects of Judaism. However, in the fourth year, when the father dedicates the child to learning the Torah, "all its fruits will be consecrated," so that in the fifth year, "thou shalt eat its fruit." From this our sages learned that the five-year-old begins to learn Scripture.[18]

It is a recognized principle in both Judaism and psychology that the child's thinking becomes refined in the second stage of development, for at this point he is able to use symbols such as words to solve problems. During this stage of preconceptual thinking, the time is ripe for the child to be taught the alphabet and the foundations of Judaism.[19]

The preschool period is believed by Jewish sages to be critical for the child's cognitive capacity in all areas of mental development, especially in his growth as a Jew. The rabbis ordained: "As soon as the child knows how to speak, his father must teach him the verses 'Hear, O Israel the Lord our God, the Lord is one' [Deut. 6:4] and 'Moses commanded us the Torah, it is an inheritance of the congregation of Jacob' [Deut. 33:4].[20] Thus, it is essential that the child be taught to speak with these first words in the Hebrew language, according to the biblical verse: "And you shall teach them to your children to speak."[21] Maimonides adds that the father then continued to teach his child "little by little, verse by verse, until he was about six or seven years old, all in accordance with his strength, whereupon he led him to the schoolteacher."[22]

Judaism stresses the importance of guiding the child's development in accordance with his individual capabilities, for as Rabbi Meir says: "Each person differs from others in three things: his voice, his appearance, and his intelligence."[23] This point is reiterated in Jewish ethics as well as Jewish law. The guiding principle for parents and teachers must be the advice appearing in Proverbs: "Guide each lad in accordance with his ways; then even when he is old he will not depart from these ways."[24] The *Sefer Ha-Musar* advises that the parent attempt to "teach his child Torah in every instance according to the strength of the child and his age level, and in accordance with his abilities."[25] The Talmud adds that the father must continue to teach his child Torah and *mitzvot* according to the child's level of understanding.

Since the talmudic sages recognized that the child at this point learns by doing and experiencing rather than by memorizing abstract ideas, the parent is urged to introduce the child progressively into observing *mitzvot* which involve active participation. Thus, as soon as the child no longer calls his mother at night, he is required to sleep in the *sukkah*. A child capable of doing so may shake the *lulav* on Sukkot and put on *tzitzit* daily; when sufficiently accomplished, he is given the privilege of reading the Torah publicly during the synagogue services.[26]

At this stage of cognitive development, the parent's role is to guide and encourage the child and to create the right atmosphere for learning. Rabbi Samson Raphael Hirsch offers practical advice to the parents of preschoolers:

> The most important factor in the child's cognitive development is the spoken word.... Therefore, it is desirable to exercise language from morning to night, to develop and prepare it to be the most efficient means for cognitive activity. The children must learn clear and correct speech from the mother.... In addition, the child must be made accustomed to expressing his thoughts and desires in clear and precise language.... The mother should also help the child develop the senses, especially those of touch, sight, and hearing ... for each symbol which the child perceives widens the horizons of his cognitive abilities.[27]

As we have seen, Maimonides advises that preschool learning should be guided by the parent until the age of six or seven, at which time the father brings the child to the schoolteacher, in accordance with the talmudic ordinance established by Joshua ben Gamla that formal instruction begin at the age of six or seven years.[28] This view, which is upheld by Rav, is based on the knowledge that the average child reaches the level of being able to perform intellectual work at the age of six or seven. In terms of the Piaget theory, the child begins formal schooling when he enters the period of concrete operations, in which his thinking becomes more sophisticated but is not yet refined completely..

Thus, according to the rabbis: "The children should be brought to learn in school at the age of six or seven according to the strength of the child and his physical development."[29] The child's "strength" refers to his cognitive development, which determines the level of learning readiness and the measure of success. The Talmud offers practical advice concerning the child's intellectual development in this period: "The rabbis ordained in Usha that each parent must teach his son with leniency up to the age of twelve years; thereafter, if the child refuses to learn, he must be compelled to do so."[30]

As the child's mental capacities are still in the formative stage up to the age of twelve, Judaism advocates that parents have a liberal attitude toward the child's level of success in schooling. Thereafter, the parent is permitted to use strict measures to require his child to learn. According to the Talmud, fathers are responsible for teaching their children Torah, *mitzvot,* a worthy occupation, and swimming.[31] Halakhah reinforces this ruling by recommending that all learning must take place with the utmost consideration for the child's innate capacities and level of development. While the child's mental capacities are in the stages of development, the parent (or teacher) must teach patiently and present that which is to be learned in an interesting and enticing way, in order to provide suitable motivation. This holds until the child attains the age of twelve or thirteen. At this age, the threshold of adolescence, "when he has learned to speak correctly and properly, and his physical senses and mental faculties have become strong enough to acquire wisdom and knowledge . . . then he apprehends some physical phenomena with his senses, and some intellectual ideas with his mental faculties, as the wise King said: 'For the Lord giveth wisdom: out of His mouth cometh knowledge and discernment' [Prov. 2:6]."[32]

Piaget's theory also holds that the child attains his most advanced stage of thinking (in the technical sense) during adolescence. In this stage of formal operations, the individual learns to function on a symbolic, abstract level—he is capable of hypothetical reasoning. The rabbis offer many technical aids to memory, which is considered essential for Torah learning.[33]

The cornerstone of the Judaic philosophy of cognition is that knowledge is gained by learning the Torah,[34] and that "the beginning of wisdom is reverence for the Lord."[35] As the child's capacity for conceptualization has matured at this stage of development, it is deemed imperative that he acquire knowledge of the Torah even against his will or despite any handicaps, for "where there is no wisdom, there is no reverence; where there is no reverence for God, there is no wisdom."[36] The Talmud teaches us that one who lacks common sense must not be pitied.[37] The father must make sure his child learns, so that when the child becomes Bar Mitzvah or Bat Mitzvah ("son or daughter of the *mitzvot*"; i.e., fully responsible for fulfilling the *mitzvot*), he or she will have the basic knowledge required to function as a Jew.

The parent's role at this stage of development, when the child has reached the fullest potential of his cognitive abilities and is capable of reasoning and deciding in all spheres of human activity, is aptly summarized by Meiri as follows:

Each parent should make sure to watch over his children's affairs and be consistent in disciplining them, whether they are grown or still young. However, the most suitable time for the parent to exercise reproof completely is when the child's cognitive abilities bloom forth until they reap fruit, and this is the age between twelve years and twenty-four, for before the age of twelve, the child's cognitive capacity is not yet developed enough to accept it, and after twenty-four years of age he does not accept willingly. In any case the father should always designate this period of his child's life to reprove and guide him.[38]

The *Alei Shor* adds to this an appropriate comment: "Happy are the parents who have succeeded in building such a strong bond between themselves and their children that when they are adolescents the children will be influenced by the parents and accept their advice and reproof!"[39] In this sense, the development of cognitive abilities, a universal process suited to each individual's unique capacities, plays a great part in ensuring the continuation of the Jewish heritage handed down through the generations.

13
Emotional Development

As we note in the talmudic dictum that "a child in his own mind is inclined to exaggerate his own importance,"[1] and the halakhic ruling that each child should be taught Torah and *mitzvot* in accordance with his strength and capabilities, Jewish sages were aware of the psychological uniqueness of children long before other societies had even acknowledged the idea of childhood as a separate and distinct phase of human development.[2]

Modern studies have shown that the child's view of things is subjective, and that the world of children is a magical and sometimes irrational blend of reality and fantasy. Psychologists explain that the child believes that his actions and thoughts can bring about events or attributes "human or supra-human causes for natural events" in the first few years of life. As the child matures he "acquires a knowledge of an objective world and is able to free his observations and his conclusions from the distortions of the primitive world."[3]

The earliest phase of emotional (or affective) development takes place in the first three years of life, a fact recognized by Judaism as well as by psychology.[4] The Midrash asks: "Who is the child of delight? The two-and three-year-old. Rav Aha adds in the name of Rabbi Levi bar Yossi: the four-and five-year-old."[5] Thus, it was recognized that until the age of three in most cases, and up to the age of five under some conditions, the child is a delightful creature living in a magical world and behaving accordingly.

In the Jewish view, and also in psychology, emotional development is linked with personality and cognitive development in terms of perception and growth of the self-concept. This is the basis for the halakhic ruling that a child should be taught Torah and *mitzvot* in accordance with his capacity, which includes his emotional, intellectual, and physical faculties.[6] Judaism also maintains, again in conformity with modern psychology, that emotional behavior is shaped by genetic predispositions as well as by environmental factors influencing the psychobiological and psychosocial aspects of development. Maimonides notes that each person has innate tendencies whether to anger, aggression, joy, fear, anxiety, optimism or pessimism, cruelty, courage, mercy, or jealousy.[7] In fact, emotional growth is a function of the soul,[8] which requires guidance in acquiring good habits in order to attain the middle course, the manifestation of mental health.[9] In light of this, parents, educators, psychologists, medical doctors, and social workers can do much to guide children toward healthy emotional development, if they follow the guidelines woven into the fabric of Judaism through various halakhic rules.

Every adult concerned with the rearing and development of children is aware of the sensitivity and complexity of the child's emotions, which range from simplicity to extremes. The child may throw a temper tantrum one day and the next day display love and tenderness; the child may be extemely aggressive in one instance and gently compassionate in another; the child may be overwhelmed with fear by a strange sight or person and overcome with joy over an unanticipated event. The process of emotional development involves "systematic changes which occur in the properties of stimuli evoking emotional reactions or in the responsiveness of children to different categories of emotional stimulation."[10] Judaism recognizes that the adult can do much to temper the child's emotions by affecting the stimuli which evoke various reactions. The following guidelines based on halakhic rulings embody subtle psychological principles intended to elicit the child's welfare and mental health.

FEAR

Fear is an emotion stimulated by a threat to the individual's self-concept, whether his physical well-being or his self-esteem.[11] Since a child experiences fear only when he is able to perceive a threat, it is linked with cognitive maturity and experience. Finally, a child's fear response is affected by cultural influences and situational factors as well as by temperament. Inherent in Judaism is the understanding that excessive fear may be the source of emotional instability and mental illness. Psychologically, historically, and philosophically, the Jewish people have acknowledged the need to repress fear or overcome it, as stated in Proverbs: "If there be fear in the heart of man, let him repress it."[12] This advice is reiterated by such philosophers as Ralbag, Maimonides, and Luzzatto, and is the theme of many works of ethics such as *Mesillat Yesharim* and *Orchot Tzaddikim*.[13]

Fear can be removed or overcome or tempered through trust—the ultimate goal being to gain courage by trusting in the Almighty. As it is written: "Trust in God and do good; dwell in the land and cultivate faith,"[14] for "he who believes in God wholeheartedly and trusts in Him with a strong trust, this trust will cause him no longer to fear terrible occurrences that might arise."[15]

How can a child learn to trust in God? In the earliest stages of life, the child cannot yet conceive of the Almighty. This fact, well recognized in Judaism, is the reason that the parent-child relationship—especially the mother-child relationship—is deemed so important in the first few years of life. When there is a strong bond between parent and child (or between caretaker and child), the child cultivates and assimilates the concept of trust, which is recognized in psychology as the basis of mental health (as clearly set forth in the works of Erik Erikson).[16] As Erikson points out, the mother is the primary representative of the world for the young child, for it is through her that the child receives food, comfort, and sustenance. If the mother relates to the child with consistency, affection, and warmth, the child will develop a sense of trust that will sustain him throughout his life. In acknowledgement of this awesome responsibility, Judaism attributes special rewards to the mother, as stated in the Talmud: "Great is the promise given to women, for the cornerstone of mental development is in their hands."[17]

This sense of trust, which is the basis of trust and faith in the Almighty and the means of combatting fear and preventing its excess, is defined in Rabbenu Bachya's *Duties of the Heart*: "It is the tranquility of the soul in the one who trusts, his hearty reliance on the one in whom he trusts, that the latter will do what is right and proper in the matter of the trust—to the extent of his ability and knowledge, for the benefit of the one who trusts."[18]

As is further explained by the Chazon Ish, trust and faith are interrelated, for "it can really be stated that faith and trust are identical. . . .Only faith is the general view of the person, while trust is his view upon himself; faith is in the realm of theory, and trust is in the realm of the practical."[19]

By experiencing trust in his relationships with his parents and later with siblings, teachers, and friends, the child develops the emotional basis for faith in the Almighty, the ultimate mechanism for combatting fear.

ANXIETY

Anxiety is a "special variety of fear experienced in response to an anticipated threat to self-esteem."[20] Anxiety is a normal element in human development. By serving as a physiological and mental preparation for danger, it is necessary for survival. Anxiety is also a basic factor in moral development, for it is one of the prerequisites for the acquisition of conscience, which is brought about by "fear of disapproval from loved persons as well as the desire to be loved."[21] Yet an absence or excess of anxiety is a symptom of pathology which may signify mental instability. The necessity of normal situational and developmental anxiety is implied in the following verse: "The child who is disciplined by his father grows to be wise, while the fool was never reprimanded."[22] Moreover, Halakhah is specific in determining guidelines parents must follow in order to prevent the excessive anxiety that may lead to pathology.

> It is forbidden to threaten a child that he will be punished at a later time, but if one sees a child doing something wrong, one should immediately punish the child or forever remain silent. The story is told of a child who ran away from school and his father frightened him by threatening to hit him. The child then killed himself.[23]

The example shows the dire consequences which may occur if a child is drawn into a state of pathological anxiety.

ANGER AND AGGRESSION

Related to these emotions (fear and anxiety) are anger and aggression, which are instigated by a threat to self-esteem or physical well-being. While anger is an active feeling of hostility against the threatening agent, aggression is behavior whose goal is the injury of that agent. In the psychological sense, aggression has been thought to be the manifestation of an innate destructive drive, or the instinctive reaction to frustration, or the learned way to respond to particular situations. In any case, it is an accepted fact both in Judaism and psychology that "the incidence of anger and aggression in children depends heavily on parental determinants," such as how children see adults and peers cope with frustration, and the rewards and punishments for anger and aggression. It has been shown that children whose parents threaten or nag them, or who condone aggression, or who are inconsistent and overcritical, display more frequent occurrences of anger outbursts and aggression.[24]

On the basis of these facts, which were common knowledge to rabbis centuries ago, a number of rules have been incorporated in the Halakhah. The Talmud warns that "it is forbidden for a man to impose terror within his home, for much damage can result from it."[25] Furthermore, when attempting to teach a child or discipline him, the parent or teacher must "talk calmly and not angrily, for things said in anger are not accepted."[26] "Even though a child may hasten to carry out something which his father has directed in anger, the father should not delude himself into thinking that his shouting has a lasting educational impact. It is only possible to educate through calm and patience, for anger and excitement should not be brought into the worship of the Almighty—this is the wisdom of education."[27] "The person who acts out of anger is like one who worships idols."[28]

The Talmud is specific on physical punishments administered by parents and teachers. "Rav stated: When you hit a child, do not hit him with anything but the string of a shoe."[29] Maimonides comes to the same conclusion (as does the Rashi commentary on that passage): teachers should strike children only in order to impose discipline, but not out of cruelty. "Therefore, the child should not be struck with sticks or whips—rather with a small string."[30] Yet another rabbi notes that when a father strikes his child, he should not strike him out of anger for what the child has done—rather, the physical punishment should be intended to prevent the child from behaving badly again in the future. Furthermore, the father should not strike the child many times—only once. Moreover, when the father feels very angry at the child, he should not strike him at all.[31]

Finally, biblical law directly forbids the administration of physical punishment to a grown child (legally a boy over thirteen and a girl over twelve—or any child who is intellectually and emotionally mature). This law is based on the commandment "You shall not place a stumbling-block before the blind."[32] By striking a grown child, the parent may instigate anger and aggression, causing the child to strike back at the parent, which is a violation of a strict biblical injunction, the fifth commandment: "Honor thy father and thy mother."

These concepts inherent in Judaic law have recently been reiterated in modern child-development research. It has been found that aggression breeds more aggression. Severe punishment for aggression, especially punishment that is like the aggressive act itself, does very little to decrease the frequency of aggressive behavior, while ignoring such behavior does not help at all. Children grow into the more sophisticated manifestations of aggressive behavior unless the environment—the home, school, and community—indicates that such behavior is not valued and will not be tolerated. This cannot be done by withdrawing love or punishing the child aggressively; rather, the child must be made to understand the necessity of developing self-control and prosocial behavior.

HATRED

Hatred is a powerful emotion of intense dislike or aversion which a child may experience in varying circumstances in his daily relationships with parents, peers, or other adults. The Halakhah is very specific in warning against hatred of fellow men, based on the commandment "You shall not hate your brother in your heart."[33] As a practical measure to help the child overcome feelings of hatred, parents and educators may train the child and explain the importance of being honest about his emotions. The child should be taught that if he feels hostility toward someone, he must not keep this feeling pent up inside him, but rather he should confront the person and discuss his feelings openly and eventually be friends with that person again.[34]

JEALOUSY

Closely related to this powerful emotion is jealousy, in which the child feels threatened "when he perceives his exclusive possession of a source of security, status or affection challenged by the needs, aspirations, and activities of others."[35] The most common form of jealousy in childhood is sibling rivalry, in which the child believes that he is competing with his brother or sister for parental affection, status in the home, or material things. This emotion has been a source of great misfortune for many children and parents from the time of our biblical ancestors to the present day. Based on the dire consequences of the sibling rivalry between the twelve sons of our forefather Jacob, Rav said: "One should never favor one child over another, for because of the worth of two *selaim* more of wool which Jacob gave to Joseph more than to his other sons, they envied Joseph, and the circumstances which followed led to the exile of our ancestors in Egypt."[36]

What can a parent do to mitigate jealousy and envy among siblings and to help children overcome or avoid these emotions? The answer to this great dilemma appears in Judaic writings from the Bible through the modern Responsa. The Judaic view, which is now supported by psychological findings, is that excessive jealousy arises in a child who feels insecure or lacks basic feelings of adequacy.[37] The logical remedy is to build the child's self-esteem by accepting him for what he is and respecting him as an individual.

SELF-ESTEEM

The principle of respecting each child as an individual is based on the verse, "When God created human beings, He made human beings in the image of God; male and female He created them."[38] According to Rabbi Eliezer, this is the great principle of the Torah. By indicating that every human being possesses qualities which have a spark of the Divine, it provides the foundation for the view that each child must be treated equally. Moreover, the Talmud advises parents and teachers alike: "Let the honor of your pupil be as dear to you as your own."[39] Also, "The honor of your friend should be as dear to you as your own."[40]

Even the youngest child has a sense of personal dignity, and according to the rabbis, this sense "motivates man more than all the desires in the world, for no child can stand to be considered less worthy than another."[41]

The child's psychological well-being, sense of identity, and self-esteem are determined to a great extent by the way his parents treat him in the early years of life. If the child develops self-esteem, he is free to relate to others in a balanced and healthy manner, without anxiety or unnecessary jealousy or envy. The Torah teaches: "Love your neighbor as yourself."[42] Rabbi Akiva teaches that this is the greatest principle of the Torah. Indeed, this passage has great implications for child-rearing. It teaches us that before one can learn to love or respect others, one must love oneself. The development of self-esteem, "feeling good in your skin," liking yourself, determines to a great extent how one relates to others and what one will make of his life. Rashi notes that "a person prefers one measure of his own to nine measures of another."[43]

The child who is envious of his brother or sister, or who feels uncomfortable among other children, or who is constantly fighting with others, is manifesting a basic insecurity within himself. Every child prefers his own success or achievement to that of another, but when the child feels no satisfaction or confidence in himself he looks elsewhere for compensation. Parents should use every opportunity to praise the child for his achievements whatever they are, to share in his joys, and to set tasks which are within his capabilities. Above all, the parent should never embarrass the child in front of others. This guideline is reiterated in the Halakhah prohibiting embarrassing a person on the grounds that doing so is equivalent to murder.[44] Parents should not rebuke their child in public or call him derogatory names. Teachers must not ask questions which they know the pupil cannot answer.[45]

A child who is respected by his parents and, consequently, develops self-esteem, acquires the psychological foundation for healthy relationships with family and friends, and eventually manifests sympathy, compassion, and justice in his dealings with others. These basic values of Judaism are dependent on the psychological foundation developed in the home in the first two years of life. Based on this, when the child has developed sufficient cognitive maturity, he is ready to "love his neighbor as himself," feeling sorrow when he perceives distress in others, or reacting with sensitivity to injustice and finally with compassion—by displaying prosocial behavior. The feelings of sympathy, justice, kindness, and compassion are basic values interwoven into the fabric of Judaism, for the Bible teaches us that Israel should walk in the ways of the Almighty.[46] How is this to be done? The Talmud teaches us: "Just as He is gracious, so you be gracious; just as He is merciful, so you be merciful. . . . Just as He is full of kindness and truth . . . so you too."[47]

The development of these emotions based on Jewish values emanates directly from parental influence more than any other factor. Although environmental elements such as family, friends, and school affect the child's self-image as well as the resulting emotional makeup, the example set by the parents and their treatment of the child are the most important determinants, as is evident from the following passage: "What the child speaks in the marketplace, he has heard from his mother or father."[48]

AFFECTION

The most crucial element in the development of the child's mental health is the impact of parental affection during the early years of life. Psychological studies have shown that if "affectionate ties to parents are either lacking or excessively strong," the child develops handicaps in his relationships with other people. "The overprotected child is isolated emotionally from other persons by physical barriers, by induced fears, and by an overwhelming dose of parental love," while the rejected child fears involvements with others because he regards himself as unworthy of love. The child who is overvalued "has such a grandiose self-concept that he develops little capacity for loving others."[49] In any case, if the parent deprives the child of affection or showers him with too much of it, the child does not develop intrinsic feelings of security and adequacy necessary to overcome fear, anxiety, jealousy, and envy or to feel compassion, kindness, and love for others.

The Judaic guideline for parents, educators, and others involved with children is simple and direct: "In dealing with children, let the left hand repel, while the right hand draws near."[50]

Parents and others responsible for rearing children must find the middle path in relating to the child. The adult must find the right measure of guidance, discipline, and love necessary to nurture the child on the way toward emotional health in "accordance with each child's way"—or temperament. Only then can the child develop the basic values of Judaism, which arise naturally from such a state of mind. In accordance with this view, the parents should take every opportunity to express their love for the child, both verbally, with loving words, and physically, with a kiss or a hug. At times when discipline is needed, the parent should find a way to make the child understand that the punishment or anger is aimed at the misbehavior, not at the child himself, and that at all times the child is loved. In addition to offering the child security and self-confidence, parental affection for the youngster ensures that discipline will be more effective. If punishment is accompanied by manifestations of love, the child will more readily accept it as aimed at his wrong acts and not against him as a person.

JOY

Parental affection and respect, as reflected in the child's emerging self-concept, also have positive effects on the child's capacity for experiencing and expressing joy. Psychological research has shown that smiling in infants is an indication of the formation of bonds of affection and attachment. As the child grows, he tends to feel joy in connection with factors that enhance self-esteem.[51] These findings are in accord with the Judaic principles of child-rearing advocating parental love and respect for the child as means to build his self-esteem so that he may function happily and free of anxieties.

The Bible ordains: "Only be happy."[52] In Psalms we find the advice to "worship the Almighty with joy."[53] This philosophy is expressed in Halakhah with the requirement that "one should not be a jester or mocker, neither should one be sad or dejected; rather one should be happy . . . happy with one's lot."[54] The Ralbag explains that happiness is preferable to sadness, for when one is happy, he is capable of learning the ways of the Lord, whereas a sad person is engrossed in his depression and unable to experience and learn properly.[55] Happiness and the capacity of experiencing joy are deemed as essential as knowledge and wisdom.[56] Ultimately, the child who is reared in a home which grants him affection, warmth, respect, and self-esteem, as well as the basic values of Judaism, will find happiness in fulfilling these values, as it is written: "He who seeks the Almighty will be filled with joy."[57]

14
Personality Development

WHAT IS THE PERSONALITY?

The child's personality, with its unique and individual features, constitutes an integral element in the Judaic perspective on child-rearing and child-development. The classic advice that each child be reared "in accordance with his ways"[1] requires that parents and teachers "learn the ways" of their children—in other words, have a reliable understanding of the child's personality.

The foundation for the Judaic psychology of personality is found in the following statement: "The main point to be considered is that man cannot sever himself from his *mazal* [the star, or agent, through which the Almighty administers human affairs]." This *mazal,* although visualized as an external mechanism, is actually an internal force in the individual. The term is a metaphor for what we refer to as "nature" or temperament. Thus, a person born with a certain temperament will have the tendency to be righteous in his behavior. Another, born with a nature of a different sort, will tend to be either a murderer, a *mohel,* or a butcher. The course of his behavior is up to the individual himself; his temperament indicates that he will shed blood, but he may do so in any of the three ways mentioned: by being evil and committing crimes, by choosing the middle road and becoming a butcher, or by following the path of the righteous and performing as a *mohel.* The purpose of the mitzvoth is that one should subjugate one's nature to the work of the Almighty as prescribed in the Torah, so that the personality develops its maximum potential for the good.

In light of this, each child must be trained in the *mitzvot* according to his personality. If this is done successfully, he will not leave the path of Judaism even in his old age. However, if in the course of *chinnukh* one tries to separate him from his nature—i.e., to make him go against his nature—the child may demonstrate obedience out of fear, but after he removes the yoke of the parent or teacher he will leave the path of Judaism, for it has been taught to him in a manner against his true nature.[2]

This view of personality is further defined by Maimonides in the following passage:

> It is not possible that man be born from his creation naturally perfected, only of high qualities, without deficiencies, lacks, and lowly qualities, just as it is impossible for a man to be born by his nature a finished craftsman. However, it is possible that he be born "predisposed" to a high or low quality, so that certain deeds will "take" to him more easily than others.[3]

Maimonides delves further into psychology when he explains:

> Pertaining to tendencies in general there are such tendencies which a man acquires at his birth, in keeping with the nature of his body; and there are particular tendencies to which a particular person is by nature prepared to acquire them more aptly than other tendencies; there are among them such which do not come naturally to a person at his birth, but which he learns from others, or by leaning toward them as a result of a thought invented by his heart, or by having heard that this particular tendency is good for him and proper to follow it, and he did follow it until it was set in his heart.[4]

This remarkable statement includes the basic definition of personality accepted by modern psychologists as well as the foundation for *chinnukh* and all of civilized culture.

A modern definition of personality by Gordon P. Allport contains the main elements described by Maimonides in the twelfth century. Allport defines personality as "the dynamic organization within the individual of those psychophysical systems that determine his unique adjustments to his environment." He states that this definition is derived from the traditions of academic psychology and is close to the concepts of John Dewey and Kurt Lewin. According to Allport, this dynamic organization consists of attitudes and traits ("those aspects of personality in respect to which most people within a given culture can be profitably compared") and values ("meanings perceived as related to the self").[5]

TEMPERAMENTAL INFLUENCES

As the preceding section indicates, the traditional Jewish view and modern psychology agree that innate factors and environmental influences both have an influence on personality development. The natural relationship between the two holds the key to the success of *chinnukh* in Judaism. The Judaic perspective on personality development emphasizes the importance of nature and nurture, utilizing both as instruments in molding man into his civilized form.

As we have seen, the child's nature "is made up of diverse entities, natures conflicting and mutually antagonistic."[6] These entities, defined by the talmudic sages as the *yetzer ha-tov* (good inclination) and the *yetzer ha-ra* (evil inclination), are "mutually antagonistic" in the battle to control the child's predispositions. In the very first stages of life, the child does not by nature possess any virtues, as is stated in Job 11:12: "Man is born as wild as a young ass." Nevertheless, the infant must be taught little by little to assume good characteristics, for "each child is stamped during his childhood with individuality [temperament] through which his relatives and directors must train him."[7]

Child psychologists who have studied this individuality reaffirm the importance of temperament in the process of child development and upbringing.[8] Modern experts in child development, like the rabbis before them, urge parents and educators to make every effort to "know the child"—to pay attention to the unique temperament which directs the child's primary reactions to the environment. As further explained by Maimonides:

> There is one man of a feverish temperament, constantly vexed, and there is another man of a calm disposition, without any angry moods—if he does display anger it is only a bit of anger in many years; one individual is too supercilious, another is too unobstrusive; one is sensual and is never satisfied in his pursuit of sensual pleasures, while another is so pure-hearted that he feels no desire even for the barest necessities of his body.[9]

In the earliest years of life, the child's predisposed temperament dominates him in a crude form. The parent and educator must identify his character traits and relate to the child on those terms. An anecdote is told of Rabbi Israel of Salant, who discerned in his granddaughter a tendency to be miserly. He immediately began to educate her in her earliest years by giving her money or candies so that she could share with others and thus root out the evil tendency.[10]

Similarly, we see in the Bible that Jacob blesses each of his twelve sons in accordance with their unique characteristics,[11] and Moses does the same with the twelve tribes of Israel.[12] Thus, Reuben is mentioned for his impetuous temperament. Simeon and Levi are scolded for their cruelty and are dealt with accordingly by being divided among the tribes; Judah is noted for his bravery and strength, and is rewarded by receiving the distinction of being the seat of the Kingdom of Israel, as well as inheriting a rich and bountiful tract of land; Zebulun, whose temperament leans toward trade (rather than study), will receive land along the ocean so that the tribe may conduct its trade and supply food to Issachar, who leans more toward study of the Torah; Issachar will receive a fruitful tract of land and will be able to learn Torah and teach his brothers the law; Dan will employ his trait as a warrior to lead the fight for all the people of Israel (especially in the battle against the Phoenicians); Gad will maintain legions of soldiers to oust enemies from the Land of Israel in accordance with his trait of courage; Asher will be blessed with land rich in olive trees as a result of his pleasant character; Naphtali's heroic nature is rewarded with an inheritance of a rich tract of land; Joseph is noted for his outstanding beauty—the envy of his brothers—and also for his piety, which entitles him to receive special blessings from the Almighty and be appointed King over his brothers; Benjamin is blessed for his qualities as a brave fighter whose descendants will bring salvation to Israel throughout history.

Thus, each of the twelve ancestors from whom the twelve tribes of Israel are descended has unique character traits which place a mark on the lives and the future of his descendants. By blessing them according to their individuality and leaving each a legacy suited to his temperament, Jacob attempts to ensure as far as possible that every one of his children and their descendants will succeed in life. Similarly, each parent-educator must discern the unique characteristics of his child and relate to him, in routine matters as well as in education, in accordance with the child's temperament. This technique will ensure the success of *chinnukh* throughout the child's life, as stated in Proverbs (22:6): "even when he grows old he will not depart from these ways." It will also grant the maximum possibility for good relationships between parent and child, thus forming a basis for mental health.

ENVIRONMENTAL INFLUENCES

Under no circumstances, however, does Judaism view the

child's personality as predetermined. The very *raison d'être* of Judaism postulates that the environmental factor has a decisive role to play in the formation of personality and behavior. In the beginning of his blessing for the people of Israel before his death, Moses proclaims the verse which is the foundation of Judaism, the first words taught to a child as soon as he learns to speak: "Moses commanded us the Torah, it is an inheritance of the congregation of Jacob."[13] As a balance to man's innate tendencies, the Almighty gave us the Torah. It is as much our inheritance as the elements of our genic endowment, and each child's development must be guided by a synthesis of the two forces. The means by which Torah becomes an integral part of the child's personality is through *chinnukh* at home and in school as well as through his environment, for "it is a natural tendency of man to be influenced in his ideas and conduct by his fellows and associates, and to follow the usage of people of his state."[14]

Judaism considers *chinnukh* the "hope for the child's future" and the means through which he learns to "conquer his evil spirit and egocentric desires, so that he is not drawn after evil and corruption; instead he will attempt to act in accordance with goodness and justice" when he reaches maturity.[15]

Yet every parent and educator responsible for rearing children is faced with a dilemma in resolving the proper proportions to attribute to the roles of nature and nurture in personality and moral development. How much can the child be influenced by ideals, by examples set by the parent or educator, by guiding rules? Where is the boundary between the child's independent will, egocentrism, and stubbornness, and the role of environmental factors in development? Maimonides states this controversy (which has marked the course of child study throughout history) in the following words:

Had the decree of God prompted man to be either just or wicked, or had there been a fundamentally inborn something to draw man to either of the paths, or to any one branch of knowledge, or to a given tendency of the tendencies, or to a particular act of all actions as the astrologists maintain by their foolish inventions, how did He charge us by the prophets to do thus and not to do such, improve your ways and do not follow your wickedness, whereas man before birth had a decree of his conduct issued, or his innate nature draws him toward a given path of conduct from which he cannot deviate? Moreover, what need would there be, under such circumstances, for the Torah altogether? And by what law, and under what system of justice, could the wicked be punished, or the just rewarded?[16]

The reply given by Maimonides forms the basis of *chinnukh*, the essence of Judaism, and the Judaic philosophy of personality development:

Know that all that man does is in accordance with His will, although our actions are really in our own keeping. . . . so was it His will that man should have the free choice of conduct in his own hands, and that all his actions should be lodged within him, and that he should be neither forced nor drawn, but he, of his own free will and accord, as God endowed him with, he exercises in all that is possible for man to do. He is, therefore, judged according to actions; if he did good, he is rewarded with good: and if he did wrong, he is punished.[17]

This free will, the core of Judaism, is further explained:

Every man was endowed with a free will; if he desires to lean toward the good path and to be just, it is within his power to reach out for it, and if he wishes to bend himself to a bad path and be evil, it is within his power to reach out for it. Thus, every man is capable of being as just as Moses our Master, as wicked as Jeroboam, wise or foolish, merciful or cruel, miser or philanthropist, and so on for all other tendencies. There is nothing to force things upon him or to decree things against him; to pull him one way or the other. It is he alone, of his own free will, with the consent of his mind, which bends to any path he may desire to follow.[18]

The free will is manifested through the individual's actions, which stem from his character traits, as is clearly stated in *Mesillat Yesharim*: "For as all of a person's worldly actions, so are his traits. It is from them that his actions flow."[19] Here we come to the core of the problem, as resolved by the *Orchot Tzaddikim*:

> According to the characteristic that he possesses, man will act: the squanderer after his squandering, the miser after his miserliness, the lover after his love, the hater after his hate. Therefore, a man who seeks to become truly God-fearing must first remove himself from all the deficient characteristics so that he is not drawn by the characteristic within him toward their nature.[20]

THE ROLE OF TORAH AND HALAKHAH IN PERSONALITY DEVELOPMENT

By teaching his child the Torah, the parent-educator gives him the ultimate resource for living a just and honest life. The Torah and its consequent Halakhah guides and commands, but the final choice is up to the individual: "I have put before you life and death, blessing and curse. Choose life, if you and your offspring would live."[21]

The Code of Jewish Law is specific concerning the prohibition of tale-bearing, slander, lying, mockery, flattery, revenge, and bearing a grudge.[22] As every parent and teacher knows, young children are naturally inclined to these vices in the early years, "for the inclination of man's heart is evil from his youth."[23] If we consider the evil inclination with reference to the psychological id (the instinctual part of the personality), the Judaic appraisal of personality development closely corresponds to psychology. The learning process, which begins in the sensorimotor stage of development and continues through the period of formal operations, constitutes the beginning of the development of the ego (the part of the personality that deals with life in a rational manner), and culminates in the development of the superego, which is based on moral rules that guide the child's actions. The final stage takes place at the time of adolescence, which corresponds to the age of twelve for girls and thirteen for boys—a stage in life when (according to Judaism) the child becomes mature enough to be responsible for his own actions and assume responsibility for fulfilling the *mitzvot*.[24] The rules that form the basis of the superego for the Jew are incorporated in Halakhah, which is based on the Torah (the 613 commandments), rabbinic legislation throughout Jewish history, and the sanctified practices of Jewish tradition. The means by which the child internalizes these rules is referred to as *chinnukh*. The root of this word in Hebrew means "to inaugurate." Thus, according to Judaic philosophy, the child begins life with a personality dominated by the id and is inaugurated by his parents, the school, and the environment into the realm of reality within the framework of the Torah. Through practice, imitation, and learning the values of Judaism, the child develops mechanisms in his personality that regulate the drives, wishes, and egocentric desires of his private magic world to maintain an equilibrium with the demands of the outer world.

The basic message inherent in the Judaic view of childrearing is that in order for the child to develop a healthy personality, *chinnukh* must be individualized. The Midrash brings our attention to the fact that "Just as no person resembles another, so each person's temperament differs."[25] Rabbi Samson Raphael Hirsch explains, in accordance with this perspective, that each parent and educator must "act in every instance according to the personal conditions of each child; to develop his characteristics and encourage his talents, while at the same time restraining his negative tendencies by directing them in the right direction rather than by destroying them."[26]

This education guideline is implicit in the advice to "rear

each lad in accordance with his ways, so that even when he grows old he will not depart from that which he is taught."[27] If we consider, as does Rabbi Samson Raphael Hirsch, that "the characteristics and tendencies which are innate will accompany the child throughout life more than the educator will," then we come to realize that "the educator can only attempt to foresee how the child will act in the future as a result of his temperament, and on this basis to guide and direct the child toward the moral goal. The success of the educator lies in the measure that the child does not sway from the path in which he was educated even when he becomes an adult."[28]

The key to the development of a healthy personality lies in the ability of the parent-educator to adapt the learning process which begins in infancy and intensifies throughout childhood to the child's temperament and dispositions, so that the values of Judaism are internalized freely and willingly. If this is the case, by the time the child reaches the age of maturity, Bar Mitzvah or Bat Mitzvah, he or she will have developed a healthy sense of identity and a strong personal conviction to choose the Jewish way of life. He or she will be ready to accept the responsibilities of Judaism and thus make a healthy contribution to society.

Part IV
Child Development in the Social Context

Introduction

Child-development in the social context involves child-rearing practices of parents, training in schools, relations with peers and siblings, and the status of the child in society. As the Torah was given for us "to live by" (Leviticus 18:5), Judaism serves as a framework for socialization which encompasses each of the processes by which a child acquires the ability to participate effectively in all aspects of social interaction.

The Torah, as an all-encompassing source of values and ideals, is the root of socialization for every Jewish child. The socializing agents include parents, relatives, teachers, friends, and others who come into contact with the child during the formative years of development. As Erikson discusses in *Identity: Youth and Crisis,* during the course of socialization, at different stages of development, the child identifies with whatever aspects of these people most immediately affect him, whether in reality or fantasy. According to Judaism this process culminates with the formation of identity in the period of adolescence, when the child is Bar Mitzvah or Bat Mitzvah. Consequently, the aim of child-rearing, within the framework of Judaism, is to instill in the child the values of Judaism, for they determine how he will understand the world: his reactions, motives, goals, and preferences.

The success of socialization is measured by the extent to which the child chooses the Jewish way of life freely and willingly upon reaching the age of Bar Mitzvah or Bat Mitzvah; as it is written: "Choose life, if you and your offspring would live" (Deuteronomy 30:19). The effects of child-development in the social context are intertwined with other dimensions of development, such as personality, emotions, and cognition. In the words of the noted psychologist Kurt Lewin: "an early build-up of a clear and positive feeling of belongingness to the Jewish group is one of the few effective things that parents can do for the later happiness of their children." Socialization, which provides the child with the foundations for the development of Jewish identity, is the most effective means of assuring the child's mental health.

15
Socialization

SOCIAL LEARNING

Socialization as a process of social learning enables the child to interact with others in accordance with the values transmitted in the framework of *chinnukh* by the prime socializing agents—parents and teachers. Since each child's experiences and interactions with others will be different, and each child reacts according to his own temperament and aptitude, the process of socialization is always unique to the individual, yet in all cases the values of Judaism, perpetuated in the Torah and administered through Halakhah, constitute the child's frame of reference on every occasion—in accordance with his ability to comprehend and to apply them in his daily relations with adults and peers.

The essence of Judaism as a frame of reference for socialization is expressed in the following rabbinical discourse:

> Rabbi Samuel bar Nachman said in the name of Rabbi Jonathan: In the Torah, Prophets and Oral Law we find that man must fulfill his obligations to people just as he must fulfill his obligations to the Almighty. Where in the Torah? As it is written: "And you shall be free of sin toward the Almighty or the people of Israel" [Num. 32:22]. Where in the Prophets? As it is written: "The Lord our God will know, and the people of Israel will know . . ." [Josh. 22:22]. Where in the Oral Law? As it is writ-

ten: "Find grace and favor in the eyes of the Almighty and man" [Prov. 3:4]. Gamliel Zoga asked Rabbi Yose bar Rabbi Nun: Which is the most clear of all? He answered: "And you shall be free of sin toward the Almighty or the people of Israel."[1]

Furthermore, we find the observation that "All who are well liked by people are well liked by the Almighty; those who are not well liked by people are not well liked by the Almighty."[2]

The Torah encompasses all human affairs in the *mitzvot*, decrees and laws.[3] The *mitzvot* are divided into two entities: *mitzvot* between man and the Almighty (constituting moral acts and faith), and *mitzvot* between man and fellow man (guides for social relations).

As we have seen, children under the age of thirteen are not liable for the fulfillment of the *mitzvot* of their own accord until they reach the age of maturity (thirteen for a boy and twelve for a girl).[4] Until that time, it is the parents' responsibility to train the children to perform positive *mitzvot* in accordance with their ability to comprehend and execute them.[5] The parent must also prohibit the child from committing transgressions or violating prohibitions, starting at age or two or three—the onset of the preoperational stage of development, when the child's ability to think becomes refined.[6] It is during this pre-adolescent period of socialization that the child learns the *mitzvot* in the home and school in the process of *chinnukh*. If *chinnukh* is successful, the child internalizes the *mitzvot* and chooses freely and willingly to execute them upon reaching the age of maturity and independent responsibility for his actions.

During this process of socialization, the child's relations with parents, peers, siblings, teachers, and other people must be guided by the *mitzvot*, which are the frame of reference for human relations in Judaism.

In the Talmud we find a summary of all the *mitzvot* pertaining to social relations:

"Thou shalt love thy neighbor as thyself" [Lev. 19:18]. Rabbi

Akiva says: "This is the most important principle in the Law." Ben Azzai says: "'This is the book of man's history . . . in the image of the Lord He created him' [Gen. 5:1]. This is a more important principle, so that you will not say, 'As I have been shamed, so my friend should be shamed with me. As I have been cursed, so my friend should be cursed with me.'" Said Rabbi Tanchuma: "If you do so, know whom you shame: for God created man in His image."[7]

The ideal Jewish education should make it clear to the child that all his social relations must be based on respect for every individual. In fact, one of the first verses a child can easily identify with is the precept: "Love thy neighbor as thyself."

Judaism recognizes the psychological principle that as the child "exaggerates his own importance,"[8] he naturally relates to others in terms of his egocentric desires and satisfactions. Perhaps this was why Rabbi Akiva chose this precept as the most important of all for socialization, for it provides the most simple and direct means of teaching the child respect for others. As the child matures, he internalizes this value and it becomes disassociated from his personal satisfaction to the extent that it becomes his natural manner of relating to others.

PEER GROUPS

We have seen that in the process of socialization the child identifies with certain aspects of the people who affect him. As the prime agents of socialization, parents and teachers have the most striking effect on the child's identity formation. Judaism provides moral codes of behavior as well as halakhic laws to which they must adhere in their relations with children (as discussed in the relevant sections of this chapter). The other significant agent of socialization in the child's life is the peer group.

Although a peer group does not socialize its members intentionally, its own dynamics make it a most influential agent in shaping the child's values, attitudes, and preferences. Since the child enjoys contact with close friends and attains emotional satisfaction from such relations, he usually internalizes the pressures and expectations of the peer group. The practical application of this fact is incorporated in Halakhah in the following guideline:

> As the nature of man is for him to be influenced in his thoughts and actions by his friends and associates, and as he naturally behaves in the tradition of his community, therefore, each person must associate himself with the righteous and be close to the wise, so that he may learn from their deeds. Also, man must separate himself from evil people, so that he may not learn from their actions.[9]

The implications of this rule are that a parent must always strive to find a good environment for his child to grow in and must at least try to find him good friends. The extent of this ruling is such that if a family finds itself in a community in which the morals are bad, the parent must do everything possible to move to a better community so that his child will grow up in a more suitable society. All attempts must be made to draw near to the "wise and their students" so that the child will be exposed to good influences in his contacts with people.[10] The choice of a peer group is a critical one in the child's life, for "the individual is known by his friends."[11] The parent who lives in a suitable community, thus making it possible for his child to associate with children and adults who follow the paths of Judaism, paves the road for the child to develop a positive orientation to Judaism.

Nevertheless, Judaism does not require that the child be isolated from the outside world. Such a situation could be very unfortunate if the child is confronted at some stage of life with different ways of life and cannot cope with the challenge. The Talmud instructs: "One should always mingle with people."[12] Even more explicit: "When you arrive in a city, act in its ways."[13] The parent must make his child aware of the differences among men, making no secret of the varying life-styles of nonobservant Jews and of gentiles. In such a manner, the child is fortified when he emerges from the shelter of his home environment and comes into contact with the outside world and its varying societies.

SIBLING RELATIONS

The influence of sibling relations on the child's socialization is a more complex matter, for the manner in which the child relates with his siblings greatly affects his self-image and developing identity. Sibling relations are directly and indirectly affected by the attitudes of the parents toward each of their children and their involvement in the relations between them. Jewish history points out many examples of sibling rivalry leading to tragedy, such as the stories of Cain and Abel, Isaac and Ishmael, Jacob and Esau, Joseph and his brothers, and Adonijah and Solomon. In most of these historic cases, we find that one or both parents showed preference, either directly or in subtle ways, for one of the children. This naturally led to feelings of jealousy between the children, with catastrophic results for them and for generations to follow. The Talmud specifically states: "One should never single out one child from the others; because of a scrap of cloth of little worth, Joseph's brothers envied him mortally,"[14] and the resulting bad relations between the brothers led to Israel's eventual exile in Egypt. The bad relations between Isaac and Ishmael, and between Jacob and Esau, have implications for the distress among nations to this day, while the jealousy between Adonijah and Solomon caused civil strife within the Jewish nation.

In addition to the ruling that parents must not favor one child over the others, Maimonides decided, based on a Torah ruling, that a child's inheritance cannot be denied to him if the parent favors another child who is better than the one in line for the property.[15] The *Reishit Chokhmah* advises parents to treat each child equally, "in food and drink, in financial affairs, presents, and inheritance." Even a favorite son cannot inherit a double portion, if he is not a firstborn.[16]

Sibling relations—the contacts between brothers and sisters—offer the child his first and most frequent kind of social exchange. The parent can do much to enhance the child's approach to relations with others. The great principle "And thou shalt love thy neighbor as thyself"[17] must first be taught in the family setting, where it is most often applicable in the first few years of life. The child who is taught early in life to respect his brothers and sisters will find it easier to relate to peers in a healthy manner.

In all instances, sibling relations should be guided by the basic rule that "each child be reared in accordance with his ways."[18] Just as the parent must relate to each child in accordance with his temperament and capabilities, so must each child be taught to accept his brothers and sisters with their strengths and weaknesses as individuals. If the child accepts the fact that "no two children are created alike,"[19] it will be more natural and less painful for him to accept a sibling's competition in any area of their relationship. The Code of Jewish Law adds an element of order in sibling relations by ruling that each person is obligated to honor his older sibiling.[20]

PLAY

Judaism acknowledges that play is a natural activity for children, necessary for growth and learning. In the early years of life, play serves as a source of emotional expression and as a focus for sensorimotor development. In the Talmud this is vividly portrayed by the story of the talmudic scholar Rabbah, who used to bring home broken crocks from the market for his child to break.[21]

In the historical sense, play also had a function in the process of learning and socialization. We have seen that little children astounded their teachers by reciting the alefbet in a game of moralization.[22] It seems that the device of teaching the alefbet in the form of a play on words and moral concepts was very popular with children. As an effective method for learning the alefbet and introducing Jewish moral concepts in a light and pleasant manner, it served two purposes at the same time. Throughout the Talmud, we find references to the use of riddles and light anecdotes as a means of enabling students to learn through a less formal framework similar to natural play activities.[23] The Talmud also mentions teachers who played with their students before the lesson to entice them to learn.[24]

By its nature as a group activity, play entails role-playing, dramatization, concentration, thought, and reenactment of life situations. Its function as a means of socialization is fulfilled as the child interacts with others in the play activity. We find examples of this aspect of play in the following talmudic anecdote:

> A story is told of Rabbi Eliezer and Rabbi Yehoshua and Rabban Gamliel, who went to Rome. They came to a site where they found children making piles of sand and saying: "This is what the Jewish people do, and they say, 'These are for *terumah* and these for *ma'aser.*'" The sages said: "It seems that there are Jewish people here."[25]

The fact that the children were reenacting a life situation in a group setting clearly indicates the role of play in socialization.

An even more striking indication of the role of play in learning and socialization appears in the following excerpt from the Talmud:

> It happened on a very rainy day that the scholars did not come to the House of Study. And the children entered there and said: "Come, let us see to it that learning should not be interrupted in the House of Study." So they said: "Why two letters—*mem*

mem, nun nun, tsade tsade, pe pe, and *kaf kaf?* From the word [*ma'amar*] to word, from a true one [*ne'eman*] to a true one, from a righteous one [*tsaddik*] to a righteous one, from mouth [*peh*] to mouth, and from the hand [*kaf*] of God to the hand of Moses." The scholars kept their eyes on these children, and they all grew up to be great men. It is said that Rabbi Eliezer and Rabbi Joshua came from this group.[26]

As play is considered a natural childhood activity necessary for learning and socialization, Judaism has incorporated it into religious customs, making it possible for children to participate in various religious festivals and ceremonies on a level suitable for them. The child thus experiences the religious occasion and comprehends the situation according to his stage of development. For example, the playful tradition of hiding the *afikoman* during the Passover Seder ceremony is intended to include the child in the religious observance in a manner that will arouse his natural curiosity and willingness to participate. Before the Shavuot holiday, children gather leaves and branches to decorate the house in honor of the revelation on Mount Sinai. Before the Sukkot holiday, children busily make decorations for the *sukkah*. On Chanukah, the children play with the *dreidel,* a game which reminds them of the historical "miracle" of the Chanukah lights in the Holy Temple. On Purim the children disguise themselves in costumes and embark on merrymaking in celebration of the salvation of the Jewish people from the evil decree of Haman. (In the Talmud, it is mentioned that children used to make Haman dolls out of scraps of cloth and wood and burn them in a hole in the ground. They would then play jumping games around it as part of the Purim frolic.)[27]

It is also recognized that children play games as part of their daily routine. Just as there are halakhic guidelines on the toys very young children may use on the Sabbath, so there are halakhic rules concerning the games that may be played on the Sabbath by older children.[28]

16
The Parent-Child Relationship

The Halakhah concerning the parent-child relationship is a most impressive illustration of the psychological subtlety interwoven in the fabric of Jewish law. Judaism recognizes that the parent-child relationship is reciprocal. The legal and moral obligations and responsibilities of the parents toward the child—matched by the obligations and responsibilities of children toward their parents—are a natural outcome of this sophisticated insight into one of the most crucial of human relations in the process of development.

PARENTAL DUTIES

The basic responsibility of the parent toward the child is decreed by the Almighty in a statement concerning our forefather Abraham: "For I have known him in order that he may instruct his sons and his household after him, that they may keep the way of the Lord to do righteousness and justice."[1] The Talmud reiterates this parental responsibility by asserting that the father is expected to "guide his sons and daughters in the straight path."[2]

The specific obligations of the father toward his child are enumerated in the Talmud as follows: "The father is obliged to circumcise his son, to redeem him (if firstborn) [Num.

18:15–16], to teach him Torah, to have him wed, and to teach him a trade. Some say he must also teach him to swim."[3] It is also the father's duty to train the children in such a manner as to inspire in them a sense of modesty.[4]

Both parents are obliged to train their children in the *mitzvot* they will be obliged to fulfill as adults.[5] This is to be carried out in accordance with the child's learning readiness and capabilities.[6]

Although the father is legally obligated to provide food for his children until the age of six,[7] the Usha ordinance extended this obligation until the children mature.[8] Maimonides states that "just as a man is obligated to sustain his wife, so he is obligated to sustain his small children."[9] The Code of Jewish Law states that the father must afford his children maintenance "until they grow up."[10] If grown children are incapable of sustaining themselves, the father is obliged to continue maintaining them.[11] Indeed, the father should provide for the needs of his wife and children before he takes care of his own necessities, as it is written: "The father must honor his wife and children with clothes and food more than what he has for himself, for they are dependent upon him, and he is dependent upon the Almighty."[12]

The parent should administer light punishment if the child is disobedient, as it is written: "He that spareth his rod hateth his son, but he that loveth him chasteneth him betimes."[13]

The parent who does not teach his children Torah is considered an "ignorant boor,"[14] while the father who does not teach his son a trade or handicraft is "as if he teaches him to be a robber."[15] The father who refuses to maintain his children is declared worse than a cruel raven.[16]

FILIAL DUTIES

The basis for filial duties toward parents appears in the Ten

Commandments: "Honor thy father and thy mother." Since this decree follows the commandment to honor the Almighty, respect for parents is compared to respect for the Almighty.[17]

The decree for children to respect their parents is reiterated in the Bible with a remarkable psychological sophistication. As it is usual for the child to fear the father more than the mother and to love and honor the mother more than the father, the Torah mentions the father first when commanding honor for parents, but mentions the mother first when issuing the commandment to revere parents.[18]

The Code of Jewish Law indicates several ways in which honor and reverence for parents is to be shown. A child must not sit in a seat reserved for parent or stand in a place reserved for him. A child must not contradict his parent. It is the child's duty, when grown, to take care of the parent if the parent needs food, clothing, or shelter.[19] Filial duty extends to the point that if one parent instructs the child to do something and the other parent expresses anger when the child performs the act, the child must not attempt to excuse himself by telling the second parent that he was carrying out the first parent's instructions, because this would cause anger between the parents.[20]

The responsibility of the child to respect his parents remains constant, without regard to the merit of the parent. The Code of Jewish Law specifies that the child must honor his parent even if the parent is evil.[21] However, if the parent instructs the child to commit a sin or to violate a *mitzvah*, the child should nevertheless fulfill the *mitzvot*.[22]

The Talmud tells many stories of exemplary obedience and respect for parents.[23] According to Halakhah, respect for one's parents is a very important mitzvah which must be fulfilled by each child. However, the commandment is not enforced by the court (as it is a mitzvah which entails its reward). On the other hand, abuse of parents is liable to punishment by the court (Shulkhan Arukh Yoreh Deah, 240,24).

CURBS ON PARENTAL INITIATIVE

The most remarkable aspect of the Halakhah concerning the parent-child relationship is the advanced psychological perceptiveness indicated by the laws guiding parental initiative. The Code of Jewish Law specifies that the father is forbidden to impose too heavy a yoke on his children and to be too exacting with them in matters concerning his honor, lest he cause them to stumble. The father should forgive his children, for he has the right to forgo his own honor.[24] In the *Sefer Chasidim,* we find the same guideline: "The father and mother should not so enrage the son that he cannot control himself and must rebel against them."[25] The rabbis urged that parents motivate filial piety through the use of *mechilah* (i.e., renouncing or waiving a right or privilege) in accordance with the talmudic conclusion stated as follows: "Rabbi Isaac ben Shila said in the name of Rabbi Mattanah, who said in the name of Rabbi Chisda: A father may forgo the honor due him."[26] Similarly, the observation that "one is jealous of everyone except of one's own son"[27] reflects the special parent-child relationship.

Although discipline is an essential factor in *chinnukh* (which is the basis for child-rearing), the dynamic nature of the parent-child relationship warrants that the parent structure his assertiveness relative to the child's ability to render service and honor. The father is warned not to impose "excessive fear into his household."[28] The Code of Jewish Law rules that it is forbidden to strike a grown child, and that the maturity of the child is based on his cognitive level and temperament.

If a child might react violently in speech or through action, even if he is not yet Bar Mitzvah (thirteen years old), the parent should not strike him. Instead, the father should admonish him with words. A parent who strikes his mature child is banned, for he has violated the Torah commandment: "You shall not place a stumbling-block before the blind."[29] The talmudic source for this ruling is as follows:

A maid-servant of the House of the Patriarch saw a man strike his mature son. She said: "Let that man be placed under the ban, for he has violated the commandment of the Torah 'You shall not place a stumbling-block before the blind' [Lev. 19:14]."
... As the *baraita* says: "'You shall not place a stumbling-block before the blind.' This refers to one who strikes his mature son."[30]

In the Tosefta, *Bava Kamma* 9:8–11, we find sources which discourage and even ban parents from striking their children to the extent that a father who beats his child is liable to be sued for assault and even must compensate the minor. Although the Bible and the Mishnah advise discipline with the rod[31] and state that "if one vigorously disciplines his son, the son loves him all the more and honors him,"[32] a parent who strikes a child "beyond what is proper" is liable.[33] As a deterrent to child abuse, a court is authorized to determine whether the father strikes the child beyond what is proper.

Judaism also offers rules and advice on preventative disciplinary measures. "The father should not so enrage his child that he cannot restrain himself but must rebel."[34] The parent should not threaten the child, but should either punish him immediately or forgive him.[35] The parent must not promise to give the child something and then not do so, for this teaches the child to lie.[36]

Parents must set an example for their children through their behavior and speech, their relations with others, and their conduct as Jews. The extremely powerful influence of the parental example and the force of imitation in the process of child-development is stated in a terse talmudic source: "A child's babbling out-of-doors comes from either its father or its mother."[37]

Judaism also recognizes that socialization is a dynamic process involving both the parent and the child, with mutual influence on each other. The parent is urged to learn from his child, for "there are times when the child is wiser than his father."[38]

SUMMARY

The parent-child relationship is embodied in Halakhah within the framework of a subtle psychological determination of the mutual nature of the bond. Parents are obliged to fulfill specific obligations toward their children, and children are obliged to render respect and honor regardless of parental merit. Yet Halakhah incorporates effective guidelines for parental assertiveness which constitute effective methods to elicit normative responses of reverence and honor from the child.

The Talmud summarizes the halakhic obligations in the parent-child relationship as follows:

> All obligations of the son upon the father, men are bound but women are exempt. But all obligations of the father upon the son, both men and women are bound. What is the meaning of "all obligations of the son upon the father"? ... Said Rav Judah: This is the meaning: All obligations of the son [which lie] upon the father to do to his son, men are bound, but women are exempt. But "all obligations of the father upon the son," etc. What is meant by "all obligations of the father upon the son"? Said Rav Judah: This is the meaning: All precepts concerning a father, which are incumbent upon a son to perform for his father, both men and women are bound thereby.[39]

As the parent's duty of maintaining his child is a more complex halakhic question, the Talmud determines as follows:

> "Happy are those who maintain justice and give charity at all times" [Ps. 106]. Our sages in Yavneh asked: Is it possible to give charity at all times? Rabbi Eliezer said to them: This concerns the person who maintains his sons and daughters while they are young.[40]

Concerning filial piety, the Code of Jewish Law summarizes the best way to honor parents as follows:

> Whoever really wants to honor his father and mother will live according to the Torah and do good deeds, for this is the greatest honor for parents, as people will say: "Happy are the mother and father who reared such a child." However, if the child does not follow the right path, his parents will bear the shame for him, and he shames them in the worst manner.[41]

In a reciprocal manner, characteristic of the dynamic nature of the relationship:

> And the father who really wants to show compassion for his children will live according to the Torah and do good deeds and will be pleasing to the Almighty and to people, and his children will be honored through him. However, whoever does not follow the right path, his children are disgraced after him, and children also die for the sins of their parents, as it is written: "The Almighty punishes children for the sins of their fathers." And there is no cruelty greater than this which he causes—that his sons should die for his sins.[42]

When parents and child fulfill their obligations toward each other, and parental initiatives toward the child are structured in accordance with the child' capability to render honor, the bond between them is healthy and strong: Under such conditions it is said: "When the children are blessed, the parents by this very token are blessed."[43]

The best testimony to the healthy bond between parent and child created through the halakhic prescriptions is described as follows in the Talmud: "The child shall keep the memory of his parents green, and whenever he speaks of them it shall be with words of loving veneration."[44] Judaism provides the most important element of a healthy parent-child relationship by affording continuous opportunities for parents to spend time with their children through mutual participation in religious observances and the experience of *chinnukh* within the family framework.

Judaism has built-in mechanisms to facilitate good relations between parent and child so that both are indeed blessed. The traditional Jewish way of life, with the presence and participation of children in the performance of rituals within the family framework and the attention they receive from their parents in the process, is the foundation for mutual respect between the two generations. In essence, the role of the home in the process of socialization, with the emphasis on parental harmony in the child's development,[45] consitutes the primary principle of education (*chinnukh*) in Judaism. The Jewish way of life integrates family relations with education as a means of continuing the heritage of Judaism from generation to generation. The celebration of Chanukah, Purim, the Seder ceremony, the blessing over the *Lulav* and *Etrog,* and the Sabbath rituals, in which the child is an active participant or even the central performer, ensures that parents and children spend time together throughout the crucial stages of development.[46] It is to this effect that we find the prophecy: "And He shall turn the heart of the fathers to the children, and the heart of the children to their fathers."[47]

One of the most beautiful and effective rituals, carried out every Friday and festival evening before the recitation of Kiddush, is "blessing the children." The father greets his children upon returning from the synagogue with an impressive symbol of love, placing his hands on the head of the child, even the youngest, and reciting the following blessings:

For boys: "May God make you as Ephraim and Manasseh."
For girls: "May God make you as Sarah, Rebecca, Rachel, and Leah."[48]

In both cases, the blessing is followed by the traditional blessing for peace:

> May the Lord bless you and protect you: may the Lord make His countenance to shine upon you and be gracious to you; may the Lord favor you and bestow peace upon you.

17
Birthdays

The tradition of celebrating the date of one's birth is an ancient one. In the Bible, it is mentioned that Pharaoh celebrated his birthday.[1] Indeed, a historical survey shows that this custom was very popular among non-Jews and in time became associated with idol worship and forbidden sacrifices. For this reason, some sages of the Mishnah forbade birthday celebrations.[2]

On the other hand, the birth dates of several outstanding figures are specifically mentioned in the Talmud, based on biblical sources. The birthday of Isaac is associated with joy and is dedicated to happiness in each generation.[3] Indeed, the Talmud attributes great importance to the birthdays of our forefathers, Abraham, Isaac, and Jacob, which are said to have occurred in the same month that the world was created.[4] The Talmud stipulates the seventh day of Adar as the date Moses was born.[5] The birthday of King David is marked yearly on Shavuot by the reading of Megillat Ruth, which ends with David's lineage.[6] The ninth of Av is a day of mourning and fasting, but it is also considered to be the birthdate of the Messiah, and special customs are observed to commemorate the occasion.[7] The most exemplary instance of a birthday celebration is that of Rabbi Simeon bar Yochai, which coincides with Lag ba-Omer. The festivity on this occasion, known as the Hillula de-Rabbi Simeon bar Yochai, is marked by a pilgrimage to the site of his tomb in Israel, accompanied by prayers, songs, and dancing. It is also the occasion for cutting the hair of boys who have reached their third birthday and thus are entering the world of the Torah.[8]

The view favoring the celebration of one's birthday is based on the Judaic philosophy that the creation of each individual is a blessing when he fulfills his task in life,[9] as it is written: "so that the Almighty will be loved through you."[10] When a person executes good deeds and fulfills *mitzvot* between man and his fellow man and between man and the Almighty, his life is a source of blessing for himself and his community.[11] Therefore, there should be happiness and celebration on his birthday and one should thank the Almighty for having created him, as is shown by what is written in the case of a righteous person: "A *tzaddik* has come to the world; good has come to the world."[12]

BAR AND BAT MITZVAH

The Jewish birthday celebration, like every other occasion and activity in Judaism connected with child development, is based on the conception that each child has the potential of fulfilling the moral, religious, and ethical values of Judaism throughout his life and is, therefore, a source of blessing for everyone around him.[13] The most impressive birthday celebration takes place when the child reaches the age of maturity: Bar Mitzvah for a boy, at the age of thirteen, and Bat Mitzvah for a girl, at the age of twelve. The sources for the rights and responsibilities incumbent upon the Bar Mitzvah boy and Bat Mitzvah girl are from the Aggadot, but the halakhic basis is stipulated by Rashi's commentary on the passage in *Avot*: "The thirteen-year-old is obliged to fulfill the *mitzvot*."[14] Rashi notes that according to biblical law, an adolescent who shows the signs of maturity (two hairs) is obliged to fulfill the *mitzvot* as an adult. Since the sages estimated that the average age of maturity is thirteen for boys and twelve for girls, these ages are designated for the onset of adulthood in religious matters,[15] such as fasting, wearing phylacteries. This is, indeed, a just cause for celebration. According to the Talmud, it is a *mitzvah* for the father to hold a feast on the day that his son is Bar Mitzvah.[16] One source maintains that the obligation stems from the fact that at this point the father terminates his duties toward the education of his son.[17] One month prior to the boy's thirteenth birthday, it is customary to educate him to don the phylacteries.

The Bar Mitzvah ceremony takes place on the first Sabbath following the thirteenth birthday (according to the Jewish calendar). The boy is called to the *bimah* in the synagogue for the public reading of the Torah. His father is also called to read the Torah and then recites the benediction: "Blessed is He who has now freed me from the responsibility of this one."[18] (The sages explain that this benediction is based on the concept that the father is responsible for his child's sins for the first thirteen years of the child's life, since they may have resulted from a parental failure to educate the youngster properly.)[19] As the ceremony continues, other members of the boy's family are called to read the Torah, and the rabbi usually delivers a "drasha" (sermon) noting the responsibilities of the boy's new legal and social status. The members of the congregation are usually served refreshments (Kiddush) following the service.

The banquet arranged by the parents following the Sabbath service (which some sages consider to be a *se'udat mitzvah*)[20] is highlighted by a talmudic discourse delivered by the boy. On this occasion, the boy thanks his parents for their devotion and love and expresses appreciation to the guests for their presence.

Although the Bat Mitzvah celebration is less formal, in some Israeli synagogues it is customary for the girl's father and brothers to be called to the public reading of the Torah on the Sabbath following the birthday. A family birthday party is usually held in honor of the occasion.

OTHER BIRTHDAY CELEBRATIONS

Many sources indicate that the sages celebrated their birthdays as an expression of joy at having been granted life and with it the opportunity to carry out good deeds in the framework of Judaism.[21] Some sages prove that the celebration of one's sixtieth birthday is a *se'udat mitzvah*,[22] and that it is customary to recite the *She-Hecheyanu* benediction on the occasion of the seventieth birthday.[23] Indeed, there is historical evidence that many sages observed the occasion with a feast.[24] In the Responsa, we find the opinion that a festive celebration is to be held on the occasion of one's eightieth birthday as a holiday and thanksgiving to the Almighty.[25]

Judaism recognizes the natural impulse of parents who wish to express their joy on the occasion of their child's birthday—from the first year on.[26] One rabbi notes in the Responsa on the subject that it is customary to recite the *She-Hecheyanu* over a fruit or new item of clothing on one's birthday. (This is because the use of the fruit or item of clothing makes it permissible to pronounce the name of the Almighty when reciting the benediction, since some authorities maintain that a birthday itself is not an occasion that warrants doing so.) It is also mentioned that the author of *Yishrei Lev* celebrated the birthday of a scholar each year with a feast.[27]

In this spirit, it is worthy for parents to plan their child's birthday as an occasion of offering thanks to the Almighty for the precious life developing under their guidance. As early as possible the child should participate by reciting the *She-Hecheyanu* blessing in accordance with the tradition. It is also fitting for a *dvar Torah* to be recited. Indeed, the festivity takes on a special meaning if the child himself delivers a short recitation of Torah verses he has learned—even if it is the first biblical passage learned by a three-year-old. As the child grows, the recitation may be more elaborate according to his abilities.

18
Religious and Non-Religious Education

The great importance attached to education in Jewish law and literature is unparalleled. The Bible clearly indicates that Judaism has always stressed the importance of study and mental growth from the cradle throughout life. Judaism strives to develop individuals who reflect the Jewish values clearly defined in the Torah: "And be it that these laws which I command unto you today, you shall teach them diligently to your children, and you shall speak of them, as you sit in your home and as you walk on your way outside, when you lie down and when you awaken."[1] This theme, which forms the legal and social basis of *chinnukh* (education based on the Torah), appears over and over again in the Bible and literature of the prophets. Of Abraham it is written: "And I have known him in order that he may ordain his children and his household after him that they may follow the ways of the Almighty to do charity and justice."[2]

THE MEANING OF CHINNUKH

Chinnukh encompasses religious as well as secular education. Religious education comprises practical *mitzvot,* Torah learning for its own sake, Jewish history, morals, and the ultimate goal of reverence for the Almighty. Secular education consists of teaching the child a trade and lifesaving techniques such as swimming, as well as all the elements of general education.

The obligation to teach children *mitzvot* is based on the biblical verses quoted above. The parent and later the school system have the responsibility of teaching the child *mitzvot* and of training the child in their observance according to his level of maturity, understanding, and strength. Consideration for the child's state of learning readiness in being taught *mitzvot* is embodied in Halakhah, based on the guideline that each child be educated in accordance with his course.[3] The requirement that the father teach his son Torah is learned from the passage: "And you shall teach your children to speak of them."[4] This requirement extends to grandsons as well, as it is written: "And you shall make it known to your son and your son's children."[5]

The child is to be taught Torah as soon as he is capable of speech. Torah learning begins at the tender age of the toddler period, when the child is taught the first two verses, "Moses taught us the Torah" and "Hear, O Israel,"[6] and it continues throughout life with the daily accumulation of knowledge of the Torah.[7]

The father must also teach his child the history of the Jewish people, especially the central events that are the foundation of the Jewish faith, such as the revelation of the Torah on Mount Sinai and the exodus of the Jews from Egypt. The basis for this area of *chinnukh* is the verse: "And you shall tell your son on that day as follows: For this reason the Almighty has brought me out of Egypt";[8] "And you shall relate to your children and grandchildren the day you stood before the Almighty on Mount Horeb."[9] This sphere of *chinnukh* begins when the child is at the suitable stage of intellectual growth, according to the passage: "rear each child in accordance with his course."[10]

Finally, the parent must rear his child in accordance with Jewish values based on Torah morals, sanctity, and reverence for the Almighty. This fundamental aspect of *chinnukh* begins with life itself, on the basis of halakhic rulings that even the youngest child should be prevented from eating prohibited foods and doing prohibited acts.[11] The root of this inauguration to Judaism is to be found in the biblical story that Moses as an infant refused to nurse from gentile women. Rashi comments that Moses was preparing himself to speak with the Shekhinah.[12] This teaches us that preparation for sanctity entails purity from the very beginning of life. The child is ordained: "Listen, child, to the ethics of your father, and do not abandon the Torah of your mother."[13]

The father's obligation of including non-religious education in his child's training is based on the talmudic insistence that "a man is responsible to teach his son a trade."[14] The reason is that if the child does not develop marketable skills which will enable him to earn a livelihood, he may turn to criminal means to maintain himself.[15] Within this category are included all branches of professions, business, or crafts which may enable an individual to support himself in adult life.[16] The role of secular education in the framework of Judaism is further indicated by the talmudic ruling that a parent may make arrangements for his child's education, including preparations to "teach him a trade," even on the Sabbath, as this is considered to be in the realm of the "affairs of heaven."[17] In fact, the obligation to teach one's child (whether a boy or girl) a marketable skill is a *mitzvah* specified in Halakhah based on Torah law, as is pointed out in the Code of Jewish Law, the writings of Maimonides, the *Mechilta,* and the Responsa of both the Rosh and the Rif.[18]

Yet the concept of *chinnukh* is even more encompassing, by its very nature as a means of inaugurating the child into life. The rabbis taught: "He who does not increase his knowledge, decreases it."[19] Indeed, the goal of *chinnukh* is to increase one's knowledge throughout life. Toward this aim, we find that *chinnukh* includes several more subjects for a total education.

One of these is the study of the Hebrew language, which is Halakhah based on Torah law, for it is written: "And you shall speak of them." This clearly indicates the obligation of the parent to teach his child Torah in the Hebrew language although translations and commentaries in other languages are valid.[20]

Child Development in the Social Context

Art and music also found their place in Jewish learning from the Torah throughout the generations up to contemporary Chasidic rabbis. The Torah singles out Bezalel and Oholiab as "wise-hearted" because of their great artistic skills, which were put to use in designing the Tabernacle.[21] Musical instruments inspire spiritual thought and accompany religious services, as indicated in Psalms.[22] The musical tradition infused in Judaism has been carried down to our century with the famous *niggunim* composed by noted Chasidic rabbis.

The obligation of parents to include physical training in the course of their child's education is rooted in Halakhah with the precept "you shall guard your lives"[23] as well as the talmudic ruling that the father is responsible for teaching his child to swim, as this is a skill which maintains physical health and may save the child's life in a perilous situation.[24]

Thus, all elements of wisdom and knowledge which enhance the child's reverence for the Almighty, build character in accordance with Jewish values, and make the child self-sufficient are incorporated in *chinnukh*. The goal of *chinnukh* is to reach the whole child and touch all dimensions of development in harmony.

PARENTS AS TEACHERS

Both parents are responsible for educating their children, as is evident from the passage: "Listen, my son, to the ethics of your father, and do not forsake the Torah of your mother."[25] This is the conclusion reached by Rashi[26] as well as by Rabbi Judah the Prince.[27]

The guiding principle in assigning the parental roles in educating the child is that the parents are each responsible for teaching those *mitzvot* which they are personally obliged to fulfill. Thus, the mother is exempt from the responsibility of teaching the child Torah, since she herself is not commanded to learn Torah for the sake of learning, but since women are obliged to learn all matters in the Torah relating to their obligations as Jews, she is responsible for teaching her children the same.[28] In addition, while it is the father who carries the main responsibility for teaching his son Torah, the mother is rewarded for bringing the child to school to learn Torah.[29]

In essence, the father is obliged to teach his children the positive precepts, as well as the prohibitions, Torah learning, Jewish history, a trade, and swimming,[30] while the mother bears the responsibility for teaching the child all the prohibitions and those positive precepts which she must carry out herself (excluding precepts that require a specific time to be fulfilled, such as *tzitzit, Sukkah, Megillah,* and the like). Through her daily contacts with her children, the mother instills in them the values of the Torah.[31]

The child, too, is responsible for his education, as it is written: "Ask your father, he will inform you; your elders, they will tell you."[32] In any case, if neither the parent nor the child provides for the child's education, the *beth din* has the authority to enforce the fulfillment of *chinnukh* (see Chapters 8, 16).[33]

PRESCHOOL EDUCATION

Preschool education, which takes place in the home, is the foundation for learning throughout life.[34] It determines to a great extent the child's intelligence and capacity for learning,[35] for "what one learns in one's youth is absorbed in the blood."[36] Furthermore: "To teach a young child is like writing on new paper, while to teach an older person is like writing upon paper which has already been written on."[37]

The detailed guidelines specified in Halakhah for preschool education in the home enable parents as teachers to "initiate" the child into the world of learning. In accordance with the ruling to teach (or initiate one into learning) according to the child's individual capability, the parent must discern the child's level of understanding and learning readiness.

Thus, when the child begins to speak, his father teaches him the verse "Moses taught us the Torah, it is the inheritance of the congregation of Jacob," and then the prayer "Hear, O Israel, the Lord our God, the Lord is One."[38] As soon as the child is capable of putting on the *tzitzit* himself, his father is to teach him the blessing for the *tzitzit*. If the child can wave the *lulav,* he is to be taught the blessing, and when the child can handle routine procedures of hygiene, he should be taught to wash his hands before eating and after taking care of his needs and to recite the relevant blessings. When the child has the ability to spread his fingers in the manner of the priests during the traditional blessing, his father is to teach him this routine.[39]

Similarly, the mother is to teach her children good behavior in accordance with Jewish values, as appropriate to their level of maturity.[40] The mother is especially suited for this purpose because she is constantly with her children and has more opportunity to teach them moral behavior.[41] The mother is also responsible for teaching her daughters the domestic arts, such as cooking, baking, washing, and weaving (see Chapters 8, 16).[42]

EDUCATION OF GIRLS

Whether girls are to be taught Torah is a somewhat controversial question, although in the course of time it has been resolved. Some sages regarded the teaching of Torah to girls as forbidden. For example, Rabbi Eliezer states: "He who teaches his daughter Torah teaches her licentiousness."[43] Maimonides explains that most females do not study Torah with the seriousness required and make use of their knowledge for vain purposes.[44] On the other hand, Ben Azzai states: "A father is required to teach his daughter Torah."[45] Other sages bring evidence that it is not forbidden to teach girls Torah, for it is written: "But he may teach his sons and daughters of the Bible."[46]

The practice that has arisen is to teach girls Torah in respect to its relevance for them concerning *mitzvot* they are obliged to fulfill. This education begins in the home and continues in school. All other Bible study by girls is voluntary, and as Maimonides comments: "women who learn Torah are rewarded less than men, for they are not commanded to do so, and the reward for something one does voluntarily is not as great as for what one does to fulfill a precept."[47]

According to the consensus, mothers begin to practice with their daughters those precepts which females are obliged to fulfill—all in accordance with the child's level of learning readiness. Girls are taught the blessings for food, washing the hands before meals and after taking care of bodily needs, washing hands upon rising and reciting the relevant blessings, reciting the blessing over challah when baking, and lighting the Sabbath candles with the appropriate blessing.[48]

EDUCATION FROM AGE THREE TO SIX

Many Jewish traditions were designed for the purpose of coordinating *chinnukh* with family religious observances. The Haggadah ceremony on Passover eve, during which the child asks the father four questions and is answered with the story of the exile of Israel from Egypt; the reading of the Megillah on Purim, with noisemakers for the children to employ upon hearing the name Haman; and the pilgrimages to Jerusalem on Passover, Shavuot, and Sukkot are just a few examples.

As Judaism recognizes the fact that young children learn by actively experiencing and participating, Halakhah has determined that children should be included in most religious observances within the family framework as soon as they display the maturity required to do so. Thus, as soon as a boy no longer requires his mother at night, he must remain with his father in the *sukkah*;[49] a child who can eat solids must be given the required portion of matzah on Passover.[50] Since children under the age of maturity are not responsible for fulfilling these precepts themselves, the goal in requiring their participation in these *mitzvot* is strictly educational.[51]

For all aspects of Torah learning, the child progresses gradually in accordance with his individual level until he reaches the age of six or seven, at which time the parent is responsible for bringing him to school to continue his education on a formal level with an authorized teacher.[52] This is preceded by a stage of informal training in the home under the guidance of the parent or a private tutor or in a nursery school directed by specialized teachers. Informal education usually commenced when the child reached the age of three, as it is written: "The first three years of life, the child is not yet ripe to learn, for he does not speak; yet in the fourth year he is dedicated to the Torah."[53] This is also learned from the fact that Abraham recognized the essence of the Almighty at the age of three.[54] By the age of three, as we have seen, the child enters the second stage of cognitive development and has acquired the capability for preconceptual thought and for conceiving of symbols.

In this stage of life, the child's entrance into the world of Torah is preceded by learning the letters of the bible—the alefbet.[55] A wonderful tradition has arisen for initiating the child into the world of learning. The Jewish sages, attributing great importance to the first impression the child received at school, attempted to instill a love of learning that would accompany him throughout life. When the time comes for the child to learn the alefbet at the age of three, the father wakes him early in the morning and takes him to the teacher. The child is wrapped in a *talit* so that he will not look upon anything unclean on the way. The ceremony takes place in the synagogue or the schoolhouse. As soon as the father and the child arrive, the father places his child in the arms of the teacher, as it is written: "Thus the teacher carries the child in his arms." The teacher then reads the alefbet to the child from a special board and the child repeats each letter. This is followed by the recitation of the verse "Moses taught us the Torah, it is the inheritance of the congregation of Jacob." Finally, the teacher recites the first verse of Leviticus and the child repeats after him. At the end of the ceremony, honey is placed on the alefbet board, and after the child recites the appropriate blessing, he licks the honey. After the ceremony, the father returns the child to his home in the same manner as the arrival, wrapped in the *talit*. It is customary to hold a festive dinner in the evening and to invite the poor to participate.[56]

After learning the alefbet the child progressively learns words and verses of prayers. "The father slowly teaches him verses of the Torah until the child reaches the age of six or seven—all in accordance with the child's capacities. Then the father brings the child to a schoolteacher."[57]

FORMAL EDUCATION

As we have seen, Jewish education originates in the home. Indeed, in the early period of Jewish history, throughout the biblical period, education originated in and was dominated by the family. The child was taught Torah, morals, general education, and a craft in the home. It was not until the talmudic period that the concept of the school evolved. One source in the Talmud credits Simeon ben Shetach with the innovation of proclaiming that all children be sent to school to learn.[58] Another source credits Joshua ben Gamla with the initiative of establishing schools in every town and village, with compulsory education for all boys above the age of six years. This had the effect of providing education for fatherless children as well. The Talmud commends this educational initiative as follows: "Verily, may the memory of Joshua ben Gamla be blessed: for were it not for him, knowledge would have been entirely forgotten in Israel."[59]

Formal education was to begin at the age of six years if the child was medically fit to receive instruction. If a medical examination indicated that the child was still too weak to attend school, the commencement of formal schooling was postponed for another year. Sending a child to school before the age of six, if he was too frail to withstand the rigors of formal instruction,[60] was considered to be endangering his life. "Rav said to Rabbi Samuel ben Shilat: Do not receive a pupil under the age of six years, but after that age stuff him like an ox."[61]

It is the duty of the mother to prepare the child for school by washing and dressing him carefully. Mothers are privileged with the duty of accompanying the child to school and are rewarded greatly for this task.[62] A mother who neglects this obligation for any reason is reprimanded.[63]

The Talmud notes that the children already had the basic background required for Torah study when they were first brought to school. In fact, the educational basis attained in the home was so strong that we find the following anecdote:

> The rabbis told Rabbi Joshua ben Levi: "Children have come to the *bet ha-midrash* and said things the like of which was not said even in the days of Joshua ben Nun. [For example:] *Alef bet* means 'learn wisdom' [*alef binah*]; *gimmel dalet*, 'show kindness to the poor' [*gemul dalim*]. Why is the foot of the *gimmel* stretched toward the *daled*? Because it is fitting for the benevolent to run after [seek out] the poor. And why is the roof of the *daled* turned away from the *gimmel*? Because he must give him help in secret lest he be ashamed of him. *He vav*—that is the name of the Holy One, blessed be He. *Zayin, chet, tet, yod, kaf, lamed*. This sequence teaches: 'And if thou dost this, the Holy One, blessed be He, will sustain [*zan*] thee, be gracious [*chen*] unto thee, show kindness unto thee [*me tiv*], give thee a heritage [*yerushah*], and bind a crown on thee [*keter*] in the world-to-come.' . . . And so on for the entire alefbet."[64]

In this example we see that children linked learning the alefbet in a formal educational setting with the Jewish values learned at home.

Although six or seven was the official registration age for beginning formal education in talmudic times, it was customary to send children to school at a more tender age.[65] Following the talmudic period, children attended the *cheder*—the Jewish religious kindergarten—at the age of five, four, and even three. This is explained by the view that in post-talmudic times the strength of man (including his capacity for knowledge) was reduced somewhat, so that it became necessary to begin teaching children Torah earlier.[66]

CURRICULUM

In essence, the guideline for curriculum in Judaism throughout Jewish history has been the following passage from *Avot*: "The five-year-old learns Torah the ten-year-old learns Mishnah, the thirteen-year-old is obliged to fulfill *mitzvot,* the fifteen-year-old learns Talmud, the eighteen-year-old marries."[67] Although this is not an immutable timetable, it outlines the basic curriculum for Judaic studies in correspondence with the child's stages of cognitive development and learning readiness as well as the priorities of Judaic literature. This basic framework is passed on from generation to generation.[68]

The study of the Bible begins with the portion in Leviticus teaching about sacrifices, for "children, who are pure, ought to learn about sacrifices, which are pure"; the child is then taught Bible, learning each book in sequence.[69] The Scriptures are taught with the aid of a translation, in order to attain the goal of learning the exact meaning of each word and its authoritative explanation whenever this differed from the literal meaning.[70] Although it was usual to learn Scripture with the Aramaic translation, the rabbis permitted the translating of the Torah into other languages for Jews who did not know Hebrew—to stress the importance of comprehending the text.[71] The translation is considered so important that "the study of the Holy Scripture leads to Targum [translation], Targum to Mishnah, Mishnah to Talmud, Talmud to practice, and practice to the fear of God."[72]

The child learns Midrash at the age of ten. At the same time, he is taught liturgy, for according to the Mishnah, "minors are obligated to say the *Tefillah* [Eighteen Benedictions] and recite the Grace After Meals."[73] This forms an important link between the school and the synagogue. Indeed, in its early history, the school was often located in the synagogue.[74] Many Orthodox yeshivot today are also based physically and spiritually in the community synagogue.

At the age of ten, the child begins to learn Mishnah and later on the Talmud. In the course of his religious education, the child also acquires much knowledge of secular subjects. Mathematics, history, geography, astronomy, biology, anatomy, and medicine are studied within the framework of the Mishnah and Talmud as well as the Bible. Since Judaism involves all of life, these subjects are interwoven in the Judaic religious texts. Knowledge of various secular subjects is required to better understand the Torah, which was given for the Jews "to live by." For example, the determination of the Jewish calendar requires knowledge of astronomy; observing the dietary laws requires knowledge of the basics of physiology and anatomy; the laws concerning the *eruv* (the distance it is permitted to carry on the Sabbath), sowing the fields, and other matters require knowledge of mathematics; and so on for a great variety of subjects related to religious purposes. The study of non-religious subjects for the purpose of better understanding the Torah, remains a controversial issue and should be discussed with the authorized Rabbi.

Apart from this, the pursuit of secular knowledge is bound up with the father's duty to teach his son a trade, preferably a pleasant and worthy profession. The time and manner in which this is taught varies with the historical period and society in which *chinnukh* takes place, yet at all times it was and should be carried out to provide the child with the best possibilities for a successful future.

There is evidence that in talmudic times formal education was terminated at the age of thirteen, as it is written: "a man must care for his son's needs until the age of thirteen; after that age he must say, 'Thank God I am rid of the penalty for this child.'"[75] This is not to say that Torah learning ends at that time, for in accordance with Halakhah, one must continue learning Torah throughout life. Yet it would seem, according to some talmudic sources, that the father's obligation toward his child's *chinnukh* is restricted to the first twelve years of life. After that age, the child himself is responsible for his Torah education.[76] The father's main task after his child reaches the age of Bar Mitzvah (i.e., adolescence) is to guide him in moral behavior, for "the time most worthy to attempt reproof to the maximum is the time when knowledge buds until it bears fruit, from the age of twelve to twenty-four years, for beforehand the child does not have the cognitive capacity to accept it, and after twenty-four years of age he does not listen."[77]

There are some differences of opinion concerning the extent of the parent's obligation to teach his son Torah;

> To what extent is a man obliged to teach his son Torah? Said Rav Judah in Samuel's name: "For example, Zebulun the son of Dan, whose father taught him Scripture, Mishnah, Talmud, Haggadah, and Aggadot." An objection is raised: "If he taught him Scripture, he need not teach him Mishnah." Whereupon Rabbah said: "Scripture means Torah—like Zebulun ben Dan, but not altogether so. Like Zebulun ben Dan, whose grandfather taught him; but not altogether so, for whereas there [he was taught] Scripture, Mishnah, Talmud, Halakhot, and Aggadot, here [i.e., as a general rule] Scripture alone suffices."[78]

At one time, the rabbis determined that if a father discerns that his child is not suited for religious study (after learning Scripture), he may bring him to a craftsman or professional to learn a trade.[79]

Despite the difference of opinion regarding the education of girls, it is agreed that daughters must be supervised and guided by the parents so that they may develop loyalty to the Torah and the nation in their task as future mothers. To that end, it is generally accepted today that girls should be taught all aspects of Judaism that are relevant to their role as women in Jewish society. This includes the *mitzvot* that women are obligated to fulfill, Jewish moral values, the history of the nation, and whatever secular subjects are necessary for them as homemakers and as workers who may have to help support the family. In essence, no distinction is made between male and female concerning *chinnukh* to the *mitzvot* pertaining to each. The Talmud points out that just as it is obligatory to train daughters to fast on Yom Kippur when they reach the appropriate age (nine years), it is imperative to educate girls in all *mitzvot* of the Torah which they are required to fulfill.[80] Secular subjects such as those required of future mothers and homemakers were always an integral part of a girl's training in the home.[81]

METHODS OF EDUCATION

Ever since the time of the Bible, a great deal of attention and consideration has been given to educational methods, in order to ensure that the men, women, and children who learn Torah comprehend what is being taught. The basic guideline for parent and teachers alike—the advice to "educate each child in accordance with his ways"—entails knowledge of child-development and careful attention to the individual to discern his capabilities, stage of development, learning readiness, handicaps, strengths, and weaknesses. This is learned from the revelation at Mount Sinai:

> Come and see how the Voice of the Almighty comes forth to each individual in Israel, each òne according to his strength, the elderly according to their strength, the young people according to their strength, the small children according to their strength, the women according to their strength, and even Moses according to his strength.[82]

In the Talmud, the term "a young child who has reached the stage of education" refers to a child who is mature enough, intellectually and physically, to be inaugurated into the world of Torah and *mitzvot*. No specific age-level is mentioned, for the rabbis recognized that this will vary with each child. Further indicative of the humanistic philosophy of education characterizing *chinnukh* are the following passages from the *Ethics of the Fathers*:

> Four characteristics are found among students: quick to learn and quick to forget, his gain is canceled by his loss; slow to learn and slow to forget, his loss is canceled by his gain; quick to learn and slow to forget, his is a happy lot; slow to learn and quick to forget, his is an unhappy lot.[83]

Furthermore, students are categorized as follows:

> (1) Those who absorb everything they hear like a sponge. (2) Those who, like a funnel, receive at one end and dismiss at the other. (3) Those who, like a strainer, allow the wine to flow out and retain the lees. (4) Those who, like a sieve, separate the bran from the fine flour.[84]

It is the task of parents and teachers to teach each child in accordance with "his own way" in order to assure maximum comprehension and retention of the material learned.

Alongside individualized instruction, we find many guidelines for those who must teach groups of children, and thus have less possibility of devoting maximum individualized attention to each student. The material should be taught in the shortest manner possible, with pauses between lessons so that the children can absorb what is being learned.[85] A student who is inattentive should be seated next to a diligent student.[86] Children can do much to help each other learn: "As one piece of iron sharpens another, so do two students sharpen each other [when they study together]."[87] Rabbi Nachman ben Isaac said that the words of the Torah are likened to wood; for just as a small splinter lights a big log, so an elementary student helps the more advanced one.[88]

Teachers (and parents) are advised to respect each child and treat him with dignity: "The honor of your pupil should be as dear to you as your own."[89] This is based on the educational philosophy that self-respect is an essential factor in intellectual and emotional development. Indeed, the rabbis recognized that "as a general rule, one's honor motivates man more than all other desires in the world."[90] By respecting the student or his own child, the teacher or parent gains the child's trust and lays the foundation for a good learning environment.

Much effort was made to ensure that the child's first experiences in the world of the Torah were pleasant, so that he would be motivated to learn. The introductory ceremony preceding the child's learning the alefbet gives him a sweet first impression of the world of learning. It is recommended that this method be continued in school. As an example, the Talmud relates that "Rabbah would first put his students into a joyous, cheerful mood before starting on the lesson."[91] Another anecdote is very instructive on this method of teaching:

Rav happened to arrive at a place where a drought had brought on famine. A public servant came before him. He said: "Let the wind blow." And the wind blew. He said: "Let there be rain." and the rain came. Rav asked him: "What is your profession?" He replied: "I am a schoolteacher, and I teach children of the rich as well as the poor. And whoever cannot pay me tuition—I do not require it of him. And I have a pool of fish, and whenever a child does not want to learn, I 'bribe' him with fish, and I persuade him and appease him until he comes and learns."[92]

In general, the rabbis advised that students pay close attention to the teacher, ask many questions, and constantly repeat aloud what they had learned.[93] Teachers make use of mnemonics to fix knowledge in the memory, as it is written: "The

Torah cannot be retained except through signs or mnemonics."[94] These are a few of the forty-eight requirements for the acquisition and retention of knowledge which are listed in *Avot*.[95]

In any case, the primary method of teaching should be one of encouragement, for as Rabbi Samson Raphael Hirsch says, "generally, prizes and encouragement are preferable to punishments"[96] in *chinnukh*. In the *Sefer Musar* we find the following passage indicative of this philosophy:

> If the child has difficulty studying, one should always appease him with things children like, such as honey and nuts and the like, and one should say, "I will give you some of these if you go to school and learn." When the child grows older and no longer desires such things, the father should tell him, "Go to school and I will buy you a nice belt and nice shoes." When the child grows older, the father should say, "I will give you some money if you learn the Grace After Meals and the prayers," and the father should buy him *tzitzit* and phylacteries to train him in the *mitzvot,* and later on, when the child grows older, he should tell him to learn with his rabbi, and so on, until the child grasps the real importance of the Torah and no longer desires all those enticements and turns to Torah learning for its own sake.[97]

In yet another source, we find the view that "encouragement influences more than punishment, praise or a prize works more successfully than threats or punishments."[98] It is advisable to grant educational prizes for learning, especially for that which the child studies voluntarily in addition to his required subjects.[99]

Teachers are required to be patient and explain everything until the student understands the subject matter.[100]

> A teacher must not become angry with his pupils if they do not understand him, but he must repeat his explanation as many times as necessary until they understand . . . nor should the

pupil say "I understand" when he really does not, but he should question over and over again until he does understand.[101]

The rabbis agreed that young children should not be taught too many subjects at once, nor any one subject too profoundly, for "if you attempt to learn too much at once you learn nothing at all."[102]

> The fool says, "There is so much Torah, when can I learn it?" and so he turns away [and studies nothing]. The wise one says, "I will study one chapter every day," and does so until he completes the Torah.[103]

Furthermore, as Rabbah said, "One should always study that part of the Torah that his heart desires."[104] An effective way to check the child's progress is by oral examination. It became the custom for the father to test his child each Sabbath by asking him to recite what he had learned in school during the week. Similarly, it is customary for any interested party to request that the child "recite a verse" to prove his proficiency in studies. The Talmud gives many examples of bright replies by children to these impromptu examinations.[105] One interesting story is related in the Midrash:

> When the decree to destroy the Jews was sealed and given to Haman, he walked through the streets with his ministers. Just then, Mordecai walked toward them and came upon three schoolchildren on their way home. Mordecai asked one of them: "Recite me your verse." The child replied: "Do not fear sudden anxiety and the wrath of evil when it comes." The second child answered, "Make plans and they will be violated. Say something and it will not come true for the Almighty is with us." The third child quoted: "And I will be with you until your old age." Upon hearing this, Mordecai became very happy. Whereupon Haman asked him: "Why are you so happy after talking to those children?" Mordecai answered: "Because of the good cheer they

brought me, so that I no longer fear your evil advice to the king." Immediately, Haman the wicked, became furious and said: "I will kill these children before all the others." After Haman prepared the tree he went to Mordecai and found him sitting in the *bet ha-midrash* with the children before him in sackcloth and ashes, learning the Torah and crying.... Haman tied them up in shackles and placed guards to watch over them and said: "Tomorrow I will kill the children and then hang Mordecai." The children's mothers brought them bread and water, but they chose to fast, and they cried so hard that their voices were heard in the heavens and the Almighty inquired: "What is this loud noise I hear like that of sheep?" Then Moses stood before Him and replied: "Lord of the Universe, these are not sheep but the little children of your people who are fasting for the third day, and tomorrow their enemy wants to butcher them." Immediately, the Almighty tore the decrees and brought on a deep slumber on Ahasuerus, as it is written: "That night the king fell fast asleep."[106]

This Aggadah points out the role of children in the life of the nation as a direct result of *chinnukh,* as well as the custom of impromptu examinations, which continues in every generation.

DISCIPLINE

According to the Talmud, parents and teachers should be most patient with children until the age of twelve years, but after that age, since the child's cognitive abilities are more developed, they can be more severe.[107] As we have seen, it is the prerogative of the teacher to use disciplinary measures to force a student to learn.[108] However, corporal punishment may be used only with inattentive or stubborn children.[109] Even then, it is forbidden to strike a child so as to hurt him. The Halakhah, as it appears in the Talmud, determines that a child must be hit only with a shoestring (i.e., a very light blow).[110] Maimonides agrees, explaining that a teacher should not discipline a student with cruelty—rather, with a light strap in order to enforce rules.[111] With older adolescents, it was forbidden to employ corporal punishment as a means of discipline, in order not to provoke the student to strike back and commit a sin.[112] Finally, the teacher must punish only those children who have the capacity to learn and are not exerting their maximum effort. A student who is not bright and cannot learn should not be punished, rather, the teacher should encourage him to persevere.[113]

In all cases, the teacher (and the parent) must feel and display warmth and fondness for children in order to create an environment for learning based on good relationships and trust. The guiding principle in finding the median between discipline and tenderness is the verse: "In dealing with a child let the left hand repel while the right hand draws near."[114] The ideal relationship between teacher and student or between parent and child is one in which the adult relates to the youngster with resoluteness concerning all matters of *chinnukh,* and with warmth, understanding, and encouragement on the personal level. This is the Judaic formula for maximum success in *chinnukh* and in all aspects of child-development (see Chapter 9).

THE IMPORTANCE OF THE SCHOOL IN JUDAISM

Judaism attributes such significance to learning in school that the world is said to exist only by the breath of schoolchildren.[115] According to the Talmud, any city in which there is no school for children to learn must be banned.[116] In fact, Rabbi Hamnuna said that Jerusalem was destroyed only because they neglected the education of schoolchidren, as is shown by the verse, "Pour it out [God's wrath] because of the children in the street" (Jer. 6:11). Why "pour it out"? Because the child is in the street instead of learning in school.[117] R. Hanan ben Pazzi indicates the role of the school in Judaism by pointing out that the verse "They that are planted in the house of the Lord" (Ps. 97:13) refers to the little children who are in school.[118]

THE ROLE OF THE TEACHER

That teachers have a very significant effect on the development of children is shown by the extensive treatment of the role and nature of the Jewish teacher in Jewish law and literature. The teacher of small children (*melammed tinokot*) has a critical effect on his pupils through his ability to train them in Torah and Jewish values. "'They that turn many to righteousness like the stars forever' [Dan. 12:3]—these are the teachers of small children."[119]

The Midrash states that there are seven categories of saints who will greet the Shekhinah in the future. Two Amoraim state separate views concerning the most beloved of all; one says it is the one who comes from the strength of the Torah and the *mitzvot*; the other declares that it is the teachers of small children, who are destined to stand to the right of the Almighty.[120]

The sacred nature of the teacher's role in the lives of children is exemplified by the Almighty, who is said to teach young children in the fourth hour of the day.[121]

The teacher was so vital to Jewish life that rabbis decreed it forbidden to live in a town in which there are no teachers for schoolchildren.[122] The following anecdote points out the value of teachers in the Jewish community:

> Rabbi Judah the Prince sent Rav Chiyya, Rav Assi, and Rav Ammi to traverse the cities in the land of Israel in order to appoint Bible and Mishnah teachers. They came to a city and found no teacher of Bible or Mishnah. They said: "Bring to us the guardians of the city." The people brought to them the senators of the town. The rabbis said: "Are these the guardians of the town? They are the destroyers of the town." "Who then are the guardians of the town?" asked the people. The rabbis answered: "The teachers of Bible and Mishnah, as it is written: 'Unless the Lord guards the city, the watchman wakes in vain' [Ps.127:1]."[123]

The Talmud goes as far as to state that "he who teaches the

son of his friend Torah, it is considered as if he has given birth to the boy."[124]

In light of the significant role of the teacher in child-development, Halakhah stipulates a detailed code of conduct for those who choose this profession:

> No teacher should be appointed for the young unless he is a God-fearing person and possesses the qualifications to teach accurately.[125]

> The Ark was overlaid with gold from within and from without; so the teacher's inner and outer self should be consistent.[126]

> If a teacher resembles a messenger of the Lord, seek instruction from him, otherwise do not.[127]

The teacher must be patient and conscientious in his work:

> The easily angered cannot teach.[128]

> A person must go on teaching his pupil until he has mastered the subject.[129]

> A person who leaves his students and goes out of the room or engages in other work while in their presence or shows carelessness in teaching them comes under the ban of Jeremiah: "Cursed be he who does the work of the Lord deceitfully" [Jer. 48:10].[130]

> A teacher of young children is liable to be dismissed immediately [if inefficient]. The general principle is that anyone whose mistakes cannot be rectified is liable to be dismissed [if he makes one].[131]

The teacher must strive for good relations with his students:

> If you see a pupil for whom learning is as difficult as iron, it is because the teacher is not pleasant to him.[132]

The teacher should strike a student only to impose discipline. And he must not strike him with cruelty, with a strap or a stick—only with a light string.[133]

The teacher must take care of his appearance:

Any scholar upon whose garment is found a stain is worthy of death.[134] (This statement, pertaining to all scholars, including teachers, concerns respect for the Torah.)

The teacher of little children must not keep late hours, so that he will not be lazy during the day to teach; he must not refrain from eating or drinking, nor eat or drink too much, for this causes inefficiency, for which he should be dismissed.[135]

The teaching schedule is clearly outlined in Halakhah:

The teacher of little children should teach all day and a small part of the night in order to train them to learn night and day. The children should not be idle except for Sabbath eve and the eve of holidays in the afternoon, and young children are not to remain idle [from learning] even for the sake of building the Holy Temple.[136]

Children should not be taught something new on the Sabbath, for it is forbidden to toil on Sabbath; rather, they must repeat on the Sabbath what they learned during the week.[137]

The more teachers there are the better:

The child should be brought from one teacher to another who is quicker in Scripture or grammar only if both are in the same town, but children are not to be sent out of town to learn, for reasons of safety.[138]

A teacher cannot prevent another teacher [from establishing a school on the same street], for the reason that "the jealousy [competition] of scribes increases wisdom."[139]

The number of pupils assigned to a teacher is twenty-five.[140]

Finally, Halakhah determines that all children without exception have the same right to education—the children of the poor as well as the children of the rich, the slow learners and exceptional children as well as the bright and average students:

> Be careful regarding the children of the poor, for it is from them that Torah does come forth.[141]

> The School of Hillel said: One should teach [Torah] to every person, for many transgressors who were drawn to the study of the Torah became righteous, pious, and worthy people.[142]

> Even if a child does not know how to read, he is not to be expelled from the class but is to sit with the others in the hope that he will eventually understand.[143]

> Teach each one according to his strength [ability].[144]

SUMMARY

For the Jewish people, learning is more than a value or a method of attaining knowledge for personal gain. As an indication of the spiritual importance of learning, the sages taught: "He who does not study deserves to die."[145] Learning is a way of life in Judaism; a continuous pursuit that should be reinforced throughout the process of human development. "He who does not increase his knowledge decreases it."[146] The focal point of learning in Judaism is the study of the Torah, which includes the Bible, the Talmud, and the commentaries, including the Responsa literature. Jewish law requires that every Jew study the Torah.[147] The content of the Torah is not limited to religious doctrine. It encompasses every aspect of human knowledge, either in a direct or an indirect form; as the sages said: "Turn it and turn it over again, for everything is in it."[148]

The basis for the child's education is in the home, where learning begins with life itself in the framework of the family. As the child develops and becomes physically capable of going beyond the primary home environment, he or she must be enrolled in school. The school is so important in Judaism that it is considered more sacred than a house of worship.[149] Moreover, while the parents are responsible for making sure that their child receives education for a life as a good Jew and a healthy contributing member of society, the teacher provides the greatest amount of content in the process of *chinnukh*. The teacher's crucial role is recognized in Jewish law by the dictum that one is to honor and revere his teacher even more than his parent, for the parent brings the child into this world, but the teacher brings him to the afterworld.[150]

19
The Rights of the Child in Jewish Law

In Jewish law the term "child" refers to the period up to the age of thirteen for a boy and twelve for a girl. Before this age of majority, the child is considered a minor insofar as legal and religious matters are concerned. After the age of majority, the child has the same legal status as an adult and is responsible for fulfilling the *mitzvot*.[1]

THE FETUS IN JEWISH LAW

As Jewish law is sensitive to the value of life, giving it the highest priority, the Halakhah regarding the fetus is sophisticated even in terms of modern law. The Talmud notes that "man was created alone to teach us that whoever destroys one individual, the Torah considers it as if he had destroyed the entire world, and he who maintains one life, the Torah considers it as if he sustains the entire world. Therefore, each person must say: The world was created for me."[2]

Within the framework of this perspective, the unborn child is viewed as a potential life and is said to possess a soul after the first forty days of conception. According to some opinions, it is permitted to desecrate the Sabbath in order to save its life. The Halakhah concerning the daughter of a priest who is carrying a child further qualifies this viewpoint; see Chapter 2.

The Halakhah concerning abortion is based on the same high value of life. As there are many complex legal and moral issues involved and each case has its unique circumstances, a competent Rabbi should be consulted when the problem arises. Halakhah deals with every case according to the factors involved (see Chapter 3), so that the Rabbi is able to make a pertinent judgement according to the individual case (see Ch. 3).

The Halakhah determining the status of the fetus during childbirth is especially poignant: "If a woman is in labor [and her life is endangered] the fetus may be removed to save her life," but "if the baby's head has emerged, it is not permitted to touch him, for one life does not have precedence over another."[3] Furthermore, if the mother dies and the baby can be saved by an immediate Caesarean section, this has to be done even on a Sabbath.[4]

LEGAL DEFINITION OF "SON" AND "DAUGHTER"

A child born of a union between a Jewish man and a Jewish woman is considered to be the son of his father. A child is considered son to his father even if the union with the woman was forbidden by Jewish law and the child is a bastard. In such a case, the child is still obligated to honor the father and is punished for striking or cursing him. He is a son to his father in matters of inheritance and laws concerning defilement if his father is a priest. Such a child also exempts his father's wife from *yibbum* (levirate marriage). A child born of a union between a Jewish man and a gentile woman is not considered a son to his father. A child born of a union between a gentile woman and a gentile man is considered son to his parents.[5]

The sons of a man's son or daughter are considered as his sons in relation to the fulfillment of the *mitzvah* to "be fruitful and multiply."[6]

In every instance in the Torah in which the word "son" appears, daughters are not included unless specifically mentioned.[7]

LEGITIMACY

A child is considered legitimate if born to a Jewish man and a Jewish woman whose union is legal according to Halakhah. An illegitimate child (*mamzer*) is one born of an adulterous union punishable by Divine punishment of premature or sudden death.[8] An illegitimate child is forbidden to marry a Jew.[9]

In cases where a child's legitimacy is doubtful or suspected, the Halakhah always considers it a permissible doubt. The most famous case, which set a precedent, involved a man named Shelumiel, who left his bride the day after their marriage to study at a certain talmudic academy. Twelve months later his wife gave birth to a child, and to remove any doubt from the father's mind, the rabbis concluded that although the normal duration of pregnancy is 271 days, "a child born twelve months after the departure of the woman's husband is legitimate."[10] In this case, it is considered that the pregnancy is prolonged. If a child is born to the mother more than twelve months after the departure of the husband, he is considered illegitimate. One source maintains that even in this case, the child is not to be declared illegitimate unless the father testifies that he has not been with his wife in the interim.[11] In any event, a child is considered legitimate even if there are evil rumors that his mother committed adultery.[12] Even if the mother herself says that the child is not from her husband, this does not render the child illegitimate.

A child is considered illegitimate only if the father declares that it is not his child.[13] If the father initially accepted the child as his and later said it was not his, the child is not considered illegitimate.[14] (The same applies to a child conceived by an engaged woman.)[15]

An illegitimate child must be circumcised on the eighth day, even if it is a Sabbath, and may be called to the Torah.[16] An illegitimate child must be declared as such to prevent marriage with a Jew later on.[17] If an illegitimate child marries a gentile, there is a legal dispute whether their child is considered a gentile and may marry a Jew if he converts to Judaism.[18] An illegitimate child is entiled to inherit his father's property if he knows his father' identity.[19] One who is known to be an illegitimate child without doubt, may not be included in the Jewish community, however, one whose status is of permissible doubt may be part of the community.[20]

RIGHTS OF THE FIRSTBORN

The son who is the first issue of the mother's womb is consecrated from birth, as it is written: "Consecrate to Me each firstborn, the first issue of the mother's womb."[21] The father must redeem him in the ceremony called *pidyon ha-ben* with the sum of five *shekalim* (see Chapter 4). The child who is "the first fruit of his father's vigor" (the father's first child) is first in line for inheritance and receives two portions of the legacy.[22] According to Halakhah, three people are qualified to declare the child a firstborn: the midwife, the mother during the first seven days after birth and the father.[23]

A child who is the firstborn to his mother but not to his father (i.e., the father has already had a child by another wife) is called *bekhor shoteh* as he is not a full-fledged firstborn. A child who is considered older because he is wiser than the older child is called *bekhor shanan*.[24]

The *bekhor shoteh* has a special status with regard to religious regulations. As we have seen, the firstborn infant must be redeemed by the father by a payment of five shekels to any *kohen* (priest) of his choice. (The reason for this stems from the fact that the firstborn were originally chosen by the Almighty to be devoted to Him as priests in the Tabernacle and Temple, but as a result of the transgression of worshipping the golden calf in the desert, the Levites were chosen to replace them.)[25] The firstborn's religious status remains codified to the extent that he is obligated to fast on the eve of Passover (as a reminder of the miracle in Egypt, when the Almighty killed all the firstborn of the Egyptians and saved the Jewish firstborn sons).[26]

The Halakhah requires that the father and not the mother redeem the child.[27] If the father is unwilling, the *bet din* may compel him to do so; if the child is nevertheless not redeemed, he is required to redeem himself when he reaches the age of Bar Mitzvah (see Chapter 2).[28]

The *bekhor* of a *kohen* or a Levite need not be redeemed. Similarly, the *bekhor* of an Israelite who has married the daughter of a *kohen* or a Levite need not be redeemed. A child born to a woman who had previously miscarried a fetus over forty days need not be redeemed, because he does not meet the requirement of being the "first issue of the womb." If there is doubt as to whether or not the child is a *bekhor*, he need not be redeemed.[29] An authorized Rabbi should be consulted.

The firstborn to the father is entitled to the inheritance privilege of receiving a double portion based on the biological relationship. Even a firstborn of a prohibited marriage (such as a *kohen* and a divorcee) or an illegitimate firstborn must receive the double share.[30] A child born after the father dies does not receive a double portion of the inheritance, as his status depends on the acknowledgment by the father that the child is his firstborn.[31] The firstborn female is not entitled to this prerogative. The *bekhor* inherits a double portion of the property belonging to the father while still alive and not what is due to his father after death.[32]

A father cannot deny his firstborn the inheritance rights, as is stated in the Bible in the case of the man who had two wives; although he loved one more than the other, he could not deny the firstborn from the hated wife the inheritance privilege, because this child was the first issue of his vigor.[33]

If the firstborn dies while the father is still alive, the next in line of the deceased son inherits the double portion.[34]

In biblical and talmudic times, the firstborn had a special status in the family. He would replace the father and maintain his brothers when necessary.[35] As a continuation of this tradition, the Code of Jewish Law specifies that one must honor an older brother, whether it is a brother from the mother or the father.[36]

THE CHILD'S RIGHT TO EDUCATION AND SUPPORT

According to biblical law, a child has the right to be educated by his parents in the ways of the Torah, Jewish values, and *mitzvot*.[37] Halakhah, specified in the Talmud, gives the child the right to be circumcised, redeemed, married, and taught a trade by his father.[38]

Although there is no biblical law requiring fathers to support their children, the child's moral right to be fed, clothed, and maintained until he is grown is embodied in Halakhah through the ordinance issued by the Sanhedrin at Usha.[39] The original ordinance gave children the right to support up to the age of six, but later rabbinical decisions raised the age up to the time that the child is fully grown.[40] (If the father does not carry out this obligation, he is compelled to do so if he is wealthy. If he is poor, he is not compelled.)[41]

Fathers must give their daughters a dowry,[42] but if a father is poor, he need not sell his property to do so.[43] (In Biblical times, the father had the right to sell his daughter, but this was only in order to marry her off, in special cases when he was penniless.)[44]

PROTECTION FROM ABUSE

Halakhah affords the child protection from abuse by his parents. (This fact is all the more admirable when we consider the historic background of child abuse in other nations during biblical and talmudic times and even in the present day.)[45]

Although parents are obligated to discipline their children in the process of *chinnukh*,[46] the discipline must be mild, in accordance with the child's strength.[47] Parents and teachers must not strike children with cruelty in the process of *chinnukh*.[48] The Talmud declares that a father who beats his child may be sued for assault, with the possibility of being liable to compensate the minor.[49] A father or teacher who injures a child in the process of *chinnukh* "beyond what is proper" may be liable, and it is up to the courts to decide.[50]

EQUAL TREATMENT

Every child in the family is entitled to equal treatment by his parents in accordance with rabbinical law, based on the biblical story that Joseph was envied by his brothers as a result of the striped coat his father had given him. In light of the tragedy that followed, the rabbis declared that parents must treat all of their children equally in all matters.[51]

In addition, a father may not deprive the firstborn of his inheritance privilege in order to give it to a younger, more beloved son.[52] Each child has an equal right to education (see Chapter 18).

PROPERTY RIGHTS

The child has a right to his own property to the exclusion of his parents. However, if the child finds something of value while he is still being supported by his father, it belongs to the father, according to rabbinical law.[53]

If a child over six years of age showed an understanding of business dealings, he was considered legally fit to dispose of movable property.[54] The Talmud states that "the purchase and sale of things by infants is legal only in small matters."[55]

THE RIGHT TO PARTICIPATE IN RELIGIOUS OBSERVANCES

A child under the age of thirteen (if a boy) or twelve (if a girl) is not obliged to fulfill all the commandments of Judaism.[56] The parents are responsible for the child's actions, and it is forbidden for them to make the child eat or do something forbidden.[57]

A child who is capable has the right to participate in the service (according to the Sephardic tradition). At the age of four or five years he ascends the *bimah* (reading desk) during the early morning service and sings the verse "The Lord is King; the Lord has reigned; the Lord will reign forever more" after the reader concludes Psalm 102. At the age of six or seven, the child advances to read the Haftarah during the service.[58]

Although according to Halakhah children are not bound to perform *mitzvot* until reaching the age of thirteen, they have the right to do so within the framework of *chinnukh,* in accordance, with their stage of development and their abilities. Thus,

> As soon as the child is free from his mother's care, he is old enough to undertake the obligation of dwelling in the *sukkah* on the feast of Sukkot. If he knows how to wave the *lulav,* he must wave one. If he understands the commandments of *tzitzit* and phylacteries and can put them on, it is his father's duty to provide him with them. As soon as he can speak, his father teaches him the *Shema,* Torah, and the sacred tongue: otherwise it were better he had not come into the world.[59]

Children nine years old should be trained to fast part of the day on Yom Kippur, and eleven-year-olds had the right to fast the whole day if capable of doing so.[60]

LIABILITY FOR TRANSGRESSIONS

A child under thirteen is not liable for transgressions in ordinary law. There is a talmudic view which determines that an individual is not entirely liable for transgressions against the Almighty until the age of twenty.[61] The exemption of children from punishment for sins in matters of damages and injuries is based on the fact that they are considered incapable of reason.[62]

According to the Bible, the Almighty punishes children until the third and fourth generation for the sins of their fathers.[63] However, in the Prophets we find the declaration that fathers will not die for the transgressions of their sons and sons will not die for the sins of their fathers.[64] Rabbi Yose bar-Chanina explains the contradiction by pointing out that this is one of the four decrees which Moses issued and the prophets canceled. "Moses said, 'The Almighty punishes children for their fathers' sins,' and Ezekiel came and canceled it thus: 'the soul which sins will die.'"[65]

If a minor eats something forbidden or does something forbidden on the Sabbath, the *beth din* is not responsible for keeping him from committing these acts, as he does not possess reason. This is the case if the child himself commits the transgression. However, an adult, and especially his parent, may not feed him something forbidden or make him do something forbidden on the Sabbath, even if he is an infant.[66]

A child who steals or injures someone or something should be punished by the *bet din* in order to prevent him from repeating the transgression. In all transgressions on civil matters, the *bet din* must keep him from committing such acts. There is no strict obligation to pay for damages if the stolen property is returned, but inside the line of justice it is fitting for the child to make payment for injuries when he grows up.[67]

A minor under the age of thirteen is not a valid witness.[68]

A child under thirteen may not deal in property or his inheritance. If a child who has no guardian deals in movable property (according to his understanding of business) and makes a mistake, he is liable just as an adult would be in this case. A minor who countersigns for someone is exempt from liability.[69]

CHILDREN'S RIGHTS IN MATTERS OF BETROTHAL

If a minor marries himself off, the betrothal is invalid. A father may not betroth a minor son.[70] Although a father has the legal right to betroth a minor daughter,[71] it is a *mitzvah* not to marry her off until after she has grown up and can choose her own spouse.[72] If a father marries off a daughter while she is a minor and she is then widowed or divorced, she becomes independent even if she is still a minor.[73] If a father decides to marry off a minor daughter, her brothers or mother may refuse.[74]

RIGHTS OF NEGLECTED OR ABANDONED CHILDREN

The abandonment or neglect of unwanted children was unknown among the Jewish people for centuries, while in other societies it was a matter of routine. The historical accounts mention the story of the attempted sacrifice of Isaac as a clear example of the denunciation of child sacrifice as an element in the worship of the Almighty. The prophet Jeremiah made a tremendous effort to uproot this evil from humanity,[75] the first great effort for children's rights. The Halakhah stipulates that anyone who kills even a one-day-old infant is guilty of murder.[76] This is a major step in determining and legalizing children's basic rights.

The unique nature of Jewish values in regard to children ensured that cases of abandonment or neglect were virtually unknown in biblical times and afterward. During the period of national crisis following the Bar Kokhba rebellion (132–135 C.E.), the problem arose with the new social reality, and thus we find in the Talmud the Halakhah that neglected or abandoned children have the right to be cared for through a guardian appointed by the *bet din*.

According to the Responsa of the Rosh (82:2) the *bet din* may appoint a guardian to care both for the child and his father if, in the opinion of the court, the parent is not capable of fulfilling his obligations toward the child. Similarly, in the best interest of the child's well-being, the *bet din* may order that the minor be removed from his parent's house and appoint a guardian to care for the child and his property.[77]

ORPHANS

Jewish law provides for the well-being of orphans as a fundamental legal and moral principle. The care of an orphan is considered an act of great justice, as is evident from the following talmudic declaration: "'Happy are they that keep justice, that do righteousness at all times.' Is it possible to do righteousness at all times? Yes. . . . This refers to a man who brings up an orphan boy or girl in his home and enables him to marry."[78]

The Bible offers three examples of the great act of *tzedakah* in caring for an orphan: the story of Abraham and Eliezer, the adoption of Moses by Pharaoh's daughter (as it is written: "Moses became her son"),[79] and Mordecai's bringing up of his orphan niece Esther (as it is written: "And Mordecai brought up Hadassah—Esther, his uncle's daughter—and when her father and mother were dead, Mordecai took her for his own daughter").[80] Indeed, the Almighty is termed the "father of the fatherless,"[81] and the community as a whole is warned not to oppress the orphan, for he who commits injustice toward orphans is to expect severe punishment.[82]

Great emphasis is placed on the good treatment of orphans

as one of the *middot* (good characteristics) which every Jew must assume. Maimonides details the attitude toward orphans expected by the community:

> A man ought to be especially heedful of his behavior toward widows and orphans, for their souls are exceedingly depressed and their spirits low. Even if they are wealthy, even if they are widow and orphans of a king, we are especially enjoined concerning them, as it is written: "Ye shall not afflict any widow or orphan." How are we to conduct ourselves toward them? One may not speak to them other than tenderly. One must show them unvarying courtesy; one must not hurt them physically with hard toil, nor wound their feelings with hard speech. One must take greater care of their property than of one's own. Whoever irritates them, provokes them to anger, pains them, tyrannizes over them, or causes them loss of money is guilty of a transgression, and all the more so if one beats them. Though lashes are not inflicted for this transgression, its punishment is explicitly set forth in the Torah: "My wrath shall wax hot, and I will slay you with the sword." He who created the world by His word made a covenant with widows and orphans that when they cry out because of violence they are answered; as it is written: "If thou afflict them in any way, for if they cry at all unto Me I will surely hear their cry!"[83]

This specification has been embodied in the Code of Jewish Law.[84] According to Maimonides, it applies to cases where a person afflicts orphans for his own ends. But it is permissible for a teacher to punish orphans in order to teach them Torah or a trade, or to lead them in the right way. And yet he should not treat them like other children, but make a distinction in their favor. He should guide them gently, with the utmost tenderness and courtesy, as it is said: "For the Lord will plead their cause."[85]

The Halakhic view of adoption is unique. As the Almighty is considered "father of the fatherless," and the legal status of parent and child is strictly a natural biological relationship, talmudic law stipulates that the *bet din* appoint a guardian (or even several guardians) to care for the orphan for all legal purposes.[86] The Scripture looks upon one who brings up an orphan as if he had begotten him.[87]

Specific laws deal with various aspects of the rearing of an orphan in matters relating to property. For example, orphans are exempt from taxation for charity even to redeem hostages, unless the intention is to make them known as charitable. However, it is permissible for the guardian to dispose of charity from the orphan's property for civil purposes or to help relatives of the orphan.[88]

A female orphan should be given priority over a male orphan in regard to support and provisions for marriage. A female orphan who is betrothed as a minor has the right to protest against the marriage.[89] A guardian who arranges a marriage for an orphan girl must provide her with a dowry of not less than fifty *zuzim*. If there are funds available, the newly married orphan should be supported as far as possible.[90] An orphan boy who wishes to marry must be given the necessary provisions for renting a home and purchasing household items beforehand.[91]

Halakhah determines that one is regarded as an orphan until he no longer requires the assistance of an adult to care for him and provide sustenance. If an adult orphan does not have an understanding of business, he is still regarded as an orphan.[92] If the appointed guardian dies, his heirs must continue to support the orphan out of the former's estate.[93]

The unique halakhic stance on adoption provides for the best interests of the child and, based on a realistic assessment of his status, makes provision for all his material and emotional needs. Although the guardian may call the child his son and the orphan may call the guardian his father, the legal arrangement prevents the tragic circumstance of disillusionment from arising through the child's being led to believe that the guardians are his real parents. The remarkable consequence of such a framework for the rearing of orphans is that the care for their material and emotional well-being is based on legal and moral factors and not on artificial documents (which by virtue of the simulated elimination of reality may cause more damage than good for the child).

In light of the legal and moral values shaping the development of the orphan child, we find in the Midrash that "the Almighty showed Moses all the treasures that are kept in heaven for the enjoyment of the righteous. When Moses asked to whom would be given the most valuable treasure, the answer was: 'To him who brings up orphans.'"[94]

MATURITY

The concept of maturity in Judaism involves halakhic, religious, moral, and psychological factors in child-development. The age of twelve for a girl and thirteen for a boy is mentioned in the Talmud as the age of majority.[95] In the *Ethics of the Fathers* we find that a child who reaches thirteen years of age is responsible for fulfilling the *mitzvot*. This follows the determined course of *chinnukh* (based on the stages of cognitive development), as is outlined in the same statement: at five years of age the boy learns Torah, and at ten years, Mishnah.[96]

Although the Torah does not specifically state that the age of thirteen for a boy and twelve for a girl is the decisive stage in reaching the status of maturity, according to rabbinical conclusions it is "Halakhah to Moses from Sinai" (based on Torah law).[97] This age is considered to be the average or estimated period in which most children show signs of puberty, i.e., two hairs.[98] Both age and signs determine the child's legal status concerning Torah laws. For Rabbinical decrees, the child enters the period of puberty at this age whether or not he shows the physical signs of majority (see Tractate Nidah).

Psychologically, this is the period in which the child is able to function, on the basis of what he has been taught, through his own reasoning and interpretation. Consequently, the child forms his own identity based on values gained through *chin-*

nukh and internalized identifications acquired through experience and social relationships. The Midrash points out that it was at age thirteen that Moses chose his moral and religious path in life by rejecting his father's idolatry. It was also at this decisive age that Jacob decided to follow the path of the Torah while Esau chose to worship idols.[99]

Halakhah determines that this age is the turning point after which the individual becomes responsible for his own actions. When the child was a minor, he was liable for punishment of sins commited by his parents, but from the age of thirteen he is liable for his own sins.[100] According to another view, the individual is punished for transgressions in ordinary law from the age of majority, while he is punished for sins against the Almighty from the age of twenty,[101] as it is written: "How many the years of man? Seventy. Subtract twenty, for which Thou dost not punish."[102] In *Yalkut Ruth*, we find the stipulation that the child is punished for his father's sins until the age of thirteen.[103]

The new legal status of the Bar Mitzvah entitles him to become a part of the *minyan* (the quorum of ten men necessary for communal prayer), to be a member of the court, to transact valid business deals, and to act as an agent. However, in fiscal matters he is limited. According to Maimonides, a thirteen-year-old can sell movable goods, but he can not sell property inherited from his father until he reaches the age of twenty full years and has shown physical evidence of maturity.[104] Another view includes even what he buys himself in this category.[105] The testimony of a thirteen-year-old (even if he shows physical signs of maturity) is not accepted in affairs of real estate, because he is not yet experienced and knowledgeable about buying and selling.[106] After the age of majority, the individual's vows are valid.[107] The age of thirteen is the official time chosen for the boy to assume personal responsibility for wearing *tefillin* (phylacteries): It was the father's duty to buy him *tefillin* in the course of *chinnukh* if the boy showed understanding of this *mitzvah*.[108] In any case, it is customary for the father to train him in the *mitzvah* of *tefillin* one month before the Bar Mitzvah. The Bar Mitzvah celebration centers on the Sabbath morning prayer service in the first week following the boy's thirteenth birthday, according to the Jewish calendar (see Chapter 17). The Bar Mitzvah boy is called up to the Torah. The boy's father is also called to the public reading of the Torah and recites the benediction: "Blessed is He who has now freed me from the responsibility of this one."

As the rabbis discerned that girls mature earlier than boys, the age of majority for girls is set at twelve. This age has been determined as the Bat Mitzvah. In the Talmud, we find the legal status of girls categorized in three stages: *ketanah,* from three to twelve years; *na'arah,* from twelve to twelve and one-half years; and *bogeret,* over twelve and one-half years.[109] The *ketanah* could be betrothed by her father, but if she was divorced or widowed she became legally independent. If her father betrothed her again, such a marriage was invalid. If betrothed by a mother or a brother, she could refuse to live with her husband. (In such a case, she was legally free to marry a *kohen* later, unlike an ordinary divorcee.)[110] The vows of a *ketanah* could be annulled by her father immediately upon pronouncement. The father had a right to her earnings and findings.

As soon as a girl reaches the age of twelve years and one day and shows two hairs, she is no longer a minor.[111] Although she is still under her father's control in matters of betrothal,[112] her vows are valid[113] and she is considered a responsible person.

The *bogeret* (twelve and one-half years) is considered an adult.[114] She is responsible for fulfilling the *mitzvot* and is liable for transgressions in common law.[114]

The legal aspect of a child's development is summarized in the Talmud as follows:

Rabbah said: There are three grades in a child. [If on being given] a stone he throws it away but [on being given] a nut he takes it, he can take possession for himself but not for others. A girl of corresponding age can be betrothed so effectively as not to be released [on becoming of age] without definitely repudiating the betrothal. *Peutot* can buy and sell movables with legal effect, and a girl of the corresponding age can be divorced from a betrothal contracted by her father. When they reach the age at which vows are tested, their vows and their sanctifications are effective, and a girl of corresponding age performs *chalitzah*. The [landed] property of his [deceased] father, however, he cannot sell until he is twenty.[115]

CONCLUSION

When we consider child-development in the context of Judaism, we find a natural yet unique synthesis between the interests and needs of the child and the Halakhah. A contemporary document which reflects the principles of child-rearing and child-development inherent in Judaism is the United Nations Declaration of the Rights of the Child.[116] In the preamble we find the assertion that "the child, by reason of his physical and mental immaturity, needs special safeguards and care, including appropriate legal protection, before as well as after birth."

The detailed rulings on child-rearing incorporated into Halakhah constitute clear recognition of children's human rights. One might say that Judaism was the original children's-rights movement, dating back centuries before the concept was known in modern civilization.[117] In all cases, Halakhah considers the special needs and rights of children and provides specifically for these within Judaism's all-encompassing legal framework. Legal rulings affecting the child's development are based on the child's physical and emotional maturation, which is generally universal in relation to age norms, and on idiosyncratic levels of cognitive growth, which require more individualized guidance. The Halakhah on the fetus, legitimacy, protection from abuse, equal treatment, property rights, neglected or abandoned children, and orphans form a comprehensive protection for the child in the critical years of development. The laws on children's rights to education, participation in religious observances, liability for transgressions, and maturity facilitate healthy development with maximum opportunity for growth in accordance with the individual's "own way."

Notes

INTRODUCTION

1. Psalms 8:10.
2. *Exodus Rabbah* 46.
3. Genesis 3:16.
4. *Eruvin* 100.
5. Genesis 18:19.

CHAPTER 1

1. *Shabbat* 152, 119a.
2. Bachya ibn Paquda, *Duties of the Heart* (Jerusalem: Boys Town, 1965), p. 152.
3. Deuteronomy 11:18.
4. Proverbs 1:8.
5. Rabbi Samson Raphael Hirsch, *Yesodot ha-Chinnukh* [Foundations of education] (Bnei-Berak: Netzach Yisrael, 1968), chap. 1, p. 45.
6. Jerusalem Talmud, *Pe'ah* 87:4.
7. Psalms 127:3.
8. Malachi 2:15.
9. *Ta'anit* 23a.
10. Psalms 45:17.
11. *Song of Songs Rabbah* 1:4.
12. Genesis 17:7.
13. *Yevamot* 64a.
14. *Kallah Rabbati* 8.
15. *Lamentations Rabbah* 1:33 on 1:6.
16. Deuteronomy 14:1.
17. Deuteronomy 1:4, Proverbs 7.
18. *Avot* 3:18.
19. *Ecclesiastes Rabbah* 5.
20. Genesis 1:28, with Rashi commentary.
21. *Nedarim* 64.

22. Genesis 30:1.
23. Genesis 30:2-3.
24. *Avot* 6:8.
25. *Zohar* I, 227b.
26. *Tanchuma,* Noah 2.
27. *Genesis Rabbah* 63:2.
28. *Ketubbot* 50a.
29. Ibid.
30. Philippe Aries, *Centuries of Childhood: A Social History of Family Life,* trans. Robert Baldick (New York: Knopf, 1962).
31. G. H. Payne, *The Child in Human Progress* (New York: Putnam, 1916).
32. Genesis 48:9.
33. *Avot* 3:18.
34. Bor. *Shabbat* 15b.
35. *Sanhedrin* 38a.
36. *Zohar* II, 276b.
37. *Ecclesiastes Rabbah* 3 on 3a.
38. *Numbers Rabbah* 11:3. Other examples may be found in Genesis 37:35; Genesis 44:29, 34; Judges 11:35; II Samuel 11:11.
39. *Sotah* 47a.
40. Aries, *Centuries of Childhood*; Lloyd DeMause (ed.), *The History of Childhood* (New York: Psychohistory Press, 1974).
41. Bachya ibn Paquda, *Duties of the Heart,* p. 151.
42. Ibid.
43. *Tikkune Zohar, tikkun* 19, 67b.
44. *Ecclesiastes Rabbah.*
45. Arnold Gesell, Frances L. Ilg, Louis Bates Amers, and Janet Learned Rodell, *Infant and Child in the Culture of Today* (New York: Harper & Row, 1974), p. 3.
46. *Bava Batra* 21a.
47. *Avot* 5:24.
48. Bachya ibn Paquda, *Duties of the Heart,* chap. 5.
49. *Sanhedrin* 38.
50. Alexander Thomas and Stella Chess, *Temperament and Development* (New York: Brunner/Mazel, 1977).
51. *Sanhedrin* 37.

CHAPTER 2

1. Genesis 1:22.
2. Rabbi Aharon Levi Halevi, *Sefer ha-Chinnukh* (Jerusalem: Eshkol, 1960), p. 1a.

3. *Shabbat* 3.
4. *Yevamot* 61b. (According to *Magen Avraham*, 153:109, the woman is also responsible for fulfilling this mitzvah.)
5. *Bereshit Rabbah*, 34:20.
6. *Yevamot* 61b.
7. *Even ha-Ezer* 25:2; *Sotah* 12.
8. *Shabbat* 30.
9. *Yevamot* 61b.
10. Deuteronomy 7:14.
11. *Nedarim* 64b.
12. *Gittin* 70a, *Bava Kamma* 8.
13. Jerusalem Talmud, *Nedarim* 11:12.
14. Genesis 30:14.
15. *Ketubbot* 10a.
16. *Nedarim* 90b.
17. Abraham Steinberg, *Hilkhot Refu'ah ve-Rofim* (Jerusalem: Mosad Harav Kook, 1978), p. 150.
18. *Responsa Minchat Yitzchak*, pt. IV, chap. 5.
19. Steinberg, pp. 150–151.
20. *Yevamot* 64a.
21. Bachya ibn Paquda, *Duties of the Heart* (Jerusalem: Boys Town, 1965), p. 153.
22. Leviticus 15:28.
23. *Niddah* 31b, *Sotah* 27a.
24. *Kitzur Shulchan Arukh* 155:8.
25. *Niddah* 31b.; *Shulchan Arukh, Yoreh Deah,* Siman 196, section 11, *Ramo*.
26. *Niddah* 43a (according to the Talmud, orgasm is necessary for successful fertilization). Needless to say, passion between man and wife is more readily aroused after a separation such as the two-week period from the beginning of menstruation until the night after immersion in the *mikvah*.
27. *Nedarim* 20. If the husband and wife have sexual relations during the wife's period of impurity, the children born will be ill-mannered (*Kallah* 2) or have skin disease (*Kallah Rabbah* 1, *Leviticus Rabbah* 15:5).
28. *Yoma* 82.
29. Ibid..
30. Exodus 21:22.
31. *Avot* 5:8.
32. *Bava Kamma* 83a, *Shabbat* 63a.
33. *Shabbat* 66b.
34. Rabbi A. Y. Sperling. *Ta'amei ha-Minhagim* (Jerusalem: Eshkol, 1957), p. 162.
35. *Niddah* 9a, 45a.
36. *Sanhedrin* 69a.
37. Genesis 17:2.

38. *Bava Batra* 119b.
39. Ibid.
40. *Yevamot* 12b.
41. *Yevamot* 42a.
42. Ibid. Another reason cited is that the Husband might crush the fetus. (Rambam, *Laws of Divorce,* Halakha 25.)
43. *Ketubbot* 16a.
44. *Niddah* 31a.
45. *Berakhot* 60a. (According to some commentaries the sex of the child is linked with the succesion of orgasm. . . .)
46. *Bava Batra* 10b, *Berakhot* 5b, *Shevu'ot* 18a, 18b.
47. Alan F. Guttmacher, *Pregnancy, Birth and Family Planning* (New York: New American Library, 1973), p. 63.
48. *Niddah* 38.
49. *Yevamot* 80b.
50. Jerusalem Talmud, *Niddah* 1:3.
51. *Responsa of Divrei Rivos,* 124; *Rabbinical Verdicts* II, *siman* 119; *Tizr. Even ha-Ezer* 4.
52. Judges 13:4.
53. *Nedarim* 20b.
54. *Ketubbot* 10b.
55. *Kitzur Shulchan Arukh* 145:14.
56. Steinberg, p. 146; *Responsa Maharit,* no. 99; *Responsa Yavetz* 1:43.
57. *Oholot* 7:6.
58. *Sanhedrin* 72b.
59. *Yad ha-Chazakah* 31; *Rotze'ah* 1:9.
60. Jerusalem Talmud, *Sanhedrin* 8:9.
61. *Mishpetei Uziel* 2:47, Sheilat Yavetz, Siman 43.
62. Steinberg, pp. 146–149.
63. *Responsa Seridei Esh* 7:137.
64. Steinberg, p. 147:14.
65. Ibid., 146:8.
66. *Ketubbot* 34a, *Yevamot* 12b, 34b, 69b.

CHAPTER 3

1. *Yalkut,* Job 905.
2. *Niddah* 13a.
3. W. M. Feldman, *The Jewish Child* (New York: Bloch, 1918), pp. 120–121.
4. *Niddah* 31.
5. Ibid.
6. Ibid.
7. *Niddah* 31b.

8. *Berakhot* 57b.
9. *Yoma* 85a.
10. *Niddah* 25a–b.
11. *Niddah* 25.
12. *Niddah* 30.
13. Ibid.
14. Ibid.
15. *Yevamot* 83.
16. *Bava Kamma* 142b.
17. *Seridei Esh* 3:96. *Refuah Leor Hahalakha,* Institute for Medical Research According to Halakha; Jerusalem, 1980.
18. *Eruvin* 100.
19. Genesis 25:17.
20. Isaiah 4:9.
21. Psalms 48:7.
22. Micah 14:10.
23. *Yoma* 20.
24. *Shabbat* 31b, 32.
25. Genesis 21:1.
26. *Sotah* 12.
27. Jeremiah 4:31.
28. *Niddah* 31.
29. Jeremiah 30:6, Isaiah 21:3.
30. *Shabbat* 129a.
31. Genesis 30:3.
32. *Yevamot* 103.
33. *Sotah* 12.
34. *Niddah* 40a.
35. Rambam, commentary on *Berakhot* 47a.
36. Rabbenu Gershom, commentary on *Berkahot* 19a.
37. *Sanhedrin* 49a.
38. Tosafot, *Avodah Zarah* 10b.
39. *Arakhin* 7a.
40. *Niddah* 28a.
41. Genesis 38:27–30.
42. *Shabbat* 128b.
43. Ibid.
44. *Shabbat* 128–129a; *Shulchan Arukh, Orach Chayim* 203.
45. Ibid.
46. *Terumat ha-Deshen,* pt. A, *siman* 148.
47. *Responsa Chinnukh Bet Yehudah,* 71.
48. Hayyim Schneid, *Family* (Jerusalem: Keter, 1973), pp. 38–41.
49. The prayers are recited before the reading of the Torah on the Sabbath ("Mi sheberakh . . .").
50. *Sotah* 11b.

51. Exodus 1:15, *Sotah* 11b, *Ecclesiastes Rabbah* 7:1.
52. *Kiddushin* 74a.
53. Ezekiel 16:4.
54. Rabbi Abraham Isaac Sperling, *Sefer Ta'amei ha-Minhagim u-Mekorei ha-Dinim* (Jerusalem: Eshkol, 1957), p. 30.
55. *Shabbat* 129a.
56. Rashi, commentary on *Shabbat* 66b.
57. Genesis 30:3, 2:23.
58. *Shabbat* 135a.
59. *Yevamot* 42a.
60. *Yevamot* 80a.
61. *Genesis Rabbah* 12:6.
62. Leviticus 12.
63. *Niddah* 31b.
64. *Kitzur Shulchan Arukh* 154.
65. Alan F. Guttmacher, *Pregnancy, Birth and Family Planning* (New York: New American Library, 1973), p. 264.

CHAPTER 4

1. *Zohar Chadash* I, 4b.
2. *Zohar* I, 93a.
3. *Zohar* III, 66b.
4. *Nedarim* 32.
5. Eliyahu Kitov, *Man and His Home* (Jerusalem: Yad Eliyahu Kitov, 1977), p. 294.
6. *Tanchuma*, Vayera 6.
7. *Nedarim* 31. (This concept is true of the other mitzvot such as Shabbat and tzitzit. . .)
8. *Tikkune Zohar, tikkun* 37, 112b.
9. Genesis 17:13.
10. Leviticus 12:3.
11. Rabbi Aharon Halevi, *Sefer ha-Chinnukh* (Jerusalem: Eshkol, 1960), p. 1.
12. Exodus 10:25., *Shulchan Arukh, Yoreh Deah,* siman 264/a.
13. *Yevamot* 4; *Shabbat* 19; *Yoreh De'ah* 266; Rambam, *Yad ha-Chazakah, Hilkhot Milah.*
14. *Kitzur Shulchan Arukh* 163:3.
15. *Kiddushin* 29a.
16. *Sanhedrin* 17a; Jerusalem Talmud, *Eruvin* 5:5.
17. Rabbi Abraham Isaac Sperling, *Sefer Ta'amei ha-Minhagim* (Jerusalem: Eshkol, 1957), p. 385.

Notes

18. Genesis 48:16. "The angel which redeemed me from all evil, bless this lad . . ."
19. *Kitzur Shulchan Arukh* 105.
20. J. D. Eisenstein, *Otzar Yisrael* (Jerusalem), 2:18.
21. Genesis 48:16.
23. Genesis 17., *Shulchan Arukh, Yoreh Deah,* siman 262/a.
23. *Shabbat* 130a–132b.
24. Sperling, p. 387.
25. *Responsa of Maharil* 85. *Shulchan Arukh, Yoreh Deah,* siman 265/6. *Pirkei D'Rabbi Eliezer*/19.
26. *Shulchan Arukh, Yoreh Deah,* siman 265/24/a.
27. Ibid., p. 386.
28. Rambam, *Hilkhot Milah.*
29. Ibid.
30. *Shabbat* 133.
31. Eisenstein, 5:172.
32. *Shabbat* 130.
33. *Kitzur Shulchan Arukh* 163.
34. *Responsa Binyan Zion, siman* 67.
35. Abraham Steinberg, *Hilkhot Refu'ah ve'Rofim* (Jerusalem: Mosad Harav Kook, 1978), pp. 217–219.
36. *Yevamot* 64b.
37. Steinberg, p. 217.
38. *Responsa Seridei Esh* 3:96.
39. Steinberg, p. 217.
40. *Kitzur Shulchan Arukh* 163:6.
41. Rabenu Aharon Halevi, *Sefer ha-Chinnukh* (Jerusalem: Eshkol, 1960), sec. 390.
42. Exodus 13:1., quoted in Kitov, p. 307.
43. Ibid.
44. Numbers 3:41.
45. If the firstborn attends a *Seudat Mitzvah,* such as a ceremony for the completion of a tractate of the Talmud, he is exempt from this obligation.
46. Halevi, sec. 234.
47. *Kitzur Shulchan Arukh* 164:3.
48. Numbers 3:47.
49. *Kitzur Shulchan Arukh* 164:3.
50. Ibid. 164:4.
51. Ibid.
52. Exodus 13:2.
53. *Niddah* 21:1.
54. *Kitzur Shulchan Arukh* 164.
55. Rambam, *Hilkhot Milah; Kitzur Shulchan Arukh* 164:3; Kitov, p. 309.
56. *Shulchan Arukh, Orach Chaim,* siman 219. The mother comes to the Synagogue at least seven days after birth.

57. *Pesachim* 65.
58. Proverbs 31.
59. Rashi notes that girls develop more quickly than boys (Ker. 50a; San. 69).
60. *Tanchuma,* Va-yakhel.
61. *Rosh Hashanah* 18a.
62. *Genesis Rabbah* 41:1.
63. *Sotah* 11b.
64. *Pirkei D'Rabbi Eliezar, ch. 48, 35; Zohar–Yisro.*

CHAPTER 5

1. Adolf Jellinek, *Beit ha-Midrash,* 11:96.
2. *Berakhot* 38 (this occurred at the end of the nursing period when the child was weaned).
3. *Ketubbot* 60b, *Iggerot Mosheh* 2:6.
4. *Ketubbot* 60a, *Yevamot* 43a.
5. *Responsa Ha'alef Lekach Shelomoh, Even ha-Ezer* 57.
6. *Chazon Ish, Mo'ed,* 60, 59, sec. 4.
7. *Minchat Yitzhak* 1:78.
8. *Yoma* 78.
9. *Sotah* 12:5, *Avodah Zarah* 20b.
10. *Leviticus Rabbah* 1:5.
11. *Shabbat* 108b.
12. *Hilkhot De'ot* 4/15.
13. *Chullin* 20b.
14. *Sanhedrin* 17b.
15. *Shabbat* 109a.
16. *Chullin* 106a.
17. *Shabbat* 41a.
18. *Shabbat* 109a.
19. Chayyim David Halevi, *Makor Chayyim* (Tel Aviv, 1965), vol. 1, 2:7.
20. Jerusalem Talmud, *Terumot* 7:4.
21. *Berakhot* 8b.
22. *Ketubbot* 110b, *Nedarim* 8b.
23. *Sotah* 47a.
24. *Bava Batra* 16b.
25. *Eruvin* 65a.
26. *Pesachim* 112b.
27. Leviticus 19:19.
28. *Nedarim* 81.

29. *Niddah* 65a.
30. *Berakhot* 40a.
31. *Orach Chayyim* 4:11.
32. *Shabbat* 123a.
33. *Mo'ed Katan* 18a, *Niddah* 17a.
34. *Kitzur Shnei Luchot ha-Berit* 61.
35. *Orach Chayyim* 260:1.
36. *Zohar* III, 79a–b.
37. *Shabbat* 41a, *Nedarim* 81.
38. *Sha'arei Teshuvah* 531:5, Leviticus 19:27.
39. Zechariah 12:4 (commentary).
40. *Kedivrei Rabbi Eliezer* 12.
41. *Tanchuma,* Ki Tissa 3; *Berakhot* 61b.
42. Jerusalem Talmud, Ch. 2 halakha 4.
43. *Genesis Rabbah* 91:10.
44. Tosefta, *Kelim.*
45. *Oholot* 12:4.
46. *Shabbat* 58, *Berakhot* 53.
47. *Genesis Rabbah* 8:10.
48. *Kelim* 25:15.
49. *Chullin* 91b.
50. *Ketubbot* 59b.
51. M. Jersil, *Emotional Development* (New York: Wiley, 1954).
52. *Ketubbot* 59.
53. *Yoma* 78.
54. *Yevamot* 43, (Ker. 60); *Iggerot Mosheh,* sec. 6; *Shulchan Arukh* 145:14.
55. Burton White, *The First Three Years of Life* (New York: Avon Books, 1975).
56. *Yevamot* 12b, 35b; *Ketubbot* 37.
57. *Ketubbot* 60.
58. *Iggerot Mosheh, Even ha-Ezer* 72:6.
59. *Ketubbot* 59.
60. Job 39.
61. Lamentations 4:3–4.
62. *Ketubbot* 59b.
63. *Ketubbot* 59–60.
64. Tosefta, *Sotah* 4:3.
65. Talmudic saying.
66. Jerusalem Talmud, *Berakhot* 9, 3.
67. I Samuel 1:21–23.
68. The International Organization for Nursing Mothers.
69. *Gittin* 89a.
70. *Avot de-Rabbi Nathan* 31:1.

71. Exodus 2:7-9; *Ketubbot* 60b.
72. Joshua Neubirt, *Shemirat Shabbat ke-Hilkhato* (Jerusalem: Feldheim, 1965), chap. 23:25.
73. *Avot de-Rabbi Nathan* 31:1.
74. *Yevamot* 42a.
75. *Ketubbot* 60b.
76. *Tanchuma*, Exodus 7:26; Yerushalmi 76.
77. *Sotah* 12, *Exodus Rabbah*, *Tanchuma* 7.
78. *Responsa of Azriel* 10:80.
79. Neubirt, chap. 23:15.
80. Ibid. chap. 23:13.
81. Ibid., 23:11, 12.
82. Ibid., 23:11.
83. Ibid., 23:15.
84. Ibid., 25:15.
85. Neubirt, 39:15.
86. *Ibid.*
87. *Ta'anit* 14a.
88. *Song of Songs Rabbah* 3.
89. Exodus 2:7.
90. *Ketubbot* 60b.
91. Tobias ben Moses Cohen, *Ma'aseh Tuviyyah*, trans. Dr. A. Levinson (London: Rimmon, 1924).
92. *Ketubbot* 60-61.
93. *Ketubbot* 65a.
94. *Yoma*, 78., *Ketubbot* 60b.
95. *Yoma* 78b.
96. *Genesis Rabbah* 47.
97. Tosefta, *Shabbat* 10:3.
98. *Zevachim* 88b.
99. Dr. Nathan Morris, *Toledot ha-Chinnukh shel Am Yisrael* [A history of Jewish education] (Tel Aviv: Omanut, 1960), p. 297.
100. Ibid.
101. Neubirt, chap. 15.
102. Eliyahu, Kitov, *Man and His Home* (Jerusalem: Yad Eliyahu Kitov, 1977), p. 288.
103. The commandments of Sabbath and *milah* are termed "an eternal sign" (Kitov, p. 294, introduction).
104. Neubirt, Introduction.
105. Both the thirty-nine basic functions carried out in the Tabernacle and the secondary acts are forbidden on Sabbath. See *Kitzur Shulchan Arukh*, p. 127: The Order of *Avot Melachot*.
106. "Be happy on your holiday" (Deut. 15:14).
107. *Chazon Ish*, 59:3.

108. *Responsa Minchat Yitzhak* 1:78.
109. Neubirt, 24:3.
110. Ibid., 24:5, 6.
111. Ibid., 13:22.
112. Ibid., 13:12.
113. Ibid., 13:8, 13.
114. Ibid., 13:15.
115. Ibid., 13:24.
116. Ibid., 14:5.
117. Ibid., 14:6, 10.
118. Ibid., 14:7.
119. Ibid., 14:11.
120. Ibid., 18:43–45.
121. *Responsa Chelkat Ya'akov,* pt. A, 66; *Responsa Binyan Tzion.*
122. Neubirt, 18: 7–9.
123. Ibid., chap. 32:40.
124. Ibid., 18:45.
125. Ibid., 25:61–62.
126. *Kiddushin* 29a; *Ketubbot* 65a, 49a; *Shulchan Arukh, Yoreh De'ah* 251d.
127. *Eruvin* 18a.
128. *Sanhedrin* 38.
129. *Gittin* 12 (Rashi).
130. Ephraim Fishel Weinberger, *Yad Ephraim* (Tel Aviv: Public Committee for Publication of the Works of Rabbi Weinberger, 1977), p. 191.
131. Isaiah 66:13.
132. Proverbs 4:3.
133. Genesis 2:16; *Sanhedrin* 56b.
134. Genesis 18:19.
135. II Samuel 12; *Ketubbot* 48, 61.
136. II Samuel 4.
137. The *bet din* is responsible for the welfare of the orphan who is abandoned and for imposing discipline if the parents fail or are unable to do so, as well as to ensure the child's legal rights in case of divorce (see below, chapter 19). If there is no father to provide for the child's education, the *bet din* must see to it that the child receives *chinnukh*. (Rambam, *Hilkhot Nachalot* 11:10; *Sukkah* 2b).

CHAPTER 6

1. *Eruvin* 83b.
2. Eliyahu Kitov, *Man and His Home* (Heb.) (Jerusalem: Yad Eliyahu Kitov, 1977), chap. 20.

3. Leviticus 11.
4. American College of Obstetrics and Gynecology, *Obstetrics and Gynecology,* December 1972.
5. *Ketubbot* 61.
6. Only orphans who had no mother or wetnurse to nurse them were fed goat's milk or cow's milk as infants.
7. *Yevamot* 42.
8. *Ketubbot* 60; *Responsa Noda Bi-Yehudah* 142:20.
9. *Responsa Iggerot Mosheh* 2:6.
10. *Ketubbot* 60.
11. Ibid.
12. Genesis 21:8.
13. *Ketubbot* 60; Jerusalem Talmud, *Ketubbot* 6.
14. I Samuel 1:24.
15. Deuteronomy 32:14, *Yevamot* 42b.
16. Deuteronomy 32:14, Proverbs 7:27.
17. *Bava Batra* 98b.
18. *Leviticus Rabbah* 12 (milk is considered beneficial for the circulatory system).
19. Genesis 49:12.
20. *Ketubbot* 60.
21. *Song of Songs Rabbah* 1.
22. *Yoma* 78.
23. Rambam, *Hilkhot De'ot,* chap. 4.
24. Isaiah 7:15.
25. *Yoma* 75.
26. *Berakhot* 40.
27. Rambam, *Hilkhot De'ot,* chap. 4.
28. *Berakhot* 40a–44b.
29. *Sanhedrin* 55.
30. *Bava Batra* 91a, *Ketubbot* 61a, *Sanhedrin* 17b, *Shabbat* 140.
31. Rambam, *Hilkhot De'ot,* chap. 4.
32. *Avodah Zarah* 11.
33. *Berakhot* 44b.
34. Ibid.
35. *Nedarim* 49a.
36. *Chullin* 84a, *Pesachim* 108b.
37. *Berakhot* 40a; *Niddah* 65; Jerusalem Talmud, *Eruvin* 111:1.
38. UNESCO, *The Child from Birth to Six Years Old* (Paris, 1976).
39. *Chatam Sofer* 5:12.
40. *Pesachim* 112a, *Ta'anit* 11a.
41. *Shabbat* 33a, *Gittin* 70a.
42. *Shekalim* 14:15.
43. Rambam, *Hilchot De'ot,* chap. 4.

44. Ibid.
45. *Ecclesiastes Rabbah* 1:18.
46. *Berakhot* 54b.
47. Rambam, *Hilkhot De'ot,* chap. 4.
48. *Bava Batra* 55a.
49. *Ketubbot* 110b.
50. *Pesachim* 42a, *Sanhedrin* 94a.
51. Rambam, *Hilchot De'ot,* chap. 4.
52. *Shabbat* 109b.
53. Ibid.
54. *Mishnah Berurah,* sec. 343; Joshua Neubirt, *Shemirat Shabbat ke-Hilkhato* (Jerusalem: Neubirt, 1965), 32:39.
55. Neubirt, 32:39; *Chazon Ish* 60:59; *Responsa Rabbi Azriel, Yud,* 172; *Responsa Har Tzevi* 60; *Responsa Rashba* 1:92.
56. *Kitzur Shulchan Arukh* 165:4.
57. *Responsa Chelkat Yaakov* 11:88–89, *Responsa Yabiya Omer, Yud,* sec. 3; *Darchei Teshuvah* 89:15.
58. *Mishneh Berurah* 45, *Be'ur Halakhah* 321:12.
59. *Chazon Ish* 58:9; *Be'er Rehovot,* sec. 11, chapter on grinding on Sabbath.
60. Neubirt, 8:14.
61. Ibid., 8:15.
62. Ibid., chap. 5.
63. Rema, 323:1, 306:7; *Mishnah Berurah* 36.
64. Rema, 328:17.
65. Neubirt, 1:44, 50.
66. *Tehillah le-David,* 318: 17 and 32; Neubirt 12:4, 13.
67. Neubirt, 12:6, 15.
68. Ibid., 9:19.
69. Ibid., 40:80.
70. *Sefer ha-Yashar, Chelek ha-Teshuvot, siman* 52; *Yoma* 77b, 78b, 82a; *Shabbat* 139a; *Eruvin* 40b; *Orchot Chayyim* 18:12.
71. *Kitzur Shulchan Arukh* 32:2–3.
72. Ibid. 32:6.
73. Ibid.
74. Ibid., 32:19.
75. Ibid., 32:11.
76. *Bava Metzia* 107b.
77. *Kitzur Shulchan Arukh* 32:32, 13.
78. Ibid.
79. Ibid., 32:17.
80. Rambam, *Hilchot De'ot,* chap. 4; *Kitzur Shulchan Arukh* 32:14.
81. Ibid.
82. *Kitzur Shulchan Arukh* 33:1–2.

83. Rambam, *Hilkhot De'ot* 4; *Kitzur Shulchan Arukh* 32:16.
84. *Kitzur Shulchan Arukh*, 32:14.
85. Ibid. 32:5.
86. Ibid. 32:1-2.
87. Ibid.
88. Ibid. 32:4.
89. Ibid. 33:9.
90. Ibid. 32:1, Commentary *Metzudat David.*
91. *Bava Metzia* 107b.

CHAPTER 7

1. *Yoma* 82a, *Niddah* 45b, *Ketubbot* 51a.
2. *Responsa Rav Pe'olim, Orach Chayyim, siman* 5; *Sod Yesharim, siman* 3.
3. Lawrence Kohlberg, "Moral Development," in David Sills (ed.), *International Encyclopedia of the Social Sciences* (New York: Crowell, Collier & Macmillan, 1968), 10:483-492.
4. *Etz Chayyim* 50:83.
5. Genesis 8:21.
6. *Sanhedrin* 91. Genesis 4-7.
7. Ibid.
8. *Avot de-Rabbi Nathan* 15.
9. Selma Fraiberg, *The Magic Years* (New York: Scribner's, 1959), chap. 1.
10. Ibid.
11. Rabbi Samson Raphael Hirsch, *Yesodot ha-Chinnukh* [Foundations of education], (Bene-Berak: Netzach, 1968), 2:52.
12. Fraiberg, p. 8.
13. Hirsch, p. 52.
14. *Responsa Rav Pe'olim*, pt. I; *Orach Chayyim, siman* 5; *Sod Yesharim, siman* 3.
15. *Hakdama Lesefer HaZohar perush Baal Sulam* by Rab Jehuda Halevi Ashlag, Tel-Aviv, 1975, pp. 29-30.
16. *Ecclesiastes Rabbah* 83:4.
17. Prayer included in the Shacharit (morning) service.
18. *Ecclesiastes Rabbah* 5.
19. Hirsch, p. 48.
20. David P. Ausubel and Edmund V. Sullivan, *Theory and Problems of Child Development,* 2d ed. (New York: Grune & Stratton, 1970), p. 175.
21. *Ecclesiastes Rabbah* 87.
22. *Sanhedrin* 91.
23. Ibid.
24. Rabbenu Bachya, *Duties of the Heart* (Jerusalem: Boys Town, 1965), pp. 158-159.

25. *Niddah* 16.
26. Rabbenu Bachya, *Duties of the Heart,* pp. 154–155.
27. Lawrence Kohlberg, "The Child as Moral Philosopher," *Psychology Today,* September 1968, pp. 29–33.
28. *Responsa Rav Pe'olim,* pt. I, *Sod Yesharim, siman* 3.
29. *Ecclesiastes Rabbah* 69.
30. Genesis 30:3,5.
31. Rambam, Introduction to the *Eight Chapters.*
32. Ibid.
33. Hirsch, p. 46.
34. Fraiberg, chap. 1.
35. Hirsch, p. 59.
36. Rabbi Ephraim Fishel Weinberger, *Yad Ephraim* (Tel Aviv: Public Committee for Publication of the Works of Rabbi Weinberger, 1977), p. 193.
37. *Berakhot* 7, *Reishit Chokhmah.*
38. *Midrash Rabbah,* Yitro, 28:2.
39. *Chagigah* 1:7, *Kiddushin* 29a, Rema Yud I.
40. *Berakhot* 48a. Children are exempt from the responsibility of reciting the *Shema* on time, for the father is not always at home with the child in order to educate him to recite the prayer on time (Rashi).
41. *Magen Avraham* 263:11, *Kitzur Shulchan Arukh.*
42. *Orach Chayyim* 313.
43. *Sotah* 47.
44. Erik H. Erikson, *Childhood and Society* (New York: Norton, 1963).
45. *Leviticus Rabbah* 2.
46. *Eruvin* 82.
47. *Tanchuma,* Genesis 7.
48. Joshua Neubirt, *Shemirat Shabbat ke-Hilkhato* (Jerusalem: Neubirt, 1965), chap. 32a.
49. *Reishit Chokhmah,* chap. on child-rearing; *Gittin* 6.
50. Rabbi Schwartz, *Beit Abba* [Father's house] (Jerusalem: Yeshivat Dvar Yerushalayim, 1979).
51. Ibid.
52. *Shulchan Arukh Yoreh De'ah* siman 245 seif 10.
53. Schwartz, p. 57.
54. *Sanhedrin* 38.
55. *Tanchuma,* Pinchas.
56. *Mesillat Yesharim.*
57. Proverbs 22:6.
58. Rambam, *Eight Chapters,* chap. 8.
59. A. Thomas, S. Chess, and H. G. Birch, "The Origin of Personality," *Scientific American* 223 (1970): 102–109.
60. Rabbi Chayyim David Halevi, *Makor Chayyim* (Tel Aviv: Halevi, 1967), chap. 76:5.

61. *Kitzur Shulchan Arukh* 165:6.
62. Halevi, 167:2.
63. Maimonides, *Eight Chapters,* chap. 4.
64. *Yalkut,* Job 896.
65. Meiri, *Kiddushin* 30.
66. *Avodah Zarah* 5.

CHAPTER 8

1. Isaiah 28:9.
2. *Kiddushin* 19:17.
3. Masaru Ibuka, *Kindergarten Is Too Late* (New York: Simon & Schuster, 1978).
4. *Alei Shor,* p. 263.
5. Meiri, *Kiddushin* 30.
6. *Avot de-Rabbi Nathan* 24.
7. Psalms 8:3.
8. Rabbi Samson Raphael Hirsch, *Yesodot ha-Chinnukh* [Foundations of education] (Bene-Berak: Netzach, 1968), chap. 1.
9. *Ketubbot* 58.
10. *Kitzur Shulchan Arukh* 165:1.
11. Ibid.
12. Deuteronomy 11:19.
13. Exodus 13:8.
14. Jerusalem Talmud, *Yevamot* 6.
15. *Shulchan Arukh,* Yoreh De'ah Rama 81.
16. *Sefer Musar,* 87.
17. Rambam, *Hilkhot De'ot* 1:6.
18. Meiri, *Chibbur ha-Teshuvah* 44.
19. Deuteronomy 5:1; Numbers 15:39; Deuteronomy 31:12, 11:19.
20. Rambam, *Hilkhot De'ot.*
21. *Responsa Beit Halevi* 1:6.
22. *Kiddushin* 31a; Exodus 31:18 (Rashi); Neubirt, 32:14.
23. Genesis 18:10.
24. *Sefer Chut ha-Meshulash.*
25. Exodus 13:8; Deuteronomy 6:20, "And you shall tell your son on that day."
26. Neubirt, 32:15.
27. Neubirt, 32:44.
28. Rema, Yud, 81:7; *Mishnah Berurah* 1.
29. Neubirt, 32:47.
30. Deuteronomy 31:12–13.

31. *Sanhedrin* 312; Rema 77:24.
32. Rema 769; *Mishnah Berurah* 13.
33. *Kitzur Shulchan Arukh* 165:7; *Avot* 5:21.
34. *Mishnah Berurah* 93; Neubirt, 32:18.
35. *Mishnah Berurah* 187:4.
36. Rambam, *Hilkhot Chametz u-Matzah,* 7.
37. *Mishnah Berurah* 472:47.
38. Rabbi Chayyim David Halevi, *Makor Chayyim* (Jerusalem, 1965), pt. I, 28:11.
39. *Kitzur Shulchan Arukh,* 165:2.
40. Neubirt, 32:25.
41. Ibid. 32:26.
42. Rambam, *Hilkhot Keriyat Shema* 4:1.
43. Rambam, *Hilkhot Chanukah,* ch. 4:3.
44. *Shulchan Arukh,* 343:8; *Rema* 596; Rambam, *Hilkhot Shofar* 2:7.
45. *Avot* 5:21 (Rashi).
46. *Mishnah Berurah* 343:4.
47. *Kitzur Shulchan Arukh* 165:3; *Mishnah Berurah* 343:4.
48. *Kitzur Shulchan Arukh* 165:3.
49. Ibid.; *Mishnah Berurah* 343:3; Neubirt, 32:32.
50. *Kitzur Shulchan Arukh* 165:1.
51. *Kitzur Shulchan Arukh* 133:19; *Yoma* 82a.
52. *Sukkah* 55 (Rashi).
53. Exodus 6:7.
54. Proverbs 1:8.
55. *Mishnah Berurah* 343:2; *Kitzur Shulchan Arukh* 165:1; Rambam, *Hilkhot Talmud Torah* 1; *Kiddushin* 29a.
56. Deuteronomy 6:7, "And you shall teach them to your sons . . ."; *Berachot* 21b.
57. *Kiddushin* 29a; Rambam, *Hilkhot Talmud Torah* 1.
58. *Megillah* 20a; Rambam, *Hilkhot Talmud Torah* 1.
59. *Chagigah* 1:7; Rashi, *Avot* 5:21.
60. *Chagiga* 2 (Rashi).
61. *Yitro Rabbah; Berachot* 17a.
62. Chatam Sofer, *Torat Moshe, Parshat Nitzavim* and *Sdei Chemed,* 8:59.
63. Rabbi Schwartz, *Beit Abba* (Jerusalem: Dvar Yerushalayim, 1979), p. 86.
64. Ibid. 86–87.
65. *Berachot* 17a; Deuteronomy 19:3.
66. *Kitzur Shulchan Arukh* 165:7.
67. Ibid.; *Bava Batra* 21a.
68. *Gittin* 6.
69. *Alei Shor* 6:261.

70. *Sotah* 47; *Sanhedrin* 107.
71. *Mesillat Yesharim* 11.
72. Proverbs 22:6.
73. Hirsch, p. 54.
74. Schwartz, p. 64.
75. Hirsch, pp. 62–69.
76. Hirsch, *Horev* (Vilna: Ram Press: 1862), p. 41.
77. *Shabbat* 156b; *Mishnah Berurah* 47:10.
78. *Magen Avraham* 263.
79. *Avodah Zarah* 3.
80. Hirsch, *Yesodot ha-Chinnukh* 2:2.

CHAPTER 9

1. *Sotah* 47a.
2. Proverbs 3:12.
3. Jeremiah 31:19.
4. *Exodus Rabbah* 1:1.
5. I Kings 1:6.
6. I Samuel 2:23, 3:13.
7. Proverbs 19:18.
8. Proverbs 29:17.
9. Proverbs 13:1.
10. Proverbs 29:15.
11. Ben Sira 1:1.
12. Deuteronomy 21:18–21.
13. Proverbs 29:17.
14. Ben Sira 13.
15. Rambam, *Hilkhot Genaivah* 1:10.
16. Leviticus 19:14.
17. *Mo'ed Katan* 17a.
18. *Responsa Binyamin Ze'ev* 407:1:5.
19. Proverbs 29:17.
20. *Gittin* 6b.
21. *Yalkut Shimoni,* Yitro 386.
22. Rambam, *Hilkhot Rotze'ach* 5:6.
23. *Responsa Rashba* 1:534.
24. *Responsa Shevut Yaakov* 3:140.
25. *Iggerot Mosheh* 14:103.
26. Ibid., *piska* 16.
27. Proverbs 23:13.
28. *Semachot* 2:4.
29. Proverbs 19:18.

30. *Bava Batra* 21a.
31. Rambam, *Hilkhot Talmud Torah* 5:2.
32. *Kitzur Shulchan Arukh* 165:7.
33. Proverbs 22:6.
34. *Ta'anit* 24a.
35. Proverbs 17:10.
36. *Responsa Seridei Esh* 3:95.

CHAPTER 10

1. *Eruvin* 100b.
2. *Genesis Rabbah* 20:15.
3. Genesis 48; *Bava Metzia* 87.
4. *Megillah* 21.
5. Deuteronomy 4:15.
6. Rambam, *Hilkhot De'ot* 4.
7. *Kitzur Shulchan Arukh* 32:1.
8. Rambam, *Hilkhot De'ot* 5–10; *Chullin* 4:2.
9. Genesis 33:3; Rashi 19:4; Rashi, Ha'azinu 33:11.
10. Be-Ha'alotkha 11:13.
11. Rabbi E. F. Weinberger, *Yad Ephraim* (Tel Aviv, 1976), p. 195.
12. Rambam, *Hilkhot De'ot* 3.
13. Ibid. 5.
14. *Kitzur Shulchan Arukh* 32a.
15. Arthur J. Vander, *Human Physiology and the Environment in Health and Disease* (San Francisco: Freeman, 1976), p. 1.
16. Ibid., Introduction; Rambam, *Hilkhot De'ot* 1:5.
17. *Kitzur Shulchan Arukh* 32:2.
18. Ibid. 32:3.
19. Ibid. 4–5.
20. Ibid. 7; Hugh Powers and James Presley, *Food Power: Nutrition and Your Child's Behavior* (New York: St. Martin's, 1978).
21. *Kitzur Shulchan Arukh* 10.
22. Rambam, *Hilkhot De'ot* 4:9; *Kitzur Shulchan Arukh* 32.
23. Vander, Introduction.
24. Rambam, *Hilkhot De'ot* 8:61; *Shabbat* 129:1; *Kitzur Shulchan Arukh* 91.
25. *Ketubbot* 65a; *Takanat Usha, Ketubbot* 49b; *Shulchan Arukh, Yoreh De'ah* 251:4.
26. *Kitzur Shulchan Arukh* 91:3.
27. *Ketubbot* 61.
28. *Kitzur Shulchan Arukh* 33:14.
29. Ibid. 33:20.

30. Ibid. 32:2.
31. Ibid. 32:6.
32. Ibid. 32:21.
33. Ibid. 32:21, 24.
34. Ibid. 32:23; Rambam, *Hilkhot De'ot* 4.
35. *Kitzur Shulchan Arukh* 32:26.
36. Ibid. 32:25.
37. *Ketubbot* 103b.
38. *Kitzur Shulchan Arukh* 32:22.
39. Ibid.
40. Lytt I. Gardner, "Deprivation, Dwarfism," in *Human Physiology and the Environment in Health and Disease* (San Francisco: Freeman, 1976).
41. Dorothy Burlingame and Anna Freud, *Young Children in Wartime* (London: Allen & Unwin, 1942).
42. J. Bowlby, *Attachment and Loss,* Vol. 1 (New York: Basic Books, 1969).
43. *Sotah* 47, *Sanhedrin* 107.
44. *Kitzur Shulchan Arukh* 165:7.
45. Ibid.
46. See above, chapter 6.
47. *Kitzur Shulchan Arukh* 163 (*Yoreh De'ah* 262:3).
48. *Yevamot* 64b.
49. *Berakhot* 8 (Rashi).
50. *Ta'anit* 27b.
51. *Shabbat* 33a.
52. *Berakhot* 40a.
53. *Sotah* 35a.
54. *Sotah* 35a, *Leviticus Rabbah* 18:4.
55. *Gittin* 69a.
56. *Bava Kamma* 82a, *Gittin* 69b.
57. Rabbi Sperling, *Sefer Ta'amei ha-Minhagim u-Mekorei ha-Dinim* (Jerusalem, 1957), p. 595.
58. Ibid.
59. Ibid., p. 590.
60. Ibid., p. 579.
61. Ibid., p. 592.
62. Ibid., p. 588.
63. Ibid., p. 592.
64. Ibid., p. 580.
65. *Avodah Zarah* 28b, *Gittin* 69a.
66. *Gittin* 69a.
67. *Ketubbot* 50a, *Shabbat* 77b, 109b.
68. *Ma'aseh Tuviyyah* (pediatrics), (Warsaw, 1846); *Orchot Chayyim* 513; Studenzki, *The Pediatrician's Book* (Warsaw, 1873).

Notes

69. Rabbi Joseph ben Yehudah Vaknin, *Sefer Musar, Perush Mishnah Avot* (Berlin: B. Z. Bacher, 1910), *Shabbat* 82a; *Encyclopedia Talmudit,* "Chakhmat hitzoniyot," par. 5; *Iggerot Ramban.*
70. Rambam, *Mishnah Nedarim* 4:45.
71. Rambam, *Eight Chapters, Bava Batra* 116.
72. Rambam, *Hilkhot De'ot,* chap. 2.
73. Sperling, *Toledot Adam,* p. 591.
74. *Kitzur Shulchan Arukh* 32:27.
75. Deuteronomy 28:28 *Eruvin* 17b, *Nedarim* 81a, *Pesachim* 111b, *Bava Kamma* 98a, Tosefta 7.
76. Leviticus 19:14.
77. Deuteronomy 27:17-18.
78. Book of Wisdom 10:21.
79. *Chagigah* 3a.
80. Rambam, Commentary to *Nedarim* 84:44.
81. *Shabbat* 134.
82. *Shabbat* 67.
83. Leviticus 8:15.
84. *Gittin* 69b.
85. *Avodah Zarah* 29.
86. *Even ha-Ezer* 5:14.
87. *Nedarim* 39b.
88. *Genesis Rabbah,* ch. 53.
89. *Kitzur Shulchan Aruch* 92:1. The Torah was given for the living (Lev. 18:5) and not for the dead (*Yoma* 85b).
90. *Tur, Orach Chayyim* 517; *Ketubbot* 39a; Joshua Neubirt, *Shemirat Shabbat ke-Hilkhato* (1979), 36:2.
91. Neubirt, 36:12.
92. *Responsa Minchat Yitzchak* 1:78; *Kitzur Shulchan Arukh* 134; *Badei ha-Shulchan* 18.
93. Rema, 176:1, *Mishnah Berurah* 6:328 and 5:343.
94. Rambam, *Hilkhot Shabbat,* chap. 2; *Kitzur Shulchan Arukh* 92:1; *Mishnah Berurah* 11:47.
95. Rema, 328:37, *Mishnah Berurah* 120:130.
96. Neubirt, 37:5.
97. Rema 327:1; *Mishnah Berurah* 4; *Responsa Minchat Yitzchak* 79, also pt. 4:124.
98. Neubirt, 37:8.
99. *Responsa Minchat Yitzchak* 79, 4:124.
100. Neubirt, 37:9.
101. *Chazon Ish* 59:4.
102. Neubirt, 37:14.
103. Ibid. 37:15.
104. Rema 176:a, *Mishnah Berurah* 6.

105. Rema 328:17, *Mishnah Berurah* 58.
106. Rema 328:17.
107. Neubirt, 40:50.
108. Ibid. 51.
109. Neubirt, 40:70.
110. Ibid. 40:2.
111. Ibid.
112. Ibid. 40:3.
113. Ibid. 34:4.
114. Ibid. 34:5.
115. Bor. *Shabbat* 151b.
116. *Chullin* 105b (according to Jewish law it is not permitted to drink liquids which have been left uncovered overnight).
117. *Bava Metzia* 107b.
118. Ibid. As examples: Rabbi Yochanan warned to avoid flies coming from patients with colds; Rabbi Zera avoided winds coming from the direction of disease-stricken areas; Rabbi Eliezer would not sit in the same room with people who had colds.
119. *Pesachim* 49a–b, *Yevamot* 64b, *Even ha-Ezer* 11 (Deut. 28:59–60).
120. *Bava Batra* 58b.
121. *Berakhot* 5b.
122. *Bava Metzia* 107b.
123. *Gittin* 28.
124. Dr. Abraham Steinberg, *Hilkhot Refu'ah ve-Rofim* (Jerusalem, Mosad Harav Kook, 1978), 74:3.
125. Rambam, Commentary on the Mishnah, *Nedarim* 4:45.

CHAPTER 11

1. Rabbi Abraham Isaac Kook. *Orot ha-Kodesh*, vol I (Jerusalem: Mosad Harav Kook, 1963), p. 65.
2. *Kitzur Shulchan Arukh* 31:1.
3. *Avot* 4:4.
4. *Tanchuma ha-Kadum*, Tazria.
5. *Genesis Rabbah* 11.
6. Micah 6:8.
7. *Kitzur Shulchan Arukh*, sec. 9.
8. Deuteronomy 4:15.
9. *Kitzur Shulchan Arukh*, sec. 32.
10. *Midrash on Psalms* 8.
11. Rabbenu Bachya ibn Paquda, *Duties of the Heart* (Jerusalem: Boys Town, 1965), pp. 157–159.

12. David P. Ausubel and Edmund V. Sullivan, *Theory and Problems of Child Development* (New York: Grune & Stratton, 1970), p. 50.
13. Ibid., p. 51.
14. Mishnah, *Eduyyot* 2:49.
15. *Bava Metzia* 87a.
16. *Tanchuma, Chaye Sarah.*
17. *Numbers Rabbah* 14:5.
18. *Bava Batra* 109b; *Sefer Chassidim* 377; *Kiddushin* 70a–b; *Derekh Eretz Rabbah* 13.
19. *Bava Metzia* 85a.
20. *Pesachim* 49 a–b.
21. *Yevamot* 64:2, *Shabbat* 134.
22. Rambam, *Issurei Bei'ah* 21:32; *Shulchan Arukh* 2:66; *Pesachim* 49:2.
23. *Bava Batra* 109.
24. *Yevamot* 64:2; Rambam, *Issurei Bei'ah* 21:30; *Shulchan Arukh, Even ha-Ezer* 2:7.
25. Rambam, Commentary on *Eduyyot* 2:9.
26. Ausubel and Sullivan, p. 50.
27. *Bekhorot* 45:2.
28. *Nedarim* 81:1.
29. Rabbi Samson Raphael Hirsh, *Horeb* (Vilna: Ram Press, 1882), and *Introduction to Education* (Bene-Berak: Netzach, 1968).
30. Deuteronomy 4:15.
31. *Kitzur Shulchan Arukh*, sec. 22.

CHAPTER 12

1. *Alei Shor* (Beer Yaakov: Otzar Hasefarim, 1965), p. 263.
2. Psalms 8:3.
3. Deuteronomy 31:12.
4. Deuteronomy 31:13.
5. Deuteronomy 31:13, *Or ha-Chayyim.*
6. Rabbi Samson Raphael Hirsch, *Yesodot ha-Chinnukh* [The Foundations of education] (Bene-Berak: Netzach, 1968), p. 64.
7. *Niddah* 30; *Midrash Tanhumei Pekudei.*
8. Berlyne, 1966, in David P. Ausubel and Edmund V. Sullivan, *Theory and Problems of Child Development* (New York: Grune and Stratton, 1971), p. 551.
9. Ausubel and Sullivan, p. 551.
10. Rabbenu Bachya ibn Paquda, *Duties of the Heart* (Jerusalem: Boys Town, 1965), p. 159.
11. Ibid., pp. 153–155.

12. Ibid.
13. *Avot* 5; Eliezer Ebner, *Elementary Education in Ancient Israel* (New York: Bloch, 1956), p. 69.
14. *Alei Shor,* p. 263.
15. *Chazon Ish* 59:3 in the name of *Tosefot Arukh ha-Shulchan,* 328:20.
16. Ausubel and Sullivan, p. 552.
17. *Ketubbot* 111.
18. *Yalkut Shimoni,* Leviticus 19:23-24.
19. Rashi on *Avot* 5:21.
20. *Kitzur Shulchan Arukh* 165;10.
21. *Sifri,* Ekev (Rashi commentary on the passage "And you shall teach them to your sons"—Deut. 11:19).
22. Rambam, *Hilkhot Talmud Torah,* Chap. 1; *Kitzur Shulchan Arukh* 165:10.
23. *Sanhedrin* 38.
24. Proverbs 22:10.
25. *Sefer Hamusar,* chap. 7.
26. *Sukkah* 42a; *Arachin* 2b; Tosafot, *Chagigah* 1:3; Mishnah, *Megillah* 4:6.
27. Hirsch, *Yesodot ha-Chinnukh,* p. 64.
28. *Bava Batra* 21a, *Ketubbot* 50a.
29. *Ketubbot* 50a.
30. Ibid.
31. *Kiddushin* 29a.
32. Bachya ibn Paquda, *Duties of the Heart,* chap. 5.
33. *Avot* 6; *Eruvin* 53a, 59b; *Ta'anit* 7a; Proverbs 3:18; *Megillah* 32a; *Kitzur Shulchan Arukh,* Appendix.
34. Psalms 179:71-72.
35. Psalms 110:10.
36. *Avot* 3:21.
37. *Sanhedrin* 92, Isaiah 27:11.
38. *Kiddushin* 30a, Meiri.
39. *Alei Shor,* p. 363.

CHAPTER 13

1. *Sukkah* 21.
2. Philippe Aries, *Centuries of Childhood,* trans. R. Baldick (New York: Knopf, 1962); Lloyd DeMause, *The History of Childhood* (New York: Psychohistory Press, 1974).
3. Selma H. Fraiberg, *The Magic Years* (New York: Scribner's, 1959), p. ix.
4. David P. Ausubel and Edmund V. Sullivan, *Theory and Problems of*

Child Development (New York: Grune & Stratton, 1970), p. 419. "One of the earliest features of affective development is the differentiation of specific emotions out of the state of general excitement that limits emotional reactivity at birth. This development occurs, roughly speaking, between the second half of the first year and the third year."

5. *Leviticus Rabbah* B.
6. *Kitzur Shulchan Arukh* 165a.
7. Rambam, *Eight Chapters,* chap. 4.
8. Ibid.
9. "The straight path is the mean disposition found in each and every tendency of the human tendencies.... Therefore have the wise men of yore commanded that man should ever review his tendencies [*Sotah* 5bc], estimate them, and direct them toward the middle path so that he will be sound in body." Rambam, *Treatise on Ethics,* chap. 1.
10. Ausubel and Sullivan, p. 419.
11. Ibid., pp. 421-422.
12. Proverbs 12:25.
13. Ralbag, commentary on Proverbs 12:15. Maimonides, *The Preservation of Youth: Essays on Health,* trans. Hirsch L. Gordon (New York: Philosophical Library, 1958), pp. 66-67. Moses Chaim Luzzatto, *The Path of the Just,* trans. Shraga Silverstein (Jerusalem: Boys Town, 1966), p. 99.
14. Psalms 37:3.
15. *Orchot Tzaddikim* (Warsaw: Isaac Breisblat), p. 37.
16. Erik H. Erikson, *Childhood and Society,* 2d ed. (New York: Norton, 1963).
17. *Reishit Chokhmah,* chap. on child-rearing; *Berakhot* 17.
18. Bachya ibn Paquda, *Duties of the Heart* (Jerusalem: Boys Town, 1965), p. 295.
19. Chazon Ish, *On Faith, Trust,* etc. (Jerusalem: Hamesorah, 1954), pp. 17-18.
20. Ausubel and Sullivan, p. 426.
21. Fraiberg, p. 11.
22. Proverbs 13:1, quoted in *Reishit Chokhmah,* chapter on child-rearing.
23. *Kitzur Shulchan Arukh* 165:7.
24. Ausubel and Sullivan, pp. 438-439.
25. *Gittin* 6b.
26. *Shabbat* 34a.
27. *Alei Shor* (Beer Yaakov, 1965), p. 261.
28. *Shabbat* 105.
29. *Bava Batra* 21a.
30. Rambam, *Hilkhot Talmud Torah,* chap. 2.
31. *Even Shelomoh* 6:4.
32. Leviticus 19:14.
33. Leviticus 19:17.

34. *Kitzur Shulchan Arukh* 29:13.
35. Ausubel and Sullivan, p. 441.
36. *Shabbat* 10.
37. Ausubel and Sullivan, p. 443.
38. Genesis 5:12.
39. *Avot* 4:12.
40. *Avot* 2.
41. *Mesillat Yesharim,* chap. 11.
42. Leviticus 19:18.
43. *Bava Metzia* 38 (Rashi).
44. *Kitzur Shulchan Arukh* 29:17.
45. Ibid.
46. Deuteronomy 10:12. "And so, Israel, what does God require of you, but to revere Him and to walk in his way?"
47. *Shabbat* 133b.
48. *Sukkah* 56.
49. Ausubel and Sullivan, p. 446.
50. *Sotah* 47a.
51. Ausubel and Sullivan, pp. 445, 449.
52. Deuteronomy 16:15.
53. Psalms 100:2.
54. *Kitzur Shulchan Arukh* 29:6.
55. Proverbs 15:13 ("A happy heart is reflected in the countenance").
56. Ecclesiastes 2:26.
57. Psalms 105:3, I Chronicles 16:10.

CHAPTER 14

1. Proverbs 22:6.
2. *Shabbat* 156a, Hagra, Proverbs 22:6.
3. Rambam, *Eight Chapters,* chap. 8.
4. Rambam, *Hilkhot De'ot* 1:2.
5. Gordon W. Allport, "Personality—Contemporary Viewpoints," in David E. Sills (ed.), *International Encyclopedia of the Social Sciences* (New York: Crowell, Collier and Macmillan, 1968).
6. Bachya ibn Paquda, *Duties of the Heart* (Jerusalem: Boys Town, 1965), 1:195.
7. Meiri, *Chibbur ha-Teshuvah* 43:11.
8. A. Thomas, S. Chess, and H. G. Birch, "The Origin of Personality," *Scientific American* 223 (1970): 102–109.
9. Rambam, *Hilkhot De'ot,* chap. 1.
10. Joel Schwartz, *Beit Abba* (Jerusalem: Yeshivat Dvar Yerushalayim, 1979), p. 89.

11. Genesis 49:4-27.
12. Deuteronomy 33:6-27.
13. Deuteronomy 33:4.
14. Rambam, *Mishneh Torah—Yad ha-Chazakah,* trans. Simon Glazer (New York: Maimonides Translation Publishers, 1927), vol. I, bk. I, p. 217.
15. Rabbi Samson Raphael Hirsch, *Yesodot ha-Chinnukh* [Principles of education] (Bnei-Berak: Netzach, 1968), p. 83.
16. Rambam, *Mishneh Torah,* pp. 410-411.
17. Ibid.
18. Ibid., p. 181-183.
19. Rabbi Moses Chaim Luzzatto, *The Path of the Just,* trans. Shraga Silverstein (Jerusalem: Boys Town, 1966), p. 153.
20. *Orchot Tzaddikim,* p. 76.
21. Deuteronomy 30:19.
22. *Kitzur Shulchan Arukh* 29:30.
23. Genesis 8:21, 4:7.
24. *Yoma* 82a; *Ketubbot* 50a (Rashi); *Niddah* 45a, 46a.
25. *Numbers Rabbah* 21.
26. Hirsch, p. 85.
27. Proverbs 22:6.
28. Hirsch, pp. 65-66.

CHAPTER 15

1. *Shekalim* 3.
2. *Avot* 2.
3. II Chronicles 19:10.
4. *Yoma* 82a, *Niddah* 45b, *Ketubbot* 50a (Rashi), *Avot* 5:21, *Sukkah* 82.
5. *Sukkah* 2.
6. *Mishnah Berurah* 323:3, *Shabbat* 121a.
7. Jerusalem Talmud, *Nedarim* 89:4; *Genesis Rabbah* 24.
8. *Sukkah* 21.
9. *Pesachim* 49; *Ketubbot* 111; Rambam, *Hilkhot De'ot* 6:1.
10. Rambam, *Hilkhot De'ot* 6:1.
11. Meiri, *Bava Kamma* 92.
12. *Ketubbot* 17.
13. *Genesis Rabbah* 48.
14. *Shabbat* 10.
15. Rambam, *Nahalot* 6:11.
16. *Reishit Chokhmah,* chap. on child-rearing; Deuteronomy 21:15-17.
17. Leviticus 19:18.
18. Proverbs 22:10.
19. *Sanhedrin* 37-38.

20. *Shulchan Arukh* 143:20.
21. *Yoma* 78b.
22. *Shabbat* 104a.
23. *Lamentations Rabbah* 1, *Niddah* 31b, *Numbers Rabbah* 22, *Shabbat* 77b, *Ecclesiastes Rabbah* 12:11, Jerusalem Talmud, *Sanhedrin* 10.
24. *Pesachim* 117a, *Ta'anit*.
25. *Sanhedrin* 87.
26. Jerusalem Talmud, *Megillah* 81; *Genesis Rabbah* 1:15.
27. *Sanhedrin* 64b.
28. A comprehensive guideline appears in Joshua Neubirt, *Shemirat Shabbat ke-Hilkhato* (Jerusalem: Neubirt, 1979), chap. 15.

CHAPTER 16

1. Genesis 18:10.
2. *Yevamot* 62b.
3. *Kiddushin* 29a.
4. *Shabbat* 65a.
5. *Kitzur Shulchan Arukh* 165:1.
6. Proverbs 1:8, 30:1.
7. *Ketubbot* 65b.
8. *Ketubbot* 49.
9. Rambam, *Hilkhot Ishut* 12:14.
10. *Shulchan Arukh, Even ha-Ezer,* 71:1.
11. *Yoreh De'ah* 251:4, *Bava Batra* 174.
12. Rambam, *Hilkhot De'ot* 5:10.
13. Proverbs 13:24.
14. *Bava Metzia* 85a, *Avot* 2:5.
15. *Kiddushin* 29a.
16. *Ketubbot* 49.
17. Deuteronomy 20:1–12, *Kiddushin* 30b.
18. Exodus 20:12, Leviticus 19:3, *Kiddushin* 31a.
19. *Kitzur Shulchan Arukh* 143:3.
20. Ibid. 6.
21. Ibid. 9.
22. Ibid. 11.
23. *Kiddushin* 31a, *Pesachim* 113a, *Bava Batra* 58a.
24. *Kitzur Shulchan Arukh* 143:17.
25. *Sefer Chasidim*, p. 37, sec. 565.
26. *Kiddushin* 32a.
27. *Sanhedrin* 105b, 82a.
28. *Gittin* 6b.
29. *Kitzur Shulchan Arukh* 143:19.

Notes

30. *Mo'ed Katan* 17a.
31. Proverbs 23:13–14, 13:24; *Makkot* 22.
32. *Tanchuma*, Exodus 1; *Exodus Rabbah* 1:1.
33. Tosefta, *Bava Kamma* 9:8–11; Tosefta, *Makkot* 2:5; *Makkot* 8a; *Bava Kamma* 6:17.
34. *Sefer Chasidim*, sec. 565, p. 372.
35. *Semachot* 2:6.
36. *Sukkah* 46a.
37. *Sukkah* 56.
38. *Yevamot* 63 (Rashi).
39. *Kiddushin* 29a–30b.
40. *Ketubbot* 50.
41. *Kitzur Shulchan Arukh* 143:21.
42. Ibid.
43. *Zohar* I, 227b.
44. *Kiddushin* 31b.
45. Deuteronomy 21:18–21 (In the case of the rebellious child, if there is no harmony between parents, as in the case of a broken home or an unstable relationship between the parents, the child is not liable for his defiance.)
46. Other examples of Jewish rituals performed in the family framework are preparations for the *sukkah*, baking challah, symbolic foods eaten on holidays, such as the honey, apple, and pomegranate served before the meal on Rosh Hashanah and the special Seder plate prepared to arouse the curiosity of the children, decorating the home with leaves for Shavuot, daughters lighting Sabbath candles from the tender age of the preschool period, and the five-year-old son eating and sleeping in the *sukkah*.
47. Malachi 3:24.
48. The historic figures mentioned are associated with piety and meritorious deeds.

CHAPTER 17

1. Genesis 40:20.
2. Y. D. Eisenstadt, *Otzar Yisrael*, vol. III, p. 112.
3. *Genesis Rabbah* 48:12; Tosafot, *Rosh Hashanah* 11; *Tanchuma*, Bo 9; *Yevamot* 72a; *Midrash Rabbah*, Pikudei 52b.
4. *Rosh Hashanah* 1–11a.
5. *Megillah* 13b, *Ta'anit* 2.
6. *Shulchan Arukh, Orach Chayyim* 409:90 (Rema); *Chagigah* 17a.
7. *Sha'arei Teshuvah* 494:7.
8. *Pesachim* 77a.
9. *Yevamot* 124, *Yoma* 86a.
10. *Yoma* 86a.

11. Rabbi E. F. Weinberger, *Yad Ephraim* (Tel Aviv: Public Committee for Publication of the Works of Rabbi Weinberger, 1976), p. 206.
12. *Sanhedrin* 113b.
13. Weinberger, p. 206.
14. *Avot* 5:25 (Rashi).
15. Ibid. Eisenstein, vol.III, p. 169.
16. *Bava Kamma* 87.
17. *Shabbat* 118.
18. *Bava Kamma* 67, 14; *Nazir* 29; Rema, *Orach Chayyim* 225.
19. *Nazir* 29.
20. Eisenstein, vol. III, 169.
21. Weinberger, pp. 202–207.
22. *Responsa Beit Yisrael* 32.
23. *Teshuvot Havot Yair* 70.
24. *Ginzei Yosef* 4 in name of Rav Yishrei Lev.
25. *Beit Yisrael* 32.
26. *Midrash Sekhel Tov* (Genesis 1–49).
27. *Ginzei Yosef* 4.

CHAPTER 18

1. Deuteronomy 6:6–7.
2. Genesis 18:19.
3. *Kitzur Shulchan Arukh* 165a.
4. Deuteronomy 11:19.
5. *Kiddushin* 29, *Kitzur Shulchan Arukh* 165.
6. Rambam, *Hilkhot Talmud Torah*.
7. *Kitzur Shulchan Arukh* 165:10.
8. Exodus 13:8.
9. Deuteronomy 4:9–10.
10. Proverbs 22:6.
11. *Kitzur Shulchan Arukh* 165:3, 5, 8.
12. Exodus 2:7.
13. Proverbs 1:8.
14. *Kiddushin* 29.
15. Ibid.
16. *Pesachim* 113a, *Magen Avraham* 156, *Kiddushin* 82a.
17. *Shabbat* 150a.
18. *Mekhilta,* Bo 124; *Kiddushin* 29 (Rif and Rosh); Rambam, *Hilkhot Rotze'ach* 5:5.
19. *Avot* 1:13.
20. *Sukkah* 83; *Sifrei,* Ekev 19. Based on the words "to speak of them" we learn that as soon as a child begins to speak his father must teach him Hebrew

through the verses of the Torah. Also, the words "to speak of them" are the biblical source which Rambam quotes to point out that learning the Hebrew language is a *mitzvah* (Commentary on the Mishnah, *Avot* 2a).

21. Exodus 28:3, 31:3-5.
22. Psalms 83:1-4, 150:3, 147:7.
23. Deuteronomy 4:15.
24. *Kiddushin* 29.
25. Proverbs 1:8.
26. *Chagigah* 2a (Rashi).
27. Rabbi, in Tosefta, *Chullin* 28a.
28. *Kiddushin* 29; *Responsa Beit Halevi* 1:6; Rambam, *Hilkhot Talmud Torah*, chap. 1.
29. *Megillah* 19; *Berakhot* 17a; *Midrash Rabbah*, Yitro 28b; *Chatam Sofer*, in *Torat Mosheh*, Nitzvim.
30. *Kiddushin* 31a, *Kitzur Shulchan Arukh* 165.
31. *Berakhot* 17.
32. Deuteronomy 32:7.
33. Rambam, *Hilkhot Talmud Torah* 1:3.
34. Ibid.
35. Burton L. White, *The First Three Years of Life* (New York: Avon, 1978).
36. *Avot de-Rabbi Nathan* 24.
37. *Avot* 4.
38. *Ta'anit* 9; Rambam, *Hilkhot Talmud Torah*, chap. 1; *Kitzur Shulchan Arukh* 165.
39. *Sukkah* 42.
40. *Eruvin* 82, *Berakhot* 17a, *Sotah* 21a.
41. Rabbi Yoel Schwartz, *Beit Abba* (Jerusalem: Yeshivat Dvar Yerushalayim, 1979), p. 15.
42. *Ketubbot* 5:5, Proverbs 31:10-31, *Yoma* 66b.
43. *Sotah* 20a.
44. Rambam, *Hilkhot Talmud Torah* 1:13.
45. Mishnah, *Sotah* 3:4; *Sotah* 20a.
46. Mishnah, *Nedarim* 3:4.
47. Rambam, *Hilkhot Talmud Torah* 1:13.
48. Rabbi Schneerson, Circular concerning lighting the Sabbath candles.
49. *Sukkah* 42a, *Orach Chayyim* 640b.
50. Rambam, *Hilkhot Chametz u-Matzah*, chap. 6.
51. Rambam, *Hilkhot Talmud Torah* 1:6.
52. Ibid., 1:3.
53. *Kiddushin* 19:17, *Yalkut Shimoni*.
54. *Nedarim* 32a; *Tanchuma*, *Kiddushin* 14; *Vayera* 22.
55. Rashi commentary on *Avot* 5:21.
56. *Kav ha-Yashar*, chap. 72.

57. Rambam, *Hilkhot Talmud Torah* 1:13.
58. Jerusalem Talmud, *Ketubbot* 8.
59. *Bava Batra* 21a.
60. Ibid., *Ketubbot* 50a.
61. *Bava Batra* 21a.
62. *Berakhot* 17a; Jerusalem Talmud, *Kiddushin* 4:2.
63. Jerusalem Talmud, *Challah* 1a.
64. *Shabbat* 104a.
65. *Bava Batra* 21a.
66. Dr. Nathan Morris, *A History of Jewish Education*, vol. 1 (Tel Aviv: Omanuth, 1960), p. 144.
67. *Avot* 5, *Ketubbot* 50a.
68. Morris, p. 143.
69. *Leviticus Rabbah* 7:3, *Gittin* 60a.
70. *Shabbat* 16a; Tosefta, *Megillah* 2:3.
71. Mishnah, *Megillah* 1:8, 2:8; *Sotah* 7:1; *Megillah* 17b.
72. *Sifrei* 161b.
73. *Mishnah Berurah* 3:3.
74. Morris, vol. 1, chap. 1:2.
75. *Genesis Rabbah* 63:14.
76. *Megillah* 19; Rambam, *Hilkhot Talmud Torah*.
77. *Kiddushin* 31 (Meiri).
78. *Kiddushin* 30a.
79. *Seridei Esh*, 3:95.
80. Joshua Neubirt, *Shemirat Shabbat ke-Hilkhato* (Jerusalem: Feldheim, 1965).
81. *Yoma* 82a, *Magen Avraham* 343a.
82. *Midrash Chazal* on the revelation at Mount Sinai.
83. *Avot* 5.
84. Ibid.
85. *Pesachim* 3b, *Chullin* 63b, *Sifrei* 1:3.
86. *Bava Batra* 21a.
87. *Ta'anit* 7a.
88. Ibid.
89. *Avot* 4:12.
90. *Mesillat Yesharim*, chap. 11.
91. *Pesachim* 117a.
92. *Ta'anit* 24a.
93. *Pesachim* 50b, *Eruvin* 10.
94. *Eruvin* 54b.
95. *Avot* 6.
96. Rabbi Samson Raphael Hirsch, *Yesodot ha-Chinnukh*, pt. II.
97. Schwartz, p. 61.
98. *Alei Shor*, p. 16:161.

Notes

99. Schwartz, p. 61.
100. *Eruvin* 54b.
101. *Shulchan Arukh, Yoreh De'ah* 246:10.
102. *Kiddushin* 17a.
103. *Leviticus Rabbah* 19, *Deuteronomy Rabbah* 8.
104. *Avodah Zarah* 19a.
105. *Chagigah* 15 a–b, *Gittin* 56a, *Ta'anit* 9a, *Ketubbot* 8b, *Eruvin* 53b, *Chullin* 9b, *Gittin* 58a, Jerusalem Talmud, *Horayot* 83.
106. *Esther Rabbah* 7:9.
107. *Ketubbot* 50a.
108. *Makkot* 8.
109. *Ketubbot* 50a (Rashi).
110. *Bava Batra* 21a.
111. Rambam, *Hilkhot Talmud Torah* 2.
112. Based on the decree, "You shall not place a stumbling-block before the blind" (Lev. 19:14).
113. *Sukkah* 29a, *Ta'anit* 7:8.
114. *Sotah* 47, *Sanhedrin* 107.
115. *Shabbat* 119b.
116. *Sanhedrin* 17b.
117. *Shabbat* 119b.
118. *Numbers Rabbah,* Numbers 3:1. Children are symbolically conceived as the flowers of the golden candlestick in the Sanctuary (*Pes. R.* 29b).
119. *Bava Batra* 8b.
120. *Leviticus Rabbah* 30b.
121. *Avodah Zarah* 3.
122. *Sanhedrin* 17, *Shabbat* 119b.
123. Jerusalem Talmud, *Chagigah* 1:7; *Pesikta Lamentations Rabbah* 2; *Midrash Psalms* 127.
124. *Sanhedrin* 19b.
125. *Shulchan Arukh, Yoreh De'ah* 245:17.
126. *Yoma* 72b.
127. *Moed Katan* 17a.
128. *Avot* 2:5.
129. *Eruvin* 54b.
130. Rambam, *Hilkhot Talmud Torah* 2:3.
131. *Bava Batra* 21b, 22a.
132. *Ta'anit* 7b–8a.
133. Rambam, *Hilkhot Talmud Torah* 5; *Kitzur Shulchan Arukh* 165:13.
134. *Shabbat* 114a.
135. *Kitzur Shulchan Arukh,* 165:12.
136. Ibid. 11, Rambam, *Hilkhot Talmud Torah* 2.
137. *Kitzur Shulchan Arukh* 165:14.
138. Rambam, *Hilkhot Talmud Torah* 2:5.

139. *Bava Batra* 71b, 22a.
140. Ibid. 21a.
141. *Nedarim* 81a.
142. *Avot de-Rabbi Nathan* 3.
143. *Shulchan Arukh, Yoreh De'ah* 245:9.
144. *Exodus Rabbah* 5.
145. *Avot* 2:6.
146. *Avot* 1:13.
147. Rambam, *Hilkhot Talmud Torah* 1; *Shulchan Arukh, Yoreh De'ah* 246:1.
148. *Avot* 5:26.
149. *Sanhedrin* 17b.
150. *Kitzur Shulchan Arukh* 144:1.

CHAPTER 19

1. *Yoma* 82a; *Niddah* 45b, 46a; *Ketubbot* 50a.
2. *Sanhedrin* 37a.
3. *Oholot* 6:7, Sanhedrin 72.
4. *Shabbat* 128b, *Yevamot* 80b.
5. Rabbi S. Y. Zevin, *Talmudic Encyclopedia* (Jerusalem: Talmudic Encyclopedia Publishing Ltd., 1973), Mishnah *Yevamot* 22a, vol. III, p. 346.
6. Genesis 48:8; *Pirkei de-Rabbi Eliezer,* chap. 36; *Ketubbot* 72b (Rashi).
7. Deuteronomy 11:19, Exodus 34:2, *Kiddushin* 29a.
8. *Yevamot* 49, 23 (excluding the son of a divorced *kohen,* who is co˙sidered *chalal*—unfit for the priesthood, but not illegitimate).
9. Deuteronomy 23:3.
10. *Yevamot* 80.
11. J. D. Eisenstein, *Otzar Yisrael* (Jerusalem), vol. 3, p. 231.
12. *Yevamot* 47, *Kiddushin* 78, *Bava Batra* 127.
13. *Sotah* 27.
14. *Mishpetei Shemuel siman* 109.
15. *Yevamot* 69.
16. Eisenstein, vol. 3, p. 232.
17. Ibid., p. 232.
18. *Kiddushin* 69.
19. Eisenstein, p. 232, vol. 3.
20. *Kiddushin,* 73.
21. Exodus 13:2.
22. Genesis 31.
23. *Kiddushin* 74, *Shulchan Arukh* 277:12.
24. *Yevamot* 15.
25. Numbers 3:12 (Rashi).

26. Exodus 13:11–13. If the firstborn participates in a feast celebrating the completion of learning a tractate in Talmud on the eve of Passover, he need not fast.
27. *Kiddushin* 29–31.
28. Rabbenu Aharon Halevi, *Sefer ha-Chinnukh*, sec. 234.
29. This is based on the rule that he who wishes to exact money from his neighbor must prove that the debt exists, so that the *kohen* must prove his case, which cannot be done in case of doubt.
30. *Shulchan Arukh, Choshen Mishpat* 277; *Bava Batra* 142b.
31. *Bava Batra* 142b.
32. *Bechorot* 88:9.
33. Deuteronomy 25:31, 21:15–17.
34. Deuteronomy 21:16.
35. Raba on Genesis 25:31, Job. 1:13.
36. *Kitzur Shulchan Arukh* 143:20.
37. Genesis 18:19; Deuteronomy 6:7, 11:19; Proverbs 2:1, 31:1.
38. *Kiddushin* 30.
39. *Ketubbot* 49a.
40. Rambam, *Hilkhot Ishut* 12; *Shulchan Arukh* 71.
41. *Ketubbot* 49.
42. *Kiddushin* 30.
43. *Responsa Rosh* 8:4.
44. Exodus 21:7; Rambam, *Avadim* 4, 2:5.
45. George Henry Payne, *The Child in Human Progress* (New York and London: G. P. Putnam's Sons, 1916).
46. Proverbs 13:24.
47. Proverbs 22:10.
48. *Bava Batra* 21; Rambam, *Hilkhot Talmud Torah*.
49. Tosefta, *Bava Kamma* 11, 9:8; *Semachot* 5, 2:4; *Kitzur Shulchan Arukh* 165:7.
50. *Makkot* 2:5, *Bava Kamma* 6:17, *Makkot* 8a.
51. *Shabbat* 10.
52. Deuteronomy 21:15–16.
53. *Bava Metzia* 12, *Responsa Maharil* 192, *Shulchan Arukh, Choshen Mishpat* 149.
54. *Gittin* 59a, 65a.
55. *Gittin* 59.
56. *Niddah* 45b, *Yoma* 82a, *Ketubbot* 50a.
57. *Avot* 5:21; *Kitzur Shulchan Arukh* 165:3–5.
58. *Pesachim Rabbah* 174a.
59. *Chagigah* 1:2, *Sukkah* 42.
60. *Shabbat* 121a, *Kitzur Shulchan Arukh* 133:19, *Yoma* 78b, 82a.
61. *Shabbat* 89.
62. *Shabbat* 89b, *Sanhedrin* 84, *Mekhilta, Sanhedrin* 52.

63. Exodus 34:7.
64. Deuteronomy 24:15, II Kings 14:5-6.
65. *Makkot* 24a.
66. *Mishnah Berurah* 343:3, 4, 7; *Kitzur Shulchan Arukh* 165:3.
67. *Kitzur Shulchan Arukh* 165:6.
68. *Sanhedrin* 52b.
69. *Gittin* 59. In order to deal in his father's property or property inherited from his father, he must reach the age of twenty (*Bava Batra* 155).
70. *Yevamot* 96, 102.
71. *Kiddushin* 41, 62. For examples in the Bible: Exodus 2:21, Genesis 29, Joshua 16:16, I Samuel 17:25.
72. *Kiddushin* 41.
73. *Ketubbot* 43.
74. *Yevamot* 13a; *Arukh ha-Shulchan* 155.
75. Jeremiah 19.
76. *Oholot* 6:7.
77. *Beit Yosef* to *Tur, Shulchan Arukh, Choshen Mishpat* 290:6; Rema to *Shulchan Arukh, Choshen Mishpat* 285:8; *Gittin* 52b.
78. *Ketubbot* 50.
79. Exodus 2:10.
80. Esther 2:7, 15.
81. Psalms 68:6.
82. Exodus 22:21-23.
83. Rambam, *Hilkhot De'ot* 6:10 (biblical quotes—Exodus 22:21-23, Proverbs 22:23, 6:10).
84. *Shulchan Arukh*, 29:29.
85. Rambam, *Hilkhot De'ot* 6:10.
86. *Gittin* 37a; *Shulchan Arukh, Choshen Mishpat* 290:1-2; *Responsa Rosh* 85:6, 87:1.
87. *Sanhedrin* 19b, *Megillah* 13a.
88. *Bava Batra* 8.
89. *Ketubbot* 67a.
90. *Ketubbot* 67.
91. Ibid.
92. Rambam, *Hilkhot De'ot* 6:10, *Responsa Terumat ha-Deshen* 62.
93. *Shulchan Arukh, Choshen Mishpat* 60:4.
94. Exodus 45, *Midrash Rabbah* 2. Other exemplary stories concerning the *mitzvah* of caring for orphans may be found in *Ta'anit* 24a, *Leviticus Rabbah* 37, *Berakhot* 18b. The Judaic view concerning adoption of gentiles is reviewed in *Responsa Minchat Yitzchak* 3:99. The general view opposes adoption of gentile children intentionally, but after the fact the children are to undergo the process of *giyur* and are accepted as any Jewish child in the community.
95. *Kiddushin* 82a.
96. *Avot* 5:25.

97. *Responsa Rosh* 47.
98. *Kiddushin* 16b, *Niddah* 52a.
99. *Genesis Rabbah* 63:10.
100. *Hilkhot Teshuvah,* chap. 1 (Rambam).
101. *Shabbat* 89a.
102. *Shabbat* 89b.
103. Eisenstein, vol. II, p. 169.
104. Rambam, *Mekach Umimkar,* chap. 29; *Bava Batra* 155.
105. Eisenstein, p. 170; *Gittin* 65.
106. Ibid.
107. *Gittin* 65.
108. *Sukkah* 42; Rema, *Orach Chayyim* 37.
109. *Ketubbot* 39a.
110. *Niddah* 46a, *Yevamot* 107, 108a.
111. *Niddah* 47a.
112. *Kiddushin* 41a.
113. *Niddah* 45b. By the age of eleven years and one day, a girl is examined to verify whether she understands the motives for her vows.
114. *Ketubbot* 39. The Code of Jewish Law stipulates specific physical examinations of the girl's breasts by a trustworthy woman to determine the child's maturity (*Arukh ha-Shulchan* 155:15).
115. *Gittin* 65a.
116. U.N. General Assembly, Res. 1386, xiv, Nov. 20, 1959.
117. P. Aries, *Centuries of Childhood,* trans. R. Baldick (New York: Knopf, 1962).

Index

Aaron, 165
Abandoned children, 260
Abbahu, R., 33, 41
Abba Saul, R., 33
Abbaye, R., 72, 83
Abel, 209
Abortion, 28–29, 35, 251
Abraham, 7, 42, 50, 76, 94, 165
Abraham Mordecai of Gur, R., 142
Absalom, 132
Adam, 18
Adolescence, 177
Adonijah, 132, 209
Affection, parental, 188–189
Affective development. *See* Emotional development
Aggression, 183–185
Aha, R., 179
Akiva, R., 187, 207
Allport, Gordon P., 193
Anger, 183–185
Anxiety, 182–183
Aphrodisiacs, 21–22
Art, 229
Artificial insemination, 22
Asthma, 148
Asube yanuke, 75

Babysitters, 89
Bachya bar Joseph ibn Paquda, 14–15, 17–18, 23, 171, 172, 182
Baer, Karl Ernst von, 31
Bar Abba, 43
Bar/Bat Mitzvah, 177, 200, 203, 216, 223–224, 265–266
Bastardy. *See* Legitimacy
Bathing, 22, 72–73, 167
Bathsheba, 25
Behavioral development, 105–106

Bekhor shanan, 254
Bekhor shoteh, 254
Ben Azzai, 207, 231
Benjamin, 39, 195
Ben Sira, 133, 134
Berit Milah
  ceremony and procedure, 45–51
  as father's responsibility, 45, 50
  of illegitimate son, 253
  of incubator baby, 52
  medical aspects, 46, 50, 51–54, 147, 165
  mohel's role, 45, 48, 49, 50
  naming of boy at, 63–64
  performed by woman, 45
  religious aspects, 43–44, 54, 162
Betrothal, 260
Bezalel, 229
Bible 1, 8, 14, 236. *See also* Torah
Birkat ha-Gomel, 60
Birthday celebrations, 222–223, 224–225
Birth stool, 38
Blindness, 75, 149
Blood transfusions, 52
"Bloody show," 37, 38
Bogeret, 266
Bowlby, J., 146
Boys. *See* Male children
Breast-feeding, 28, 71, 77–78, 81–82, 93–94
Breech presentation, 37
Butter, 95

Caesarean section, 37, 53, 59, 252
Cain, 209
Cannibalism, 12
Chalitzah, 11, 21
Chanina, R., 73

307

Chanukah, 124, 212, 220
Chazon Ish, 182
Chewing properly, 144
Child abuse, 12, 256–257
Childbirth
   blessing of thanks after, 60
   breech presentation, 37
   Caesarean section, 37, 53, 59, 252
   contractions and labor, 35–37
   death during, 36
   father's prsence during, 41
   fetus' status during, 252
   forceps delivery, 53
   Lamaze method, 37
   Leboyer method, 39, 41
   nonviolent, 39, 40–41
   religious aspects, 35
   on Sabbath, 38, 252
   woman's status after, 38–39
   woman's status during, 38
   see also midwives
Child development, 1–2, 16–18, 107
   process of, 159
   stages of, 16–18, 107–110
   study of, 14–15
Childhood, conceptions of, 7–8, 12, 14
Childhood diseases, 141, 147–150
Child-rearing, Jewish, 1, 2, 7, 9, 19, 104, 159–160
Children's rights, 251–260
   to education and support, 256
   against abuse, 256–257
   to own property, 257
   to religious observances, 258
Children's toothpaste, 75
Chinnukh. See Education
Chisda, R., 96, 216
Chromosomes, 27, 32, 164
Circumcision. See Berit Milah
Clothing, 74
Cognition, in Jewish thought, 171–172

Cognitive development, 159, 169
   stages of, 172–178
   parental role, 170, 173, 174, 175, 176, 177
Cohn, Tobias Ben Moses, 149
Colds, 14
Concrete operations, period of, 16, 176
Conscience, development, 182. See also Moral development
Contraception, 30, 78
Corporal punishment, 135–136, 183, 184, 217, 244–245, 257. See also Discipline
Coughing spells, 148
Cradle cap, 152
Cribs, 76
Cuddling and fondling, 77

Dampness, and health, 74
Dan, 195
Dark, fear of, 152
Daughters, drowning of, 12
David, King, 12, 132, 154
Deaf-mutes, 150
Deafness, 149
Demons, 46
Derech eretz, 125
Development play, 72, 83, 210–212
Deviant behavior, 114. See also Juvenile delinquent
Dewey, John, 193
Diaper rash, 87, 152
Diapers, 88
Diarrhea, 148, 152
Diet and nutrition, 72, 93, 95–98, 143–145
   and disease, 148
   foods to avoid, 101–102
   and impotence, 22
   of nursing mother, 81–82
   during pregnancy, 27–28

Index

Diptheria, 148
Discipline, 13, 111, 127, 131–140, 147, 182, 184, 189, 214, 216–217, 244–245, 257
Divorcees, 22, 26, 28
Dogs, 25
Duda'im 21

Early childhood education. *See* Education
Education, 112, 169, 226–227, 234
    early childhood, 117–130, 175, 230–231, 232
    methods and motivational techniques, 127, 239–244
    parental role, 13–14, 125, 129
    and personality development. *See* Personality development
    religious aspects, 118, 119, 120, 121, 122–125, 126, 206, 233–234, 236
    See also Schools; Teachers
Eggs, 95, 96
Eli, 132
Eliezer, R., 32, 71, 94, 186, 211, 218, 231
Elijah's chair, 47
Elkanah, 79
Embarrassing someone, 187–188
Embryo, 31–33, 35. *See also* Fetus
Emotional development, 159, 179–190
Environment, 159, 166–168, 180, 195, 196
Epilepsy, 149
Erikson, Erik, 1, 173, 181, 203
Eruv, 89, 152, 237
Esau, 209
Ethrog, 28
Eve, 35
Even tekoma, 25
Evil spirits, 73

Exercise, 76, 145, 167
Eyes, 75, 149
    secretions from, 52

Faith, 182
Fear, 147, 181
Family, Jewish, 9, 11, 21, 125. *See also* Parental obligations; Parent-child relations
Fasting
    by child, 125, 258
    by minor boy, 100
    by minor girl, 239
    during pregnancy, 24–25
    during parturition, 28–29
    by nursing mother, 38–39, 81
Fathers, obligations of
    circumcision, 45. See also *Berit Milah*
    redeeming firstborn, 56, 59. See also *Pidyon ha-Ben*
    supporting family, 142, 176
    as teacher, 118, 120, 123, 126, 227–228
Feeding schedules, 79
Feinstein, Moses, 94, 136, 138
Female children
    birth of, 42, 60–61
    education of, 120, 228, 231–232, 238–239
    naming of, 63–64
    responsibility for *mitzvot*, 104
Fetus, 11, 17, 151
    development of, 26, 28, 31, 108
    sex of, 26–27
    status in Jewish law, 35, 251
Filial obligations, 214–215, 216, 252
Firstborn son, 54–55, 59
    redemption of, 213. See also *Pidyon ha-Ben*
    rights of, 254–255
Fish. *See* Meat and fish

Food preparation on Sabbath, 87
Food storage, 97, 145
Forbidden foods, during pregnancy, 24
Forceps delivery, 53
Foreskin, 50
    burial of, 46
Formal operations, period of, 16
Free will, 197
Fresh air and sunshine, 74, 145–146
Freud, Sigmund, 1
Fruits and vegetables, 96

Gamliel, R., 141, 154, 211
Gamliel Zoga, R., 206
Gargling, 75
Garlic, 21
Gematria, 42
Genotype, 164
Gentiles, 209
German measles, 29
Germinal predetermination, 32
Gershom, Rabbenu, 37
Giddul banim, 7
Girls. *See* Female children
Grain foods and cereals, 95. *See also* Diet and nutrition
    Gumco Clamp, 53

Hair, care of, 75
Hair-cutting, of boys, 75–76, 162
Hamm (scientist), 31
Hamnuna, R., 245
Hanan b. Pazzi, R., 245
Hands, washing of, 72, 73, 100, 167, 231
Hannah, 23, 79
Hatred, 185
Head, shape of, 41
Health, physical, 141–142, 154, 161–162. *See also* Mental health
Hebrew language, 126, 228, 237

Hemophilia, 53, 147, 165
Heredity, 32, 164, 166, 191
    and personality development, 180
    See also innate temperaments
Heritage, Jewish, 9, 10
Hillel, 40
    school of, 21, 71, 94
Hirsch, Samson Raphael, 8, 86, 107, 110, 118, 129, 167, 175, 199, 242
Home, Jewish. *See* Family, Jewish
Honey, 95
Human life, value of, 12, 18–19, 35, 51, 251
Huna, R., 21

Impotence, 21, 22
Incubator baby, 52, 59
Infant care, 71–72, 73, 87
Infant sacrifices, 12
Infertility, 20, 22
Inheritance rights, 255
Innate temperaments, 191, 193–194
Insect bites, 73, 149
Intestinal worms, 148
Isaac (patriarch), 12, 50, 165, 209
Isaac, R., 26
Isaac b. Shila, R., 216
Ishmael, 132, 209
Israel of Salant, R., 194
Issachar (Jacob's son), 195
Issachar, R., 13

Jacob, 11, 12, 165, 186, 194, 209
Jaundice, 52, 147
Jealousy, 186
Jochebed, 25, 36
Jonathan, R., 13, 205
Joseph, 12, 165, 186, 195, 209
Joshua, R., 71, 94
Joshua b. Chananya, R., 119
Joshua b. Gamla, R., 14, 176, 234
Joshua b. Karcha, R., 83

Joshua b. Levi, R., 235
Joy, 190
Judah (Jacob's son), 194
Judah, R., 10, 22, 135, 218
Judah b. Tema, R., 172
Judah the Prince, R., 25, 105, 108, 150, 229
Justinia, 25
Juvenile delinquency, 114, 139. *See also* Rebellious son

Kartemi, 21
Kashrut, laws of, 92–93, 97, 144
Katan, 14
Katz, Tuviyyah, 149
Ketanah, 266
Kissing, of infants, 73
Kitov, Eliyahu, 55
Kohanim, 34, 56–57, 59
Kook, R. Abraham Isaac, 161
Kvaterin, 47, 50

Labor. *See* Childbirth
Lag ba-Omer, 162, 222
La Leche League, 79
Lamaze method, 37
Language development, 95
Learning readiness, 117–120. *See also* Cognitive development; Physical development
Leboyer method, 39, 41
Leeuwenhoek, Anton van, 31
Legitimacy, 27, 253
Levi (Jacob's son), 194
Levi, R., 76
Levi b. Yossi, R., 179
Levirate marriage, 11–12, 21, 252
Lewin, Kurt, 193, 203
Life, value of. *See* Human life, value of
Lilah, 108

Lilith, 46
Love, 13–14, 146
Luzzatto, Moses Hayyim, 181

Magic and fantasy, in child's thinking, 179
Maimonides, Moses, 29, 72, 76, 95, 96, 119, 126, 134, 135, 143, 149, 159, 175, 180, 181, 193, 197, 209, 214, 231
Majority, age of, 104, 109
Malaria, 73
Male children, 54
 birth of, 35–36, 42
 first hair-cutting of, 75–76, 162
 See also *Berit Milah*; Firstborn son; *Pidyon ha-Ben*
Mamzer, 253. *See also* Legitimacy
Manna, 95, 96
Manoah's wife, 28
Marital partners, selection of, 165–166
Marital relations, 21, 23–24
Mattanah, R., 216
Maturation, 17, 264
Mazal, 191
Meals, conduct during, 100–101
Measles, 148
Meir, R., 9, 80, 107, 174
Meat and fish, 21, 96, 97. *See also* Diet and nutrition
Meiri, Menahem b. Solomon, 115
Menopause, 25
Menstruation, 23, 25
Mental faculties, 8
Mental health, 114, 159, 180
Metzitzah, 49, 50
Midwives, 37, 39
Mikveh, 23, 27, 42
Milk, 93–94, 95, 98
 mother's, 93
Minors, 14, 258, 260

Miscarriages, 59
  prevention of, 25
Mitzvot, educational function of, 104, 175, 206
Modesty
  in dress, 163
  in marital relations, 24
Mogen Clamp, 53
Mohel, 45, 46, 48, 49, 50
Moral development, 108–109, 182–183
Moses, 165
Mothers, obligations of, 110–111, 126–127, 181–182, 229–230, 231, 235. *See also* Parental obligations
Mother's milk, 93
Motor coordination, 76
Mouth, rinsing of, 73, 75
Multipara, 26
Music, 229

Na'arah, 266
Nachmanides, Moses, 133
Nails, care of, 75
Names, Hebrew, 61–63
  for boys, 64–66
  for girls, 66–68
Naming ceremonies
  for boys, 61
  for girls, 63–64
Naphtali, 195
Neglected children, 260
Neonate
  average size of, 41
  care of, 40
Neonatal jaundice, 52, 147
Neubirt, Y. Y., 155
Nonobservant Jews, 209
Niddah, 42
Nonviolent birth, 39, 40–41
Nursing. *See* Breast-feeding
Nutrition. *See* Diet and nutrition

Odors, during pregnancy, 25
Oholiab, 229
Oil, anointing infant with, 72, 87
Olal, 14
Orphans, 21, 80, 261–264
Outings, 74, 88–89, 167
Overeating, 96
Ovum, 31

Papa, R., 32
Parental obligations, 8, 42, 74, 142, 167, 213, 218
  disciplinary, 132–133, 135
  educational, 170, 206, 229–230
  religious, 170, 206
  as role models, 129, 217
  See also Fathers, obligations of; Mothers, obligations of
Parent-child relations, 10, 11, 110–114, 213–221.
Parents, reverence for, 215, 252. *See also* Filial obligations
Passover, 55, 100, 232
  Seder, 121, 123, 212, 220
Peer groups, 207–209
Periah, 48
Personal hygiene, 72. *See also* Bathing; Hands, washing of; Washing
Personality
  defined, 191, 192, 193
  development of, 8, 16–18, 191–200
  educational influences, 195–197, 198
  environmental influences, 195–196
  in Jewish thought, 191–192
Peru u-revu, 11, 20, 21
Phinehas, 166
Phylacteries. *See Tefillin*
Physical faculties, 8
  development of, 16–18, 161–168
  purpose of, 102–104, 166–167
Piaget, Jean, 1, 16, 173, 176, 177

Index

Pidyon ha-Ben, 54–59, 254
Placenta, 33
Play. *See* Development play
Positive reinforcement, 138, 242–243
Postpartum care, 42
Prayer
   and sex of unborn child, 27
   in cases of illness, 150–151
   for safe childbirth, 39
   for cure to sterility, 22–23
Pregnancy, 23–28, 108, 251. *See also* Miscarriages
Premature birth, 41. *See also* Incubator baby
Preoperational period, 16, 173, 206
Prenatal development, 31. *See also* Fetus
Preschool education. *See* Education
Primpipara, 26, 36
Procreation, as *mitzvah,* 20–21
Puah, 37, 39
Public bath facilities, 73
Purim, 124, 212, 220, 232

Rabbah, 36, 135, 210, 243
Rachel, 11, 20, 23, 36
Ralbag, 181, 190
Rattles, 83
Rav, 17, 78, 135, 138
Rebecca, 20
Rebellious son, 133–134
Reischer, R. Jacob b. Joseph, 135
Respect, for children, 113, 129, 187–188
Reuben, 194
Rosh Hashanah, 124

Sabbath, 12, 25, 36, 123, 220
   regulations pertaining to:
   babysitters, 89
   bathing child, 73, 87
   Berit Milah, 45, 46

breast-feeding, 80–81
Caesarean section, 37, 252
childbirth, 38
diaper care, 74, 88
feeding children, 98–99
food preparation, 99
infant care, 85–87
medical care, 151–153
outings, 88–89
saving life of fetus, 35, 151, 251
the sick, 154–155
sterilizing bottle, 99
teeth care, 75, 87–88, 95
toys and games, 83–85
Safra, R., 26
Samson, 28
Samuel, Mar, 27, 33, 74, 78, 94
Samuel b. Nachman, R., 205
Samuel b. Shilat, R., 17, 235
Sandak, 47
Sarah, 7, 20, 23, 25, 36
Schools, 125, 176, 234, 245
   curriculum and methods, 236–239
   See also Education; Teachers
Secular studies, 228–229, 237
Self-concept, 180, 181
Self-esteem, 186–188
Semen tests, 22
Sensorimotor development, 210
Sensorimotor stage, 16, 124, 173
Sex, determination of, 26–27, 33
shalom zakhor, 45–46
Shammai, 100
   school of, 21
Shatnez, 74
Shavuot, 212, 232
Shiphrah, 39
Shosbinim, 47
Sibling relations, 186, 209–210
Simeon (Jacob's son), 194
Simeon b. Shetach, R., 234
Simeon b. Yochai, R., 76, 162, 222

Skin eruptions, 75
Sleep, 76, 167
Socialization
    Judaic aspects, 203, 205–207
    parent-child relations, 217
    peer group, 207–209
    play, 210–212
    siblings, 208–210
    as social learning, 205
Solid food, 71, 95–96
Solomon, 209
"Son" and "daughter," defined, 252
Sore throat, 153
Soul, 35
Spacing, of children, 79
Sperm, 31
Spock, Benjamin, 1, 173
Sterility, 21
Stress, 146–147
Studentzki, M., 149
Sukkot, 124, 175, 212, 220, 232
Swaddling, 40
Swimming, 176

Taf, 14
Talismans, 25, 35
Talking, 71, 95, 119
Tamar, 38, 39
Tay-Sachs disease, 29
Teachers, 135, 240, 241, 242, 244, 245, 246–249, 257
Teeth, care of, 75, 87–88, 95
Teething, 148
Tefillin, 163, 265–266
Theft, 259
Tinnok, 14, 71
Toilet training, 17
Tonsillitis, 148

Torah, 21, 121, 198, 203, 227. *See also* Bible
Tosfa'ah, Rabbah, 27
Toys, 72, 83–85. *See also* Developmental play
Transgressions, liability for, 259
Trust, 182
Tza'ar giddul banim, 11, 141
Tzitzit, 123, 126, 163, 175

Umbilical cord, 40

Vachnacht, 46

Wagschal, R. S., 155
Washing, 73. *See also* Hands, washing of
Water, 96
Weaning, 78, 94–95
Weinberg, R. Yechiel Jacob, 139
Wetnurses, 77, 80
Widows, 21, 26, 28
Wine, 21–22

Yehoshua, R., 211
Yetzer ha-ra, 105, 115, 193
Yetzer ha-tov, 105, 109, 110, 112, 115, 193
Yochanan, R., 9, 21, 37
Yochanan b. Beroka, R., 20
Yom Kippur, 25, 38, 81, 100, 125, 258
Yonek, 14
Yose, R., 83
Yose b. Chanina, R., 259

Zebulun, 194
Zipporah, 45
Zutra, Mar, 27